Tradition and Composition in the
Epistula Apostolorum

T0324364

HARVARD THEOLOGICAL STUDIES
57

CAMBRIDGE, MASSACHUSETTS

Tradition and Composition in the

Epistula Apostolorum

Julian V. Hills

DISTRIBUTED BY

HARVARD UNIVERSITY PRESS

FOR

HARVARD THEOLOGICAL STUDIES

HARVARD DIVINITY SCHOOL

Tradition and Composition in the
Epistula Apostolorum

Harvard Theological Studies 57

Series Editors:
François Bovon
Francis Schüssler Fiorenza
Peter B. Machinist

Second Printing with new preface and expanded bibliography.

Library of Congress Cataloging-in-Publication Data

Hills, Julian Victor.
    Tradition and composition in the Epistula Apostolorum / Julian Hills.
        p. cm. -- (Harvard theological studies ; no. 57)
    Originally published: Minneapolis : Fortress Press, c1990.
    Includes bibliographical references.
    1. Epistle of the Apostles.   I. Title
BS2900.A7H55 2006
229'.93--dc22

                                                2006021327

Contents

Preface to the Second Printing

This study has its origins in the Harvard Divinity School graduate seminar, "The Gospel of John and Related Early Christian Literature," which Helmut Koester directed in the spring of 1980. Initial research on the *Epistula apostolorum* prompted me to begin investigating this most Johannine of Christian dialogues with regard to the development both of this particular dialogue as well as of the church order genre. However, upon officially beginning the project two years later, I learned that a number of unedited Ethiopic manuscripts contained the writing; much preliminary textual work would have to precede the broader comparative task.

In light of this and other discoveries at the level of the text and its translation, I greatly reduced the scope of the present undertaking — or, rather, sharpened its focus. Thus in this study I set myself the more modest goal of describing as closely as possible the writing's communal setting and theological purpose, to the extent that the author's compositional method and use of traditions speaks to them. To put it in terms very familiar to students of the New Testament, I was taking on an exercise in the "redaction criticism" in fashion since the 1950s but now applying it outside the biblical canon.

Since that time, however, the context of biblical studies had begun to change in two ways. First, the recently recovered Qumran scrolls and so-called Nag Hammadi Library were greatly expanding the range of documents essential to understanding the context of early Christian faith and reflection. Second, the academy and the churches — not to mention individual seekers — were stretching the horizons of the historical-critical method to include fresh questions about social make-up, gender, and all manner of diversity in patterns of belief communal life associated with the Jesus tradition.

Discovery encouraged re-discovery, that is, the re-examination of writings both long known and recently found. For various reasons the "apocryphal" was once more in vogue; and I delighted to find it so at Harvard. Among other writings, the *Epistula apostolorum*, unknown to European scholars before the 1890s, might now receive a fresh reading. Yet, as Montague Rhodes James shrewdly recognized, "even to the enthusiast not everything need be important because it is uncanonical" (*Apocrypha Anecdota* [TS 2/3; Cambridge:

Cambridge University Press, 1893; reprinted Nendeln: Lichtenstein, 1967]
ix). So what would it take to render this apocryphal *Epistle of the Apostles*,
which (not incidentally!) happens to remain a part of the liturgical life of
the Ethiopic church, if not more *important* to western scholars then at least,
perhaps, more *interesting*? In the Conclusion, I suggest that what matters is
character: the text not only as a repository of traditions and useful linguistic
data but also as a witness to the actual lives of people of faith in some specific
place back in those early post-New Testament decades. I hope these pages,
along with the work of others, can continue to supply, if not a full character
sketch, at least the beginning of a silhouette.

Let me make brief mention of the editions and translations of the *Epistula
apostolorum* that I quote in this study (the bibliography contains full publication details). Unless otherwise noted, I take English quotations from the cur-
rently standard translation of Hugo Duensing's German version, first issued
in the Kleine Texte series in 1925 and reprinted in the third and subsequent
editions of the Edgar Hennecke and Wilhelm Schneemelcher compendium,
Neutestamentliche Apokryphen (ET *New Testament Apocrypha*). I refer to
the Coptic text by codex page (in roman numerals) and line number in Carl
Schmidt, *Gespräche Jesu mit seinen Jüngern*, 1*–26* (the asterisks indicate
page numbers in the Appendix) and to the Ethiopic by page and line number
in Louis Guerrier and Sylvain Grébaut, "Le testament en Galilée," 1–96. In
neither the Coptic nor the Ethiopic have I normalized orthographic irregularities (variant spellings, dialectical anomalies). To the conventional section or
chapter numbers I have added "verse" numbers for more precise location;
generally each verse comprises one sentence. Transliteration of the Ethiopic
text follows the principles enunciated in Thomas O. Lambdin, *Introduction
to Classical Ethiopic (Ge'ez)*, 1–12.

I shall always be grateful to Helmut Koester, my dissertation adviser; to
the late George W. MacRae, S.J., John Strugnell, and Bishop Krister Stendahl. Each of these my teachers inspired and encouraged me throughout my
time in Cambridge. My thanks are likewise due to Bernadette Brooten and
Margaret Miles, editors of the series in which the study first appeared; and
now especially to François Bovon, for including this slightly revised version
of it in the Harvard Theological Studies series.

Julian V. Hills
Marquette University
Milwaukee, Wisconsin

Preface

This dissertation has its origins in the Harvard Divinity School graduate seminar, "The Gospel of John and Related Early Christian Literature," directed by Helmut Koester in the spring of 1980. Initial research on the *Epistula apostolorum* prompted me to begin investigating this most Johannine of Christian dialogues in the context of the development both of the dialogue and of the church order genre. But when this project was officially begun two years later, I learned of the existence of a number of unedited Ethiopic manuscripts containing the writing; much initial textual work would need to be done before the broader comparative task could be undertaken.

In light of this and other discoveries at the level of the text and its translation, the scope of the present undertaking was substantially reduced. Thus in this study I set myself the more modest goal: as far as possible to describe the writing's communal setting and theological purpose as they may be learned from the author's compositional method and use of traditions.

My thanks are due to Helmut Koester, my dissertation adviser; to the late George W. MacRae, S.J.; to John Strugnell; and to Krister Stendahl, now Bishop of Stockholm. Each of these my teachers inspired and encouraged me throughout my time in Cambridge, and to each for his distinctive contribution and example I shall always be grateful.

Preliminary mention should be made here of the editions and translations of the *Epistula apostolorum* quoted in this study. Unless otherwise noted, quotations in English are from the standard translation of Hugo Duensing's German, in Edgar Hennecke and Wilhelm Schneemelcher, eds.; R. McL. Wilson, trans. ed., *New Testament Apoc-*

rypha (2 vols.; Philadelphia: Westminster, 1963–65) 1. 191–227. Quotations from the Coptic text are by codex page (in Roman numerals) and line number in Carl Schmidt, *Gespräche Jesu mit seinen Jüngern nach der Auferstehung* (TU 43; Leipzig: Hinrichs, 1919) 1*–26*. Quotations from the Ethiopic text are by page and line number in Louis Guerrier and Sylvain Grébaut, eds. and trans., "Le testament en Galilée de Notre-Seigneur Jésus-Christ," PO 9 (1913) 141–236 (fascicle pp. 1–96); where the text can be improved, the location in Guerrier is still given. To the chapter numbers in Hennecke-Schneemelcher verse numbers have been added; with few exceptions, the length of a verse coincides with that of a full sentence. Thus citations given in full include (1) chapter and verse, (2) Coptic codex page and line, and (3) Ethiopic page and line numbers; e.g. *Ep. apost.* 16.2 (IX 3, 59/4). Where the Coptic is defective, the reference notes this as follows: *Ep. apost.* 19.3 (--, 61/7). In such cases it is not to be assumed that the Ethiopic reading is a later addition to the text. Transliteration of the Ethiopic text is according to the principles described in Thomas O. Lambdin, *Introduction to Classical Ethiopic (Geʿez)* (HSM 24; Missoula, MT: Scholars Press, 1978) 1–12. In neither Ethiopic nor Coptic quotations have orthographic irregularities been normalized.

I wish to thank the editors of this series, Bernadette Brooten and Margaret Miles, and Fortress Press for accepting this monograph for publication; and for permission to make such changes in style and documentation as were deemed necessary to make the study accessible to a wider readership.

Julian Hills
Marquette University
Milwaukee, Wisconsin
June 20, 1988

Abbreviations

Abbreviations used in this volume for sources and literature from antiquity are the same as those used in *HTR* 80:2 (1987) 243–60. Some abbreviations are adapted from that list and can be easily indentified. In addition, the following abbreviations have been used:

AAWG	Abhandlungen der Akademie der Wissenschaften in Göttingen
Anton	*Antonianum*
Asc. Isa.	*Ascension of Isaiah*
Athanasius	
De incarn.	*De incarnatione*
BCH	*Bulletin de correspondance hellénique*
BG	(Codex) Berolinensis Gnosticus
BNZW	Beihefte zur Zeitschrift für die neutestamentliche Wissenschaft und die Kunde der älteren Kirche
ChrW	*Die christliche Welt*
Commodian	
Carm. apol.	*Carmen apologeticum*
Const. apost.	*Constitutiones apostolorum*
Corp. Herm.	*Corpus Hermeticum*
Crum	W. E. Crum, *A Coptic Dictionary* (Oxford: Clarendon, 1939).
CTM	Calwer Theologische Monographien
Cyprian	
Quod idol.	*Quod idola dii non sint*
Cyril of Jerusalem	
Catech.	*Catecheses illuminandorum*
GGA	*Göttingische gelehrte Anziegen*
Gos. Bart.	*Gospel of Bartholomew*
Hatch-Redpath	Edwin Hatch and Henry A. Redpath, *A Concordance to the Septuagint, with Supplement* (3 vols. in 2; Oxford: Clarendon, 1897–1906).
Hippolytus	
Apost. Trad.	*The Apostolic Tradition*
C. Gaium	*Capita contra Gaium*

Hippolytus (cont'd)
   Comm. in Cant.   *Commentarium in Canticum canticorum*
   Comm. in Dan.   *Commentarium in Danielem*
   C. Noet.   *Contra Noetum*
   De antichr.   *Demonstratio de Christo et antichristo*
   frg. in Pss.   *fragmenta in Psalmos*
   HomPastRev   *Homiletic and Pastoral Review*
   HPB   *Historisch-politische Blätter für das katholische*
                   Deutschland
Inf. Thom.   *Infancy Gospel of Thomas*
Irenaeus
   Adv. haer.   *Adversus haereses*
Jerome
   De vir. ill.   *De viris illustribus*
Josephus
   Ant.   *Jewish Antiquities*
   Ap.   *Against Apion*
Justin
   1 Apol.   *First Apology*
   De res.   *De resurrectione*
   Dial.   *Dialogue*
Lactantius
   Div. inst.   *Divinae institutiones*
   Epit.   *Epitome*
LitZentr   *Literarische Zentralblatt*
Mart. Poly.   *Martyrdom of Polycarp*
Melito
   Pass. Hom.   *Passover Homily*
Moulton-Milligan   James Hope Moulton and George Milligan,
                   The Vocabulary of the Greek Testament Illustrated
                   from the Papyri and Other Non-Literary Sources
                   (London: Hodder & Stoughton, 1924 – 29).
NThS   *Nieuwe Theologische Studiën*
Orac. Sib.   *Sibylline Oracles*
Origen
   Comm. in Matt.   *Commentarii in Matthaeum*
   C. Cels.   *Contra Celsum*
Pap. Eg.   *Papyrus Egerton*
Ps.-Cl.   *Pseudo-Clementines*
   Hom.   *Homilies*
   Recog.   *Recognitions*
Ps.-Cyprian
   De rebapt.   *De rebaptismate*
Ps.-Hippolytus
   De consumm.   *De consummatione mundi*
   frg. in Pss.   *Fragmenta in Psalmos*

P.S.I.	G. Vitelli, M. Norsa, et al., ed., *Papiri greci et latini* (Florence: Pubblicazioni della Società Italiana, 1912–).
PTS	Patristische Texte und Studien
4QEn	Fragments of *1 Enoch* from Qumran Cave 4
ROC	Revue de l'Orient chrétien
Soph. Jes. Chr.	*Sophia of Jesus Christ*
SWAW	Sitzungsberichte der Wiener Akademie der Wissenschaften

Tertullian

Apol.	*Apology*
Adv. Marc.	*Adversus Marcionem*
Adv. Prax.	*Adversus Praxean*
De bapt.	*De baptismate*
De carn.	*De carne Christi*
De cor.	*De corona*
De res.	*De resurrectione*
Test. Dom.	*Testamentum Domini*
WS	*Wiener Studien*
ZAegSpr	*Zeitschrift für Aegyptische Sprache*

Short Titles

Information appears here for frequently used works which are cited by short title. A few short titles do not appear in this list, but in each instance full bibliography is given on the page(s) preceding such references.

Black, *Book of Enoch*
> Matthew Black, ed., *The Book of Enoch or I Enoch* (SVTP 7; Leiden: Brill, 1985).

Brown, *Epistles of John*
> Raymond E. Brown, *The Epistles of John* (AB 30; Garden City, NY: Doubleday, 1982).

Bultmann, *History*
> Rudolf Bultmann, *The History of the Synoptic Tradition* (rev. ed.; New York: Harper & Row, 1963).

Bultmann, *Theology*
> Rudolf Bultmann, *Theology of the New Testament* (2 vols.; London: S.C.M., 1952–55).

Butterworth, *Hippolytus: Contra Noetum*
> Robert Butterworth, ed. and trans., *Hippolytus of Rome: Contra Noetum* (Heythrop Monographs 2; London: Heythrop College, 1977).

Cameron, *Other Gospels*
> Ron Cameron, ed., *The Other Gospels: Non-Canonical Gospel Texts* (Philadelphia: Westminster, 1982).

Charles, *Book of Enoch*
> R. H. Charles, ed., *The Ethiopic Version of the Book of Enoch or I Enoch* (Anecdota Oxoniensia; Oxford: Clarendon, 1906).

Deissmann, *Bible Studies*
> Adolf Deissmann, *Bible Studies* (1923; reprinted Winona Lake, IN: Alpha, 1979).

Dillmann, *Lexicon*
> August Dillmann, *Lexicon Linguae Aethiopicae* (1865; reprinted Osnabrück: Biblio Verlag, 1970).

Duensing, *Epistula Apostolorum*
> Hugo Duensing, ed. and trans., *Epistula Apostolorum: nach dem äthiopischen und koptischen Texte* (KlT 152; Bonn: Marcus und Weber, 1925).

Ehrhardt, "Eine neue apokryphe Schrift"
> A. Ehrhardt, "Eine neue apokryphe Schrift aus dem 2. Jahrhundert," *HPB* 165 (1920) 645–55, 717–29.

Funk, *Didascalia et constitutiones apostolorum*
> Francis Xavier Funk, ed., *Didascalia et constitutiones apostolorum* (2 vols.; Paderborn: Schoeningh, 1905).

Geffcken, *Oracula Sibyllina*
> Johannes Geffcken, ed., *Die Oracula Sibyllina* (GCS 8; Leipzig: Hinrichs, 1902).

Goodspeed, *Early Christian Literature*
> Edgar J. Goodspeed, *A History of Early Christian Literature* (rev. Robert M. Grant; Chicago: University of Chicago Press/Phoenix, 1966).

Guerrier, "Le testament"
> Louis Guerrier and Sylvain Grébaut, "Le testament en Galilée de notre-Seigneur Jésus-Christ," PO 9 (1913) 141–236 (fascicle pp. 1–96).

Gundry, *Matthew*
> Robert H. Gundry, *Matthew: A Commentary on his Literary and Theological Art* (Grand Rapids: Eerdmans, 1982).

Hornschuh, *Studien*
> Manfred Hornschuh, *Studien zur Epistula Apostolorum* (PTS 5; Berlin: de Gruyter, 1965).

James, *Apocryphal New Testament*
> Montague Rhodes James, *The Apocryphal New Testament* (Oxford: Clarendon, 1924).

Kelly, *Creeds*
> J. N. D. Kelly, *Early Christian Creeds* (3d. ed.; London: Longmans, 1972).

Koester, *Introduction*
> Helmut Koester, *Introduction to the New Testament* (2 vols.; Philadelphia: Fortress, 1982).

Lipsius-Bonnet, *Acta apostolorum apocrypha*
> Richard Adelbert Lipsius, ed., Maximilian Bonnet, rev., *Acta apostolorum apocrypha* (2 vols. in 3 parts; 1891–1903; reprinted Hildesheim: Olms, 1959).

Mansoor, *Thanksgiving Hymns*
> Menahem Mansoor, *The Thanksgiving Hymns* (STDJ 3; Grand Rapids: Eerdmans, 1961).

McNeile, *St. Matthew*
   Hugh Alan McNeile, *The Gospel According to St. Matthew* (1915; reprinted Grand Rapids: Baker, 1980).

Meeks, *First Urban Christians*
   Wayne A. Meeks, *The First Urban Christians* (New Haven: Yale University Press, 1983).

Perkins, *Gnostic Dialogue*
   Pheme Perkins, *The Gnostic Dialogue: The Early Church and the Crisis of Gnosticism* (Theological Inquiries; New York/Ramsey/Toronto: Paulist, 1980).

Robinson and Koester, *Trajectories*
   James M. Robinson and Helmut Koester, *Trajectories through Early Christianity* (Philadelphia: Fortress, 1971).

Schmidt, "Eine bisher unbekkante altchristliche Schrift"
   Carl Schmidt, "Eine bisher unbekkante altchristliche Schrift in koptischer Sprache," SPAW (1895) 705–11.

Schmidt, *Gespräche Jesu*
   Carl Schmidt and Isaak Wajnberg, *Gespräche Jesu mit seinen Jüngern nach der Auferstehung: Ein katholisch-apostolisches Sendschreiben des 2. Jahrhunderts* (TU 43; Leipzig: Hinrichs, 1919).

Vanovermeire, "Livre que Jésus-Christ a révélé"
   Pedro Vanovermeire, "Livre que Jésus-Christ a révélé à ses disciples" (Dr. Theol. diss., Institut catholique de Paris, 1962).

De Zwaan, "Date and Origin"
   J. de Zwaan, "Date and Origin of the Epistle of the Eleven Apostles," in H. G. Wood, ed., *Amicitiae Corolla: A Volume of Essays Presented to James Rendel Harris, D. Litt., on the Occasion of His Eightieth Birthday* (London: University of London Press, 1933) 344–55.

Introduction

From the earliest decades of the Christian church, the "good news of Jesus Christ," preached and taught in diverse ways and in diverse communities, was given literary expression in a variety of genres, for example the sayings collection, the letter, the gospel, and the apocalypse. Among the genres which flourished both before and after the establishment of a canon of NT scriptures the "revelation dialogue" enjoyed wide popularity, especially among gnostic Christian groups.

Typically the revelation dialogue had two distinctive features. First, its putative chronological setting was the interim, of varying or unstated length, between the resurrection and the ascension. This period, which is reflected in only a minor way in the NT (cf. Matt 28:10, 18 – 20; Mark 16:6 – 7; Luke 24:13 – 35, 36 – 49; John 20:11 – 29; Acts 1:3 – 8; 1 Cor 15:3 – 8), became the temporal setting for teaching which was declared to be new, uniquely saving, and reserved for a chosen apostle or group of apostles.

The second distinctive characteristic of the revelation dialogue was its dialogue form, anticipated in part by the "controversy dialogues" and "scholastic dialogues" in the Synoptic Gospels, in part by the longer dialogues in the Gospel of John, in part also by a long tradition of dialogue literature both Jewish and Greek. The authors of revelation dialogues employed a minimum of narrative; as far as possible, everything was in the direct speech of the risen revealer and his conversation partners, the apostles. Thus the spoken and recorded words of the risen Lord took implicit precedence over the events in the life of the earthly Jesus.

How then is the modern reader, more familiar with the contours of the canonical gospels, and informed by a century and a half of historical-critical gospel scholarship, to do justice to works whose temporal and formal frameworks have only distant analogies in canonical and in later, patristic writings? Precisely what new demands does the revelation dialogue make of the modern reader?

One approach, well established in historical-critical scholarship, has been to detect and isolate specific sources or traditions, and to make these, together with similar sources and traditions in other Jewish and early Christian literature, the focus of attention. A second approach, similarly well established, has been to recover the ideas or "doctrines" present in the text, and to place these within the known framework of the development of Christian dogma.

The majority of modern studies on the revelation dialogues, as on noncanonical literature in general, have taken one or other, and sometimes both, of these approaches. The former has been of special value in the study of documents whose composition cannot be dated even approximately; form- and tradition-historical observations permit the relative dating of specific sources and traditions, regardless of the date of the final 'host' document. The contribution of the latter approach has been to assist the description of the early Christian 'history of ideas,' unencumbered by questions concerning the specific circumstances under which any particular document came to be written.

Neither approach, however, will claim to do for the noncanonical writings what recent investigation, especially redaction criticism, can claim to have attempted for the NT gospels: to describe the life-setting, not merely of *the traditions* which lie behind a specific text, but of *the author and his or her community.*

The communities of the NT evangelists saw the production of what would later be reckoned canonical *texts.* But no corresponding assessment follows, that there was anything necessarily normative, that is, canonical, in those Christian communities themselves. It is thus in the reality of Christian *community*, whether of the first or of the second or third centuries, whether judged by a later generation to have been in the mainstream or on the fringes, that common ground may be located: between, on the one hand, the revered literary monuments of the canon and, on the other, writings which informed, encouraged, and sustained other, and *prima facie* surely no less faithful, early Christian groups.

The possibility is beginning to be explored, that the same techniques of analysis that have revealed something of the situation and the character of the authors and communities of the NT gospels might do the same for hitherto apocryphal (literally, "hidden") writers and their communities. In the context of such exploration the historic distinction between the canonical and the noncanonical may be found to give room to a new appreciation, not only of the diversity, but also of the integrity, the theological insight, and the earnestness of extra-canonical evangelists.

Among these other passionate witnesses to early Christian life and thought is the unknown author who composed the revelation dialogue to which its first modern editor gave the title *Epistula apostolorum*, or the "Epistle of the Apostles." This text, apparently the only surviving product of the particular communal reality and theological vision that inspired it, is the subject of this study.

The *Epistula apostolorum* is one of a number of early Christian writings which claim to present the revelation of the risen Christ to his disciples in the period between the resurrection and the ascension. For more than a millennium—since its disappearance from Greek-, Latin- and Coptic-speaking Christianity—this writing was familiar only to the Ethiopian Church, until in 1895 Carl Schmidt announced to the world of scholarship the discovery of a Coptic "catholic-apostolic epistle."[1] In 1908, one year after Louis Guerrier made known his plans to publish a previously unedited Ethiopic "Testament of our Lord,"[2] a Latin palimpsest fragment of the work was published by Josef Bick.[3] Guerrier's text and French translation appeared in 1913,[4] Schmidt's Coptic text, with German translation of both versions, commentary, and essays, in 1919.[5]

Schmidt's study, combining a careful reconstruction of the often fragmentary Coptic manuscript with a thorough discussion of the standard introductory questions, remains the indispensible starting point for investigation of the *Epistula*. Schmidt placed the writing in Asia Minor, and dated it 160–170 CE.[6] His judgment that the author knew and used the NT writings[7] has generally been accepted by subsequent scholars. His survey of such

[1] Schmidt, "Eine bisher unbekannte altchristliche Schrift in koptischer Sprache," SPAW (1895) 705–11.

[2] Guerrier, "Un 'Testament de Notre-Seigneur et Sauveur Jésus-Christ' en Galilée," ROC 12 (1907) 1–8. M. R. James identified Guerrier's "Testament" with Schmidt's epistle in "The 'Epistola Apostolorum' in a New Text," JTS 12 (1910–11) 55–56.

[3] "Wiener Palimpseste, I. Teil: Cod. Palat. Vindobonensis 16, olim Bobbiensis," SWAW 159 (1908) 90–99 with Plate 4; see also Edmund Hauler, "Zu den neuen lateinischen Bruchstücken der Thomasapokalypse und eines apostolischen Sendschreibens im Codex Vind. Nr. 16," WS 30 (1908) 308–40; and Carl Schmidt, "Eine Epistola apostolorum in koptischer und lateinischer Überlieferung," SPAW (1908) 1047–56.

[4] Guerrier and Sylvain Grébaut, "Le testament en Galilée de Notre-Seigneur Jésus-Christ," PO 9 (1913) 141–236 (fascicle pp. 1–96). Note the review by Anton Baumstark in TRev 13 (1914) 165–69; see also Baumstark's studies, "Alte und neue Spuren eines außerkanonischen Evangeliums (vielleicht des Ägypterevangeliums)," ZNW 14 (1913) 232–47; and "Hippolytos und die außerkanonische Evangelienquelle des äthiopischen Galiläa-Testaments," ZNW 15 (1914) 332–35.

[5] *Gespräche Jesu mit seinen Jüngern nach der Auferstehung: Ein katholisch-apostolisches Sendschreiben des 2. Jahrhunderts* (TU 43; Leipzig: Hinrichs, 1919). Isaak Wajnberg contributed the new translation of the Ethiopic.

[6] Ibid., 402.

[7] The evidence is collected and assessed in ibid., 213–50.

broad topics as the christology, the soteriology, and the eschatology of the writing enabled him to identify countless parallels to the theology of the *Epistula* in other early Christian literature. In short, Schmidt began the task of reconstructing the theological milieu of the *Epistula*'s author and community.

The *Epistula* was hailed as a major discovery. Kirsopp Lake described it as "a document comparable with the Didache or the Odes of Solomon for its additions to our knowledge of the second century."[8] Adolf Deissmann, reviewing a number of recent papyrus finds including the Heidelberg *Acta Pauli*, described Schmidt's Coptic text as "historically the most valuable."[9] A flurry of reviews,[10] an enthusiastic response to the fresh translation by Hugo Duensing,[11] and the number of published articles on the new work[12] indicated that the *Epistula* had caught the imagination of the academic world. But within ten years interest had waned. Occasionally cited as a leading example of Quartodecimanism, as an orthodox representative of the characteristically Gnostic "revelation dialogue" genre, and as the earliest extant witness to the book of Acts,[13] the *Epistula* took its place among a host of minor witnesses to second-century Christianity.

[8] Lake, "The Epistola Apostolorum," *HTR* 14 (1920) 16.

[9] Deissmann, *Light from the Ancient East* (1922; reprinted Grand Rapids: Baker, 1980) 44.

[10] See H. J. Cladder, in *TRev* 18 (1919) 452–53 (suggests the date 147/48); J. de Zwaan, in *NThS* 2 (1919) 281–86 (suggests Syrian provenance, and a date ca. 190); A. Ehrhardt, in *HPB* 165 (1920) 645–55, 717–29; Gustav Krüger, in *LitZentr* 71 (1920) 817–20; M. R. James, in *JTS* 21 (1920–21) 334–38; Gustave Bardy, in *RB* 30 (1921) 110–34 (suggests Egyptian provenance and a third-century date); Anton Baumstark, in *TRev* 20 (1921) 260–65; Leopold Fonck, in *Bib* 2 (1921) 244–45; Hans Lietzmann, in *ZNW* 20 (1921) 173–76 (prefers an earlier date, but suggests Egyptian provenance); Hans von Soden, "Die Erforschung der vornicänischen Kirchengeschichte seit 1914," *ZKG* 39 (1921) 140–47; Hugo Duensing, in *GGA* 184 (1922) 241–52 (principally concerned with matters of text and translation); Felix Haase, in *OrChr* n.S. 10/11 (1923) 170–73; and Walter Till, in *ZAegSpr* 63 (1928) 92.

[11] *Epistula Apostolorum: nach dem äthiopischen und koptischen Texte* (KIT 152; Bonn: Marcus und Weber, 1925). Note the reviews and notices by Rudolf Bultmann, in *ChrW* 39 (1925) 1064–65; Carl Schmidt, in *OLZ* 28 (1925) 855–59 (suggests a number of corrections in the translation of the Coptic); Ernest B. Allo, in *RB* 36 (1927) 305–6; and B. Vandenhoff, in *TRev* 26 (1927) 345–46.

[12] H. Schumacher, "The Discovery of the 'Epistola Apostolorum,'" *HomPastRev* 22 (1921–22) 856–65; idem, "The 'Epistola Apostolorum' and the New Testament," *HomPastRev* 22 (1921–22) 967–75; idem, "The Christology of the 'Epistola Apostolorum,'" *HomPastRev* 22 (1921–22) 1080–87, 1303–12; idem, "The 'Epistola Apostolorum' and the 'Descensus ad Inferos,'" *HomPastRev* 23 (1922–23) 13–21, 121–28; Alfredo M. Vitti, "De 'Epistula Apostolorum' apocrypha," *VD* 3 (1923) 367–73 and *VD* 4 (1924) 210–18; T. Schneider, "Das prophetische 'Agraphon' der Epistola apostolorum," *ZNW* 24 (1925) 151–54; Jakob Delazer, "Disquisitio in argumentum Epistolae apostolorum," *Anton* 3 (1928) 369–406; and idem, "De tempore compositionis Epistolae apostolorum," *Anton* 4 (1929) 257–92, 387–430.

[13] See Arthur Darby Nock, "The Apocryphal Gospels," *JTS* n.s. 11 (1960) 63; and Philipp Vielhauer, *Geschichte der urchristlichen Literatur* (Berlin: De Gruyter, 1975) 407.

It was more than thirty years before the next major examination of the *Epistula* appeared.[14] In 1962, under the direction of Jean Daniélou at the Institut catholique de Paris, Pedro Vanovermeire completed a dissertation, as yet unpublished, entitled "Livre que Jésus-Christ a révélé à ses disciples." The goal of Vanovermeire's work was intimated in the sub-title: "A study of the apocryphon known as the 'Epistula Apostolorum,' first witness to the literary influence of the Fourth Gospel on Christian literature of the first half of the second century." The thesis of direct literary dependence of the *Epistula* on the Gospel of John is not developed until late in Vanovermeire's study, and serves principally to support the general consensus.[15] But for the first time Vanovermeire's study raised serious questions as to the unity of the text.

Detecting what he believed to be a catechetical groundplan beneath the present text of the *Epistula*, Vanovermeire sought to show that the original writing had been expanded by the addition of chap. 2 (where the apostles are listed by name), chap. 4 (the story about Jesus and the schoolmaster), chap. 31 (the call and mission of Paul), chaps. 34–36 (an apocalypse), and chaps. 39–50a.[16] Relieved of these additions, the *Epistula* displays "all the vigor of its witness to apostolic catechesis in its evangelical section, and to Jewish-Christian theology in its apocalyptic section."[17]

A third major monograph, Manfred Hornschuh's *Studien zur Epistula Apostolorum*, appeared in 1965.[18] Though reaching very different conclu-

---

[14] In the period between 1929 and 1962 two influential articles on the *Epistula* were published: J. de Zwaan, "Date and Origin of the Epistle of the Eleven Apostles," in H. G. Wood, ed., *Amicitiae Corolla: A Volume of Essays Presented to James Rendel Harris, D.Litt., on the Occasion of His Eightieth Birthday* (London: University of London Press, 1933) 344–55 (arguing in detail for the position outlined in *NThS* 2 (1919) 281–86 [see above, n. 10]); and Léon Gry, "La date de la parousie d'après l'Epistula Apostolorum," *RB* 49 (1940) 86–97.

[15] Vanovermeire, "Livre que Jésus-Christ a révélé," 274–92. See J. H. Bernard (*The Gospel According to St. John* [2 vols.; ICC; Edinburgh: T. & T. Clark, 1928] 1. lxxvii) who states: "The Fourth Gospel was very familiar to the author of this imaginative work"; and W. von Loewenich (*Das Johannes-Verständnis im zweiten Jahrhundert* [Gießen: Töpelmann, 1932] 57–59) who gives numerous examples of alleged dependence. The question of the *Epistula*'s use of John was again raised in Melvyn Raymond Hillmer, "The Gospel of John in the Second Century" (Th.D. Diss., Harvard University, 1966) 28–50. He similarly concluded that the *Epistula* "has used the Gospel of John and has used it extensively" (p. 50).

[16] Vanovermeire, "Livre que Jésus-Christ a révélé," 161–63. According to Vanovermeire, *Ep. apost.* 2 is to be rejected because chap. 1 speaks not of individuals but of the "council of the apostles"; *Ep. apost.* 4 is an interpolation from the *Infancy Gospel of Thomas*; *Ep. apost.* 31 interrupts the natural connection between chaps. 30 and 32; *Ep. apost.* 34–36 have been added from the "Testament of our Lord in Galilee"; and *Ep. apost.* 39–50a merely repeat earlier material.

[17] Ibid., 163.

[18] Hornschuh, *Studien zur Epistula Apostolorum* (PTS 5; Berlin: De Gruyter, 1965). The *Studien* comprise pages 113–259 of Hornschuh's dissertation, "Die Anfänge des Christentums in Ägypten" (Rheinische Friedrich-Wilhelms-Universität, Bonn, 1959). See the reviews and

sions from those of Schmidt regarding the place (Egypt)[19] and date of composition (ca. 120), Hornschuh's special interest was in the theological influences upon the author, in the portrait of Paul within the apostolic circle, in the use of the NT, and in doctrinal issues. In favor of an early date Hornschuh claimed to find the influence of Essene thought, the citation of Jewish apocryphal writings as authoritative, the treatment of the NT gospels as not yet canonical books, an acquaintance with free-floating Synoptic tradition, an ancient credal form (in chap. 5), and the apparent lack of an ecclesiastical hierarchy.[20] Not least are Hornschuh's *Studien* of value for bringing into the discussion a wider range of comparative materials than had been accessible to Schmidt.

Characteristic of the works of Schmidt, Vanovermeire, and Hornschuh are the twin concerns, first, with the standard introductory questions of date and provenance, and second, with the theological themes of the *Epistula* against the background of well-known hellenistic Jewish and early Christian writings. The *Epistula* has been quarried for traditions and religious ideas comparable with isolable traditions from other writings. With the exception of Hornschuh's chapter on *Ep. apost.* 43 – 45 (on the parable of the wise and foolish virgins)[21] there has been virtually no attempt at *exegetical* study of substantial portions of the text. The investigation of separable traditions— sayings, quotations, credal formulae—has yet to be complemented with an investigation of the author's *compositional method* and *editorial theology*. For this reason the character of the work, of its author, and especially of its community, is little known.

notices by Walter J. Burghardt, in *TS* 26 (1965) 443 – 44; M. van Esbroeck, in *AnBoll* 83 (1965) 417 – 18; Otto Betz, *ThLz* 91 (1966) 516 – 18; Jean Daniélou, in *RechSR* 54 (1966) 283 – 85; G. C. Stead, in *JTS* n. s. 17 (1966) 171 – 73; Pedro Vanovermeire, in *RHE* 61 (1966) 539 – 41; and Gilles Quispel, in *VC* 22 (1968) 61 – 63.

[19] Hornschuh, *Studien*, 103 – 15. Hornschuh (pp. 99 – 101) conveniently summarizes Schmidt's arguments for Asia Minor: (1) the association of Cerinthus with Asia Minor; (2) the *Epistula*'s preference for the gospel of Matthew; (3) the priority given to the 'Ephesian' apostle John in *Ep. apost.* 2; and (4) the Quartodeciman observance of Easter. Against these Hornschuh (pp. 103 – 15) sets the following: (1) the surviving versions (Coptic, Ethiopic, Latin) put the *Epistula* in the "Roman-Egyptian circle"; (2) the Quartodeciman argument is not decisive, especially if the *Epistula* is of an early date; (3) there are parallels between *Ep. apost.* 21 and later Egyptian liturgy; (4) mention of Martha as one of the women at the tomb is found elsewhere only in Egypt and Rome, e.g., in an amulet and in Hippolytus *In Canticum canticorum*; (5) evidence in the *Epistula* of Western readings of the NT (against Burnett Hillman Streeter, *The Four Gospels: A Study of Origins* [London: Macmillan, 1924] 70 – 71, who interprets the Western readings as supporting an Ephesian origin); (6) the form of the credal statement in *Ep. apost.* 5; (7) the "typically Egyptian" religious milieu; (8) the literary form of the *Epistula*; and (9) the author's preference for the Gospel of John.

[20] Hornschuh, *Studien*, 116.

[21] Ibid., 21 – 29; first published, as "Das Gleichnis von den zehn Jungfrauen in der Epistula Apostolorum," in *ZKG* 73 (1962) 1 – 8.

At least two obstacles have stood in the way of an exegetical approach to the *Epistula*. The first is the nature and condition of the extant witnesses. The original Greek is lost. The Coptic (Achmimic) is preserved in a single, mutilated fourth- or fifth-century manuscript in the Institut Français d'Archéologie Orientale, Cairo;[22] it lacks all or most of chaps. 1 – 6, 21 – 22, 31 – 38, and 49 – 51. Fortunately the pages are numbered, and it has therefore been possible to determine that its length matched that of the Ethiopic.[23] Schmidt's printed text depends on much reconstruction, most of which was completed before he learned of the Ethiopic version.

In Ethiopic the *Epistula* has been transmitted as an appendix to the *Maṣhafa Kidān*. ("Book of the Covenant"), which is an expansion (best known in its Syriac version, the *Testamentum Domini*) of the *Apostolic Tradition* of Hippolytus. For his *editio princeps* of the Ethiopic, Guerrier used five manuscripts, three in Paris[24] and two in London.[25] To this evidence Isaak Wajnberg, Schmidt's colleague, added readings from an uncatalogued Stuttgart manuscript.[26] In 1973 Ernst Hammerschmidt catalogued a manuscript in the monastery on Lake Ṭana in Ethiopia.[27] Since 1976 six additional manuscripts have become accessible through the Ethiopian Manuscript Microfilm Library, Addis Ababa, and the Hill Monastic Manuscript Library, St. John's University, Minnesota.[28] It is now possible to see within the Ethiopic manuscript tradition two distinct groups of witnesses,

[22] For a description of the manuscript, see Schmidt, *Gespräche Jesu*, 4 – 6. The present director of the I. F. A. O., Dr. Paule Posener-Krieger, to whom I am grateful for a microfilm copy, has informed me that the papyrus has suffered considerable wear since Schmidt studied it (private letter, 10. 8. 1983).

[23] The evidence is graphically presented in Vanovermeire, "Livre que Jésus-Christ a révélé," 149 – 51.

[24] Antoine d'Abbadie, *Catalogue raisonné de manuscrits éthiopiens* (Paris: L'Imprimerie impériale, 1859) no. 51 (pp. 60 – 63); no. 90 (pp. 100 – 101); and no. 199 (pp. 199 – 201). To these manuscripts Guerrier assigned the sigla A, B, and C respectively.

[25] William Wright, *Catalogue of the Ethiopic Manuscripts in the British Museum Acquired Since the Year 1847* (London: Longmans, 1877) no. 361 = Br. Mus. Or. 793 (pp. 270 – 75); and no. 362 = Br. Mus. Or. 795 (pp. 275 – 77). Guerrier assigned the siglum L to the first of these; I shall identify the second with the letter K.

[26] Stuttgart Or. fol. 49, assigned the siglum S by Wajnberg. This manuscript of the *Kidān* was used by August Dillmann in his *Lexicon linguae aethiopicae* (1865; reprinted Osnabrück: Biblio Verlag, 1970); Dillmann briefly described the contents of the manuscript on p. viii.

[27] Hammerschmidt, *Äethiopische Handschriften vom Ṭānāsee I* (Verzeichnis der orientalischen Handschriften in Deutschland 20/1; Wiesbaden: Steiner, 1973) no. 35 (pp. 163 – 67). This manuscript will be referred to as MS T.

[28] William F. Macomber and Getatchew Haile, *A Catalogue of Ethiopian Manuscripts Microfilmed for the Ethiopian Manuscript Microfilm Library, Addis Ababa, and for the Hill Monastic Manuscript Library, Collegeville, Minnesota* (8 vols.; Collegeville, MN; St. John's University, 1976–) project nos. 370; 1945; 2358; 6025; 7021; and 7204. I have assigned to these manuscripts the sigla M, N, O, P, Q, and R respectively.

which will be referred to as families 1 and 2. Fam. 1 (MSS ABCKNOT) is generally superior to fam. 2 (MSS LMPQRSV; MSS QR often follow fam. 1). The strongest representative of fam. 2 is MS L, which Guerrier chose, on orthographic grounds, as the base for his edition.[29] Although there remain frequent minor disagreements between the Coptic and Ethiopic versions, at many places the translation can be revised, revealing much that was previously lost. As for the fifth- or sixth-century Latin fragment, reprinted by Schmidt in his edition of the *Epistula*,[30] it is of value chiefly because it bears witness to the longer, Ethiopic reading in *Ep. apost.* 17.5–8.

Thus the nature of the manuscript evidence may be cited as one impediment to exegesis. The second is the genre of the writing and the expectations deriving from it. Whether the *Epistula* is properly to be classified as a "letter," a "gospel," a "revelatory dialogue," or an "apocalypse,"[31] its widely presumed relationship both to its sources and to contemporary writings has suggested that it is but a rehash of well-known texts and traditions. This impression is encouraged by the many NT references supplied with the standard English translation of the *Epistula*.[32]

To be sure, literary sources are involved, but examination of their use does not lead to the conclusion that the author's community recognized an authoritative canon of NT scripture. In ways to be explored below, the same freedom in handling traditional materials is evident in the *Epistula* as even in the NT gospels; only in the *Epistula* the frame of reference is more overtly polemical and, indeed, ecclesiastical. For the time being the way remained open, through the literary dialogue, to adapt, to revise, even to contradict received formulations in the name of the risen Lord. With the *Epistula* it is therefore still possible to speak of development, here characterized specifically as traditions in dialogue with a second-century community. Precisely the critical questions of tradition and composition raised by the Gospel of John are met, in starker form, in the *Epistula apostolorum*.

The question of the *Epistula*'s date and provenance will not be reopened in this study. Great uncertainty accompanies hypotheses regarding the chronology and geography of every anonymous or pseudonymous early Christian writing, even those for which there is a massive history of interpretation.[33] I

---

[29] Guerrier departed from MS L in only twenty-three readings.

[30] Schmidt, *Gespräche Jesu*, 21–22.

[31] These possibilities are considered in Vielhauer, *Geschichte*, 685–86; see also Julian Hills, "The *Epistula Apostolorum* and the Genre 'Apocalypse,'" SBLASP 25 (1986) 581–95.

[32] The most accessible ET is presently Richard E. Taylor's translation of Hugo Duensing's German, in *NTApoc* 1. 191–227; this ET is reprinted in Ron Cameron, ed., *The Other Gospels: Non-Canonical Gospel Texts* (Philadelphia: Westminster, 1982) 133–62.

[33] See, e.g., Werner Georg Kümmel, *Introduction to the New Testament* (rev. ed.; Nashville: Abingdon, 1975) on Mark (p. 98); on Matthew (p. 119); and on Luke: "We can say for certainty only that Lk was written outside Palestine" (p. 151). Uncertainty is much greater in relation to

shall therefore presuppose only the present consensus, that the *Epistula* was composed in the mid-second century in Asia Minor, in Egypt, or in Syria. My intention is to show that the author of the *Epistula* has reshaped and transmitted traditions in the name of the risen Christ to specific communal ends. It is toward the identification of these communal concerns via their theological expression that this study is primarily directed. Philological, form-critical, and other exegetical perspectives will be brought to bear on specific passages in the text, and as far as possible through them on the situation which stands behind the *Epistula* as a compositional unity.

In Chapter One I shall argue that the *Epistula* is a dialogue both in its conception and in its intended function. In Chapters Two through Six I shall attempt to show how the author's distinctive theology, deriving from the unique historical circumstances of the *Epistula*'s community, has fashioned a catalogue of traditional materials into a literary whole unified by its dialogue form.

---

the second- and third-century apocryphal literature, e.g., the majority of the Nag Hammadi tractates.

1

The Epistula Apostolorum: Dialogue and Gospel

The purpose of this chapter is to explore the structure of the dialogue in *Ep. apost.* 13–51. As a preface to this endeavor the opening chapters will be examined briefly, because from them the "Epistle of the Apostles" derives its modern title,[1] and from them some preliminary clues may be gathered as to the function of the dialogue. These clues are not completely self-evident since *Ep. apost.* 1–12 presents the reader with an astonishing array of materials: an epistle (1–2), a hymn (3), a miracle catena (or "list," in 4–5), an exhortation (6–8), and an account of the appearance of the risen Lord to three women and to the disciples (9–12).

According to Hugo Duensing's translation, the *Epistula* begins as follows (--, 48/1):

> What Jesus Christ revealed to his disciples as a letter, and how Jesus Christ revealed the letter of the council of the apostles, the disciples of Jesus Christ, to the Catholics.[2]

[1] Duensing (*NTApoc*, 1. 191) states that "the title is not transmitted but can be inferred."

[2] Unless otherwise noted, quotations in English are from the standard translation of Hugo Duensing's German, in Edgar Hennecke and Wilhelm Schneemelcher, eds.; R. McL. Wilson, trans. ed., *New Testament Apocrypha* (2 vols.; Philadelphia: Westminster, 1963–65) 1. 191–227. Quotations from the Coptic text are by codex page (in Roman numerals) and line number in Carl Schmidt, *Gespräche Jesu mit seinen Jüngern nach der Auferstehung* (TU 43; Leipzig: Hinrichs, 1919) 1*–26*. Quotations from the Ethiopic text are by page and line number in Louis Guerrier and Sylvain Grébaut, eds. and trans., "Le testament en Galilée de Notre-Seigneur Jésus-Christ," PO 9 (1913) 141–236 (fascicle pp. 1–96); where the text can be improved, the location in Guerrier is still given. To the chapter numbers in Hennecke-Schneemelcher verse numbers have been added; with few exceptions, the length of a verse coin-

This translation specifies that we have to do with a letter; in fact, with a "revealed letter." Thus Hornschuh states that "the Epistula Apostolorum is a letter," and that it appeals to the "heavenly letter" motif frequent in revelatory literature.[3] Now it is true that the Latin fragment bears the superscription "Epistula," but this in itself is insufficient warrant for the translation of the Ethiopic word *maṣḥaf* as "letter." Both Guerrier[4] and Wajnberg[5] translated the word "book," and of its many meanings this is the most common.[6] However, the simple substitution of "book" for "letter" does not fully explain *Ep. apost.* 1.1.

Vanovermeire has made the plausible suggestion that *Ep. apost.* 1.1 preserves both the first line of the work and its superscription. He translates the first phrase: "The Book which Jesus Christ revealed to his disciples," and posits as the original Greek: Ἀποκάλυψις Ἰησοῦ Χριστοῦ ἣν ἔδωκεν τοῖς ἀποστόλοις.[7] Though this specific translation and its retroversion are debatable, the principle on which they are based is sound: the first phrase of the *Epistula* is also its title as, for example, in the *Gospel of Truth* (NHC 1, 3) and the *Gospel of the Egyptians* (NHC 3, 2). The obtrusive "and" which follows in Duensing's translation can be left untranslated (as often in Ethiopic);[8] the adverb "how" (*za-kama*) can be understood as the equivalent of a relative pronoun, "what";[9] and finally, as Vanovermeire suggests, the first phrase in the Ethiopic, *za-kašata*, could well stand for the Greek

---

cides with that of a full sentence. Thus citations given in full include (1) chapter and verse, (2) Coptic codex page and line, and (3) Ethiopic page and line numbers; e.g., *Ep. apost.* 16.2 (IX 3, 59/4). Where the Coptic is defective, the reference notes this as follows: *Ep. apost.* 19.3 (--, 61/7). In such cases it is not to be assumed that the Ethiopic reading is a later addition to the text.

[3] *Studien*, 4–5 and n. 7, where examples are cited in *Acts Thom.* 110.40–54 and in *Gos. Truth* (NHC 1, 3) 19.34–20.1.

[4] "Le testament," 48.

[5] In Schmidt, *Gespräche Jesu*, 25.

[6] Dillmann, *Lexicon, s.v. ṣaḥafa* (1268). The word can mean "letter," as it does, e.g., in Isa 39:1; Esth 3:13; and 2 Pet 3:16. But for "letter" Ethiopic more often has *malʾekt*, e.g., in the titles of all the NT Epistles. Unless otherwise noted, the Ethiopic NT cited is *Wangēl Qeddus za-ʾEgziʾena wa-Madxānina ʾIyasus Kerestos* (London: British and Foreign Bible Society, 1979). On the shortcomings of this edition and its predecessors see Bruce M. Metzger, *The Early Versions of the New Testament* (Oxford: Clarendon, 1977) 229–32.

[7] Vanovermeire, "Livre que Jésus-Christ a révélé," 112; he compares Rev 1:1.

[8] See, e.g., the opening sentence in the Ethiopic version of *4 Baruch* (reprinted from August Dillmann's *Chrestomathia* in Thomas O. Lambdin, *Introduction to Classical Ethiopic (Geʿez)* [HSM 24; Chico, CA: Scholars Press, 1978] 276): *wa-kona* "(And) it happened . . ." (see the ET of the Greek in *OTP* 2. 418).

[9] This can be shown from the *Epistula* itself. In 30.2 (XXVI 8, 72/4) the Coptic has: "<O Lord,> who will believe us . . . while we . . . tell the powers and the signs *that* <you> have done"; for the Coptic relative pronoun (ⲉⲧ-, "that, which") the Ethiopic has *za-kama*; similarly, in 30.3 (XXVI 9, 72/6) the Coptic has: "*what* he has done through me," which = Ethiopic *za-kama gabra beya*.

ἀποκάλυψις (revelation).[10] Hence *Ep. apost.* 1.1 is best treated as title and incipit, a summary—perhaps by a later hand—of the writing as a whole:

> The Book of the Revelation of Jesus Christ to his Disciples: The Book of what Jesus Christ revealed through the council of the apostles, the disciples of Jesus Christ, for all people.[11]

As soon as the second person plural begins to be used genuine epistolary language appears. Two instances are of special note. In *Ep. apost.* 1.4−5 (--, 48/6) Duensing translates:

> As we have heard (it), kept (it), and have written (it) for the whole world, so we entrust (it) to you, our sons and daughters, in joy and in the name of God the Father, the ruler of the world, and in Jesus Christ. May grace increase upon you.

This translation reveals a significant item of epistolary vocabulary; it conceals another. The first phrase ("As ... world"), like the first verb in the second ("we entrust"), is supplied by Duensing with the pronoun "it"— referring either to the gospel (1.3) or to the entire book/letter (1.1). Since Duensing's "As" is the Ethiopic *za-kama* (as in 1.1), there is no need to supply an additional pronoun. The first phrase therefore yields the sense: "What we have heard and remembered, we have written for the whole world." This leaves "so we entrust (it) to you" with no antecedent; and this is correct, for there is no conjunction present in the text. If the reading *ᵓamāxdannākemu*,[12] adopted by Guerrier, is rejected in favor of the fam. 1 reading *ᵓammāxnākemu*,[13] *Ep. apost.* 1.5 reads as follows: "We greet you, our sons and daughters, in the name of God, the ruler of the entire world, and in Jesus Christ. May grace abound upon you."[14]

---

[10] See Gal 1:12: δι᾽ ἀποκαλύψεως Ἰησοῦ Χριστοῦ = *ba-za-kašata lita ᵓIyasus Kerestos*.

[11] Cf. Rev 1:1−3. Duensing's "to the Catholics" (*NTApoc* 1. 191) is derived from the Ethiopic "for all" (*la-kʷellu*).

[12] From *ᵓamāhdana*, "to commend, entrust, commit" (Dillmann, *Lexicon, s.v. hadana* [139]).

[13] From *ᵓammexa*, "to greet" (Dillmann, *Lexicon, s.v. ᵓammexa* [734]). This verb translates ἀσπάζεσθαι, e.g., in Rom 16:21, 22, 23; 1 Cor 16:19, 20; Phil 4:22.

[14] The verb ἀσπάζεσθαι, "to greet," is not commonly found at the beginning of a letter. But it is attested in the prescripts of Ignatius *Magnesians*, *Trallians*, *Romans*, and *Philadelphians*; and William R. Schoedel has observed with reference to ἀσπάζεσθαι in Ignatius that "in this period it had begun to appear not only at the end but also at the beginning of letters just after the salutation" (*Ignatius of Antioch* [Hermeneia; Philadelphia: Fortress, 1985] 103). Schoedel refers to Heikki Koskenniemi, *Studien zur Idee und Phraseologie des griechischen Briefes bis 400 n. Chr.* (Annales Academia Scientiarum Fennica B 102/2; Helsinki: Suomalainen Tiedeakatemia, 1956) 149, where examples are cited from 2d−4th century papyri. What is unexpected in the *Epistula* is the position of the greeting, before chap. 2. The wording of the greeting, "May grace increase upon you," is similar to the greetings in Dan 4:1 and 6:25, and to 1 Pet 1:2; 2 Pet 1:2.

In *Ep. apost.* 7, having warned of the danger of Cerinthus and Simon and predicted their fate, the apostolic authors continue (8.1 [I 8, 53/7]):

Ethiopic	Coptic
Because of that we have not hesitated with the true testimony of our Lord and Saviour Jesus Christ.	Because of that we have not hesitated to write to you concerning the testimony of our Saviour Christ.

The Coptic verb here translated "hesitate" (ⲭⲛⲟ = Sahidic ⲭⲛⲁⲁⲩ) is the regular equivalent of the Greek ὀκνέω.[15] This verb, when followed by an infinitive, is found in contemporary Greek as "an epistolary formula."[16] In addition to a number of secular examples of the formula,[17] three passages in roughly contemporary religious writings are of special note since they show the incorporation of this epistolary convention into the preface not of a *letter* but of a theological *treatise*.

In *Corp. Herm.* 11.1 Nous addresses Hermes with the following exhortation and assurance:

> Mark well my discourse, O Hermes Trismegistus, and remember what I have said. As for me, *I shall not hesitate to declare* (εἰπεῖν οὐκ ὀκνήσω) what I am inspired to say.[18]

In the second fragment of his "Exegesis of the Sayings of the Lord," Papias of Hierapolis (*apud* Eusebius *Hist. eccl.* 3.39.3) states:

> *I shall not hesitate* (οὐκ ὀκνήσω) *to set down* (συγκατατάξαι)for you, together with the interpretations, what I have carefully learned and remembered. . . .[19]

In Irenaeus *Epideixis* 1 the author addresses his "dear Marcianus" in this epistolary fashion:

---

[15] Crum, *s.v.* ⲭⲛⲁ(ⲁ)ⲩ (776a).

[16] Moulton-Milligan, *s.v.* ὀκνέω (444b).

[17] Two uses are of special interest: "Do not hesitate to write . . ."; and "I/we have (have not) hesitated to write. . . ." Examples in Moulton-Milligan and in Henry A. Steen, "Les clichés épistolaires dans les lettres sur papyrus grecques," *Classica et Mediaevalia* 1 (1938) pp. 129 (= *P.S.I.* 621, 5); 130 (= *P.S.I.* 971, 23); and 159. Cf. also *P. Zen.* 59029, 3: ὠκνοῦμέν σοι γράφειν (C. C. Edgar, ed., *Zenon Papyri: Catalogue général des antiquités égyptiennes du Musée du Caire* [5 vols.; Cairo: Service des antiquités de l'Égypte, 1925 – 40] 1. 50 – 51).

[18] Greek text and French translation in A. D. Nock and A.-J. Festugière, *Corpus Hermeticum* (4 vols.; Collection des universités de France; Paris: Les Belles Lettres, 1945 – 54) 1. 147.

[19] Greek text in F. X. Funk and Karl Bihlmeyer, *Die apostolischen Väter* (SAQ 2/1/1; 3d ed.; rev. Wilhelm Schneemelcher; Tübingen: Mohr-Siebeck, 1970) 134.

Would it were possible for us to be always together. . . . As it is, since we are at the present time distant in body from each other, *we have not delayed*, so far as may be, *to commune with you a little in writing*, and to set forth in brief the preaching of the truth, to confirm your faith.[20]

Thus while the *Epistula*'s deference to the letter form is more than superficial, precisely this form is imitated in the prologues to contemporary treatises.[21] As is clear from these examples, an epistolary prologue explicitly or implicitly establishes, first, a collegial relationship between author and reader, and, second, the reader's need of accurate testimony to the truth.

In the *Epistula* this need is stated as a matter of urgency. The "false apostles" Simon and Cerinthus are said to have "come to go through the world" (cf. Job 1:7) bearing death and contamination (*Ep. apost.* 1.1; 7.1–3). Since both of these figures flourished before the end of the first century this warning is unlikely to indicate the actual situation to which the *Epistula* is responding. As Gustave Bardy remarked, Simon and Cerinthus were "already legendary types";[22] and there is little if anything in the text that can be shown specifically to oppose the heresy associated with either or both of them.[23] Indeed, one searches in vain for unambiguous guidance as to the purpose the *Epistula* was designed to serve. In the absence of a single thematic thread and accompanying editorial viewpoint, the reader is left with a series of brief expositions on doctrinal, historical, and ethical topics, held together by the frail glue of the dialogue form.

[20] English translation (from the Armenian) in Joseph P. Smith, *St. Irenaeus: Proof of the Apostolic Preaching* (ACW 16; London: Longmans, Green, 1952) 47.

[21] The comparative net may be cast wider. A number of the Nag Hammadi writings, for example the *Treatise on the Resurrection* (NHC 1, 4), the *Apocryphon of John* (NHC 2, 1), the *Hypostasis of the Archons* (NHC 2, 4), and esp. the *Letter of Peter to Philip* (NHC 8, 2), have epistolary frames or prefaces.

[22] Review of Schmidt, *Gespräche Jesu*, in *RB* 30 (1921) 118. Similarly Eduard Schwartz suggested that Noetus was for Hippolytus "not much more than a name" (quoted in Robert Butterworth, *Hippolytus of Rome: Contra Noetum* [Heythrop Monographs 2; London: Heythrop College, 1977] 110).

[23] A case can be made that the antidocetic teaching in the *Epistula* and the description of the Lord's descent through the heavens (*Ep. apost.* 13) combat the Simonian myth. See Robert M. Grant, *Gnosticism* (New York: Harper, 1961) 28; and Hans Jonas, *The Gnostic Religion* (2d ed.; Boston: Beacon, 1958) 103–11. Raymond E. Brown (*The Johannine Epistles* [AB 30; Garden City, NY: Doubleday, 1982] 766) rightly notes the significance of the pairing of Simon and Cerinthus: "one later strain of opinion about Cerinthus makes him a gnostic; and for the church fathers Simon Magus was the father of gnosticism."

The *Epistula* and the Dialogue Genre

Dialogue, Sayings Traditions, and Exegesis

It was the thesis of Manfred Hornschuh that the writer of the *Epistula* deliberately attacked the Gnostic revelation dialogues with an orthodox work of the same genre.[24] This position has received renewed support from Helmut Koester[25] and from Ron Cameron, and has proved a good working hypothesis.[26] But in a conscious imitation of a genre, the reader might legitimately expect an orderly presentation of topics and instructions, and Koester, following Schmidt, has suggested that an ordering principle is to be found in the creed.[27] Despite the merits of this proposal, in the *Epistula* the lack of internal cohesion is the more remarkable. Material central to the author's credal and antidocetic teaching is routinely interrupted by any of a number of recurring themes, for example, by the commission to preach and the keeping of the commandments, and by much discussion of the usefulness of dialogue.

Alongside this lack of thematic discipline is the consistency which the *Epistula* exhibits with regard to its dialogue form. So that the best exegetical use may be made of this consistency, the *Epistula* must be placed among contemporary dialogues. Pheme Perkins observes that

> Unlike the lively drama of the Platonic dialogue or the more pedantic style of the philosophic dialogue employed by a Cicero or Augustine, the Gnostic dialogue does not aim at an exchange of ideas and an examination of philosophical positions.[28]

She therefore states that "the philosophic dialogue tradition can hardly have been a source for Gnostic composition."[29] Alternative influences may be Jewish apocalypses, Hermetic writings,[30] or the *erotapokriseis* ("questions and answers") dialogues.[31] Perkins concludes that the Gnostic type of dialogue, exemplified by such writings as the *Apocryphon of John* (NHC 2, 1), the *Gospel of Mary* (BG 8502, 1), the *Apocalypse of Paul* (NHC 5, 2), the *First Apocalypse of James* (NHC 5, 3), the *Sophia of Jesus Christ* (NHC 3, 4;

---

[24] Hornschuh, *Studien*, 92–97.

[25] *Introduction to the New Testament* (2 vols.; Philadelphia: Fortress, 1982) 2. 237.

[26] *Other Gospels*, 131–32.

[27] "One Jesus and Four Primitive Gospels" (in idem and James M. Robinson, *Trajectories Through Early Christianity* (Philadelphia: Fortress, 1971) 203.

[28] Perkins, *The Gnostic Dialogue: The Early Church and the Crisis of Gnosticism* (Theological Inquiries; New York/Ramsey/Toronto: Paulist, 1980) 19.

[29] Ibid.

[30] See Kurt Rudolph, "Der gnostische 'Dialog' als literarisches Genus," in Peter Nagel, ed., *Probleme der koptischen Literatur* (Wissenschaftliche Beiträge der Martin-Luther-Universität, Halle-Wittenberg, 1968/1 [K2]) 85–107.

[31] See Heinrich Dörrie and Hermann Dörries, "Erotapokriseis," *RAC* 6 (1966) 342–70.

BG 8502, 3), the *Pistis Sophia*, and the *Books of Jeu*, "is widespread enough and stable enough in its characteristics to be recognized as an independent literary genre."[32]

Helmut Koester has proposed a classification of dialogue types according to the traditional materials contained in them.[33] He identifies three groups among the dialogues: (1) those in which the dialogue form is a secondary literary product; (2) those in which the dialogue functions as instruction and/or a liturgy of initiation; and (3) those whose function is the exposition of sayings of Jesus. Koester places the *Epistula*, together with the *Sophia of Jesus Christ* and the *First Apocalypse of James*, in the first group.[34]

This evaluation has to do primarily with the dialogues' access to and use of sayings traditions. It does not deny the presence of traditional materials in type-1 dialogues, and therefore the possibility of detecting editorial work even in secondary dialogues is not excluded. More importantly, the dialogues' narrative and rhetorical frameworks remain the common denominator among dialogues of all types, and it is here that a fresh look at the *Epistula* as a dialogue must begin.

As will be seen in detail shortly, the author of the *Epistula* has shown unusual care in observing certain formalities in both narrative and discourse. The writing is indebted to many of the literary conventions of the day, to a far greater extent than the repeated "We said" and "he said" alone would indicate. Identification of key dialogical features will permit the isolation of some major editorial concerns; only then may attention be focused profitably upon the traditional materials within the speeches. Thus, three literary levels are to be distinguished in *Ep. apost.* 13–51:

1) the narrative framework and literary conventions of the dialogue genre;
2) theological concerns editorially linked to the conventions of the dialogue; and
3) traditional materials and their redaction.

The task of the rest of this chapter is to explore levels 1 and 2. This approach, rather than the immediate isolation of discrete traditions, will furnish clues as to why and how those traditions were collected and incorporated into a whole unified by its literary superstructure. The present task includes an overview of some of the dominant literary forms and an assess-

---

[32] Perkins, *Gnostic Dialogue*, 26. Rudolph ("Der gnostisches 'Dialog,'" 103–6) includes a wider circle of dialogues in the discussion, including the *Dialogue* of Justin and Bardesanes *Dialogue of Destiny* (or *Book of the Laws of the Countries*).

[33] Koester, "Dialog und Spruchüberlieferung in den gnostischen Texten von Nag Hammadi," *EvTh* 39 (1979) 532–56.

[34] Ibid., 534–50.

ment of the nature of the authority to which the author explicitly and implicitly appeals. The goal of the following discussion, therefore, is to lay the groundwork for the exegesis of smaller units.

The Narrative Introductions to the Speeches

Beginning in *Ep. apost.* 13, the narrative structure around the dialogue is maintained with considerable regularity. The Lord speaks sixty times, the disciples fifty-seven. With only minor variations (the addition of conjunctions and adverbs) the formulas of introduction are (1) "He [± answered and] said to us," and (2) "We said to him." Not once in the narrative is the verb "to ask" employed, although there are inevitable similarities between the *Epistula* and the classical *erotapokriseis*.[35] This simple introductory pattern has analogues in early sayings collections, such as the *Gospel of Thomas*[36] and the *Apocryphon of James*; elsewhere in the dialogue literature such regularity is the exception. In the *Book of Thomas the Contender*, for example, the ten speeches of Thomas share nine different introductions; the fifteen speeches of Jesus share seven introductions.[37] The *Dialogue of the Savior* is probably nearest to the *Epistula* among Christian writings. The introduction "the Lord said" appears with twenty-nine of the forty-six speeches of the Lord, and "[a named disciple] said" with thirty-one of the forty-nine speeches of the disciples. Even closer to the *Epistula* are a Jewish apocalypse and a later Christian dialogue. In *2 Baruch* the fourteen speeches of God share only three, almost identical, introductions while the twelve speeches of Baruch are always prefaced with the introduction, "and I answered and said." In Bardesanes *Dialogue of Destiny* the author speaks twelve times with Avida, each time quoted with the simple introduction "Bardesanes said [± to him]"'; all ten of Avida's speeches have "Avida said [± to him]."[38]

At this most superficial level, therefore, we are dealing with an editorial

---

[35] The flexibility of the *erotapokriseis* form is well illustrated in John T. Fitzgerald and L. Michael White, *The Tabula of Cebes* (SBLTT 24; Chico, CA: Scholars Press, 1983) 11–16.

[36] James M. Robinson ("LOGOI SOPHON: On the Gattung of Q," in idem and Koester, *Trajectories*, 91) compares the introductions in the *Gospel of Thomas* and in Mark 4:1–34, finding the "rather set quotation formula" to be characteristic of sayings collections. Bertil Gärtner (*The Theology of the Gospel according to Thomas* [New York: Harper, 1961] 24) rightly observes, however, that in the *Epistula*, inasmuch as "the disciples ask doctrinal questions, and Jesus answers them . . . the dialogue is entirely predominant."

[37] Cf. the *Apocryphon of James*, where the disciples have eight speeches, seven introductions; the Lord, eleven and seven. In the *Apocryphon of John* John has ten speeches which share four introductions; the Lord, twelve and eight. In the *Sophia of Jesus Christ* the disciples have thirteen and seven; the Savior, fifteen and eight.

[38] Syriac text and ET in H. J. W. Drijvers, ed., *The Book of the Laws of Countries. Dialogue on Fate of Bardaiṣan of Edessa.* (Assen: Van Gorcum, 1965).

option available to the authors of dialogues. At this compositional level the *Epistula* has some close companions among dialogues of all classes. Yet to be accounted for, however, are the adverbs which are often found with the *Epistula*'s introductions. Here the relationship between the two versions becomes problematical, for the Coptic and Ethiopic adverbs do not always correspond to their counterparts in the other recension.[39] Since it is impossible to be certain which Greek or Coptic adverbs may be reflected when the Ethiopic text stands alone, any such speculation might appear hazardous. But a marked consistency in the Coptic text suggests that the choice of the introductions was not made indiscriminately.[40]

First, in all fourteen cases where the Coptic text has ⲧⲟⲧⲉ (then) in an introduction,[41] it is before a speech of the Lord.[42] The presence of this adverb is not indicative of a particular generic heritage. The *Book of Thomas the Contender*, for instance, has ⲧⲟⲧⲉ twice before speeches of the Lord (139.31; 143.8), not at all before speeches of the disciples; the same is true of the *Apocryphon of John* (27.24, 33). But in the *Dialogue of the Savior* the speeches of both the Lord (136.5) and the disciples (137.11) have ⲧⲟⲧⲉ. It is absent from the introductions in the *Apocryphon of James*, the *First Apocalypse of James*, and *Hermas*. In the *Sophia of Jesus Christ* only the apostles' speeches are prefaced with ⲧⲟⲧⲉ (103.22; 108.16; 112.19). In the *Epistula*, therefore, we have to do with a stylistic choice whereby the author has distinguished the speeches of the Lord from those of the disciples. The reason is not clear; possibly it is to emphasize the Lord's initiative.

---

[39] This is attributable in the main not to scribal interference with the text but to the nature of the languages. Useful descriptions of Coptic and Ethiopic as translation languages can be found in J. Martin Plumley, "Limitations of Coptic (Sahidic) in Representing Greek," and Josef Hofmann, "Limitations of Ethiopic in Representing Greek," in Metzger, *Early Versions* , 141–52 and 240–56, respectively.

[40] Conscious choice of one introduction over another has recently been observed in the parables of *1 Enoch*. David Winston Suter (*Tradition and Composition in the Parables of Enoch* [SBLDS 47; Missoula, MT: Scholars Press, 1979] 137) has found that "the form used seems to be dictated by the length of the question or answer that follows."

[41] 12.3 (XIV 15; the Lord's preface to the dialogue); 14.3 (VII 1); 14.5 (VII 5); 17.4 (X 3); 25.2 (XIX 2); 25.6 (XIX 13); 25.8 (XX 1, reconstruction); 28.4 (XXIII 6); 30.3 (XXVI 7); 39.4 (XXVIII 8); 41.3 (XXXI 11); 42.9 (XXXIV 2); 43.14 (XXXVI 7, reconstr.); 45.2 (XXXVII 9).

[42] This statement requires only minor modification if we look beyond the extant Coptic. In *Ep. apost.* 45.7 (XXXVIII 5) Schmidt reconstructs [ⲧⲟⲧⲉ ⲡⲁ]ⲭⲉⲛ ⲛⲉϥ ⲝ ⲉ ("Then we said to him"). In the Ethiopic of 17.5 (59/12) and 21.6 (65/11), where the Coptic is lacking, speeches of the disciples are introduced with *wa-ʾemze* (then). This is especially difficult to explain since of the fourteen ⲧⲟⲧⲉ-introductions in the Coptic only one (25.6 [XIX 13, 68/6]) is strictly reproduced in the Ethiopic; the other thirteen are all found as *wa-* (and). Greek τότε is frequently not mirrored in the Ethiopic NT, e.g., in Matt 9:37; 22:21. Further evidence is found in *1 Enoch*, a work perhaps translated into Ethiopic directly from Greek. In the surviving Greek fragments, τότε before verbs of speaking in the present or aorist is variously expressed (e.g., by *ʾamēhā*, *weʾeta gizē*, *wa-*), but never with *wa-ʾemze*.

There is a second adverb that augments the simple introductory formula: ⲡⲁⲗⲓⲛ (again), found six times in the extant Coptic. Here too the word's use is restricted; it is found only before speeches of the disciples.[43] In other dialogues the use of ⲡⲁⲗⲓⲛ or its equivalent offers almost no comparative data. The single introductory ⲡⲁⲗⲓⲛ in the *Book of Thomas the Contender* is before a speech of the Savior (140.8); in the *Sophia of Jesus Christ* it is used before speeches of the Lord (97.24) and of the disciples (106.9); it is absent from introductions in the *Dialogue of the Savior*, the *Apocryphon of James*, and the *Apocryphon of John*. What is discovered in the *Epistula*, therefore, is a second stylistic consistency.

A third preliminary observation concerns the use of the verb ⲟⲩⲱϣⲃⲉ (to answer, reply). Occurring sixteen times in the extant Coptic, and always with the verb "to say," it is with one exception found only before speeches of the Lord;[44] the exception is the first reply of the disciples, in *Ep. apost.* 14.2 (where, however, the Ethiopic has only "We said").[45] Again, other dialogues offer no comparable date. This, then, is a third literary discipline of the author's choosing.

The Narrative Asides

As striking as the consistency with which the speeches are introduced is the scarcity of interpretive or circumstantial narrative. I shall refer to the few narrative comments as "asides" by analogy with stage drama, in which an actor addresses the audience "aside" from the main action.[46] The first aside is at the start of the dialogue: "What he revealed is this that he said" (13.1). Thereafter the dialogue pauses briefly five times when it is reported: "When/After he had said this [to us] . . ." (*Ep. apost.* 20.1; 22.1; 25.4; 40.5; 51.1). It is tempting to see in this phrase an attempt to mark the end of sections within the writing. There is an obvious analogy in the recurring phrase

[43] 19.16 (XII 1); 23.1 (XVII 2); 25.1 (XVIII 14); 29.5 (XXIV 12); 29.7 (XXV 7); 40.3 (XXX 13). The number of occurrences rises to eleven when the evidence from the Ethiopic text is included where the Coptic is lacking. For four of the six Coptic uses of ⲡⲁⲗⲓⲛ , the Ethiopic has "and." Once (25.5 [XIX 11, 68/5]) the Ethiopic has "again" (except in MSS CNO) where the Coptic lacks it. In any case, ⲡⲁⲗⲓⲛ is exclusively the disciples' word.

[44] 14.2 (VII 1); 14.5 (VII 5); 16.3 (IX 4); 20.3 (XIV 3); 25.2 (XIX 2); 29.6 (XXV 1); 30.3 (XXVI 7); 39.2 (XXVIII 3); 41.1 (XXXI 7); 41.3 (XXXI 11); 41.6 (XXXII 4); 42.9 (XXXIV 3); 43.12 (XXXVI 3); 45.2 (XXXVII 10); 46.3 (XXXIX 2).

[45] Seven further instances of "He answered" are found in the Ethiopic where the Coptic is lacking; there is only one exception, in *Ep. apost.* 21.8 (--, 66/2). In 28.3 (XXIII 1) Schmidt reconstructs ⲁⲛⲁⲛ [ⲁⲛⲟⲩⲱϣⲃⲉ ⲡⲁⲭⲉⲛ] ⲛⲉϥ ("We answered and said to him"). Of the sixteen certain uses in the Coptic text, the Ethiopic exactly corresponds only eight times; but twice it has the phrase against the Coptic (30.1 [72/1]; 42.2 [84/6, in fam. 2 MSS only]), both correctly before speeches of the Lord.

[46] The term "aside" has been applied to editorial comments, e.g., in the Gospel of John; see John J. O'Rourke, "Asides in the Gospel of John," *NovT* 21 (1979) 210–19.

"And when Jesus had finished . . ." with which the five great discourses in Matthew's gospel are editorially signalled (Matt 7:28; 11:1; 13:53; 19:1; 26:1). But the summary statements in the *Epistula* do not mark a change in subject matter, and their position in the text would make for very unequal section lengths. Thus while contributing nothing to our knowledge of the work's overall structure or compositional scheme, these phrases illustrate more of the narrative fare with which the intensity of the question-and-answer exchange might temporarily be relaxed.[47]

Four further narrative asides are found, in chaps. 24, 25, 31 and 43. First, in *Ep. apost.* 24.4, after the disciples have declared their questioning to be in faith, they report to the reader: "And <he> was angry with us, saying to us. . . ." This expression is not characteristic of the writing; it is not representative of the relationship between the disciples and the Lord elsewhere, and appears here merely as a traditional *topos* of dialogue.[48]

The second interjection is of more interest. In *Ep. apost.* 25.4 one of the extended narrative introductions already referred to is augmented with this comment of the disciples (XIX 10, 68/4):

Ethiopic	Coptic
wa-ʾemza zanta yebēlana kona	ⲛ̄ⲧⲁⲣⲉϥϫⲉ ⲛⲉⲓ̈ ⲗⲉ ⲛⲉⲛ
feššuḥana ʾesma ba-yawhat tanāgarana	ⲁⲛ̄ⲡ̄[ⲉⲩ ⲫ ⲁ ⲛⲉ ϫ ⲉ] ⲁ ⲛ ⲭ ⲛ ⲟ ⲩ ϥ
And when he had said this to us,	But when he had said this to us
we were glad,	we were <glad
for he had spoken to us in gentleness.[49]	that> we asked him.[50]

This reaction to the words of the Lord has important parallels in other dialogue literature. In *Ap. Jas.* 11.6–7 the disciples remark: "And when we heard these words, we became glad."[51] A closer parallel to the Ethiopic reading is in the *Ascension of Isaiah*. The seer, having been informed of his destination by his angelic guide, remarks (*Asc. Isa.* 7.6): *wa-tafaššāḥku ʾesma ba-yawhat tanāgarani* ("And I rejoiced because he spake courteously with me").[52] This phrase is presumably a rendering of the Greek preserved in the

---

[47] The phrase "When/After he had said this [to us]" is very frequent in the *Pistis Sophia*.

[48] In *Ep. apost.* 35.1 the Lord predicts: "Then my Father will become angry because of the wickedness of men," a passage indebted to the apocalyptic writing incorporated into *Ep. apost.* 34–36. Cf. Mark 1:43; Luke 14:21; *Pap. Eg.* 2 2r,50; also 4 Ezra 10:5.

[49] Four MSS, including MS O, omit "for he had spoken to us in gentleness"; but the line length of the fragmentary Coptic text requires that something be read after "we were glad."

[50] This translation of the Coptic is according to Schmidt, *Gespräche Jesu*, 81 n. 10; cf. ibid., 12*, for Schmidt's original reconstruction. He notes that there is space at the end of the line for the "in gentleness" of the Ethiopic text.

[51] Cf. *Ap. Jas.* 12.18: "When we heard these words, we were distressed." Unless otherwise noted, quotations from Nag Hammadi codices are from James M. Robinson, ed., *The Nag Hammadi Library in English* (San Francisco: Harper & Row, 1977).

[52] Text and ET in R. H. Charles, *The Ascension of Isaiah* (London: Black, 1900) 104, 47.

Greek Legend 2.8: καὶ εὐφράνθην πάνυ ὅτι πραέως ἐλάλησέν μοι.[53] The close verbal resemblance between the Ethiopic of the *Ep. apost.* 25.4 and the *Ascension of Isaiah* suggests some literary relationship between the two writings; it is difficult to say in which direction.[54]

Finally, in *Ep. apost.* 43.5, during the discourse on the Wise and Foolish Virgins, the Lord is about to give the names of the wise ("Now hear their names") when the disciples reflect: "But we wept and were sad about those who had fallen asleep [Eth.: for those who had been shut out]." Considerations both internal and external will show this comment to be an important one.[55] For now it is enough to note that this is the only occasion within the body of the dialogue when the pattern of exchange between the speakers is disturbed. Other narrative material noted above merely creates inconsequential intervals between speeches. In 43.5 the rhythm is broken, so that the author is even obliged to repeat the introduction, "He said to us," after the interruption. Expressions of grief, however, are not uncommon in other dialogues. For example, in *Herm. Sim.* 3.1.1 Hermas, shown some sheep entangled in thorns, laments, "When I saw them . . . I grieved for them . . . ," after which the dialogue resumes.[56] The *Ap. Jas.* has two such asides, "We had been grieved at the words we have mentioned before" (11.8–10) and "When we heard these words we were distressed" (12.18). The conclusion seems warranted, therefore, that the disciples' distress is a response sanctioned by the dialogue tradition.[57] That the *Epistula* makes special use of it will be seen below to be part of the author's adaptation of the genre to specific communal ends.

---

[53] Ibid., 143. For the relation between the *Ascension of Isaiah* and the *Greek Legend* see ibid., pp. xxvii–xxviii.

[54] A third aside appears in Duensing's translation of *Ep. apost.* 31.9 (--, 73/11): "'As you have learned from the Scriptures that your fathers the prophets spoke concerning me and it is fulfilled in me'—this certain thing he said—'so you must become a leader to them.'" The phrase "this certain thing he said" looks like a scribal gloss on what is already a confused construction. New manuscript evidence suggests, however, that the confusion can be resolved as follows: "As you have learned from the scriptures that your fathers the prophets spoke about me, and through me it has been fulfilled, so too they have said this and it is likewise being fulfilled: 'Become leaders to them [Paul and the gentiles].'"

[55] See below on *Ep. apost.* 9–12 (Chapter Three) and on *Ep. apost.* 43–45 (Chapter Six).

[56] See also *Herm. Vis.* 3.1.9; *1 Enoch* 86.69; 90.3, 41. Unless otherwise noted, quotations from the apostolic fathers are from Kirsopp Lake, ed. and trans., *The Apostolic Fathers* (2 vols.; LCL; Cambridge, MA: Harvard University Press; London: Heinemann, 1912–13).

[57] Perkins (*Gnostic Dialogue*, 41) notes that grief is especially common at the beginning (before the Lord appears) and end (at the time of the Lord's departure) of dialogues. Cf. also Matt 17:23; 18:31; 26:22.

The Rhetoric of Dialogue

The narrative introductions and asides described above account for all of *Ep. apost.* 13–51 (except for the ascension scene in chap. 51) not in direct speech.[58] The economy of this narrative structure is striking, but in the speeches it is more than compensated for by the presence of frequent, and often protracted, remarks and exchanges about the dialogue itself: the purpose, the privilege, and the necessity of the disciples' conversation with the risen Lord. At this point our attention is still not yet on the traditional substance of the discourses, but on the structure of the dialogue at one stage removed from the narrative introductions. Important clues will be gathered here about the overlap between traditional units and their new settings.

There is as yet no standard system for the classification of the fixed and variable characteristics of literary dialogues. Perkins' work promises a fresh approach. She observes that

> we need to attend to the genre requirements that bring together a number of common elements in a collection of dialogues whose content suggests that they derive from different contexts and hold diverse theological views.[59]

What is called for, therefore, is a rudimentary inventory of the dialogues' component parts. This will be now be attempted for the speeches in the *Epistula*. The object is to observe the intersection of traditional *rhetorical* devices and traditional *thematic* material. Where the conventions of dialogical rhetoric and separable theological *topoi* overlap, we shall be in a position to see the author at work.

The Rhetoric of the Revealer

Three times the Lord *rebukes* the disciples for their failure to understand:

> How long do you still ask and inquire? (22.2)
> Until what day do you ask? (24.4)
> How long are you still slow of heart? (35.3)

In each case the rebuke serves only a dramatic function. Never is it suggested that the disciples' failure to understand will disqualify them from the blessing of the revelation.[60] Other dialogues have similar reproaches made with references to time, for example:

---

[58] In *Ep. apost.* 18.1–2 the Ethiopic text has in indirect discourse what the Coptic has in direct speech.

[59] Perkins, *Gnostic Dialogue*, 30.

[60] Cf. the reproaches in the Gospel of John discussed in C. H. Dodd, "The Dialogue Form in the Gospels," *BJRL* 37 (1954) 54–67, esp. p. 62.

She answered and said to me, "How long will you be stupid and foolish, and ask everything and understand nothing?" (*Herm. Vis.* 3.6.5)

He answered and said to me, "How long are you foolish?" (*Herm. Vis.* 3.10.9)

"Are you still," said he, "silly and foolish?" (*Herm. Sim.* 9.14.4)

Twice in the *Epistula* the Lord *invites* the questions of the disciples:

Ask me concerning what you wish, and I will speak well with you. (20.4)

What you wish, say to me, and I will tell it to you without grudging. (24.5)

To these invitations Schmidt cited close parallels, again from *Hermas*:[61]

Hear then, . . . I shall reveal everything to you. (*Herm. Vis.* 3.3.2; cf. *Sim.* 5.5.1)

Ask, therefore, what you will about the tower, and I will reveal it to you. (*Herm. Vis.* 3.3.3)

Since you ask accurately concerning all things, I will explain this also to you. (*Herm. Man.* 4.3.3)

Indeed, Schmidt was so impressed with the formal correspondence between the *Epistula* and *Hermas* that he suggested there must be a relationship of literary dependence between them.[62] But examination of other revelation dialogues shows that these invitations are part of the standard morphology of the genre:

If you ask about anything, I will tell you. (*Soph. Jes. Chr.* 113.1−2)

Speak openly and do not fear. I will reveal all things which thou seekest. (*Pistis Sophia* 1.19)

Question that which thou dost wish to question, and I will reveal it with assurance and certainty. (*Pistis Sophia* 2.83)

A third rhetorical feature is the revealer's *approval* of the recipients of revelation:

I know that you are listening and your heart is pleased when you hear me. (20.3)

I know that in faith and from your whole heart you question me. Therefore I am glad because of you. (25.2)

Parallels in the cognate literature reveal this motif as part of the dialogical stock-in-trade:

---

[61] Schmidt, *Gespräche Jesu*, 206−8.
[62] Ibid., 208.

I praise you because you ask about the great aeons. (*Soph. Jes. Chr.*
108.20–22)

Everything which I have said to you you have understood and received in faith.
(*Dial. Sav.* 142.11–13)

Finally there is an occasional *general exhortation*, again entirely separable
from its context and usually prefacing further discourse on the same topic:

Have confidence and be of a peaceful heart. (19.13)

Do not be grieved. (32.4)

The "Amen" Sayings

One additional rhetorical feature within speeches of the Lord has to be considered here, namely the introductory formula "Truly I say to you." The
examination of this introduction may serve as a test case of the combination
of traditional, self-contained units and the freer or novel formulations to
which the author of the *Epistula* has given literary expression. Familiar from
the NT gospels,[63] this phrase is found in the *Epistula* only in its Synoptic
form, that is, with one "Amen," despite the writing's widely recognized
Johannine atmosphere.[64] As a self-contained declaration and introduction, the
formula is only rarely syntactically tied to its context in the Synoptic Gospels,[65] and never in John.

In the Synoptic Gospels the Amen introduction often serves as a logion
marker, that is, as a preface to a previously contextless dominical saying
(e.g., Mark 10:15; 11:23).[66] Its range extends from proverbial to personal
sayings (e.g., Mark 9:1; 13:30; 14:25). It is used to emphasize specific parts
of a speech or saying (Mark 9:41). An Amen saying can be complemented
with another saying which has its own formal introduction (Matt 18:18). In
the Fourth Gospel, on the other hand, the Amen sayings are primarily of the

---

[63] It appears in Matthew, thirty-one times; in Mark, fourteen times; in Luke, sixteen times; and
in John, twenty-five times (figures for sing. and pl. "you" are combined). For discussions of the
introduction's origin and use in the NT and early Christian literature, see Victor Hasler, *Amen:
Redaktionsgeschichtliche Untersuchung zur Einführungsformel der Herrenworte "Wahrlich ich
sage euch"* (Zürich/Stuttgart: Gotthelf, 1969); Klaus Berger, *Die Amen-Wörte Jesu. Eine Untersuchung zum Problem der Legitimation in apokalyptischer Rede* (BZNW 39: Berlin: De Gruyter,
1970); idem, "Zur Geschichte der Einleitungsformel 'Amen, ich sage euch,'" *ZNW* 63 (1972)
45–75; and John Strugnell, "'Amen, I say to you' in the Sayings of Jesus and in Early Christian
Literature," *HTR* 67 (1974) 177–82.

[64] The Johannine form is found once in the Ethiopic text (42.2 [84/7]).

[65] In Mark 14:9 the connecting particle δέ is found; in Matthew the formula is attached to its
context with γάρ five times; and in Matt 18:19 the Amen introduction, already used in 18:18, is
repeated with πάλιν.

[66] See the discussion and examples in Rudolf Bultmann, *The History of the Synoptic Tradition*
(rev. ed.; New York: Harper & Row, 1963) 323.

logion or nondiscursive type, although they include both personal and proverbial material (see John 12:24; 13:16).

The Amen introduction attached to a saying was not inseparable from it. Thus Mark 8:12 ("No sign shall be given to this generation") is reproduced and altered (from Q) in Matt 16:4; 12:39 (= Luke 11:29) without the introduction.[67] However, many sayings persist with their Amen,[68] while others are supplied with it.[69] The provisional conclusion is warranted, therefore, that what distinguishes sayings with the Amen introduction from those without it is not their dominical origin, the particular dominical association with the formula notwithstanding.[70] Rather the Amen gives a saying a special authority or solemnity, and its use is at the discretion of each writer. The methodological consequences of this are two. First, the introduction cannot be assumed to preface a traditional saying; and second, the Amen can serve as an indication of an author's special theological concerns.

A brief review of some dialogues confirms this judgment. In the *Apocryphon of James*, for example, the preface is found eight times; it occurs twice in the *Book of Thomas the Contender*; and in the *Pistis Sophia* fifty-six times! The *Apocryphon of James* has the introduction with sayings concerning possession of or entry into the kingdom (five times); with a biographical statement (10.15–17: "Had I been sent to those who listen to me..."); with a woe and a blessing (13.8–13); with a proverb-like comparison (10.1–3 "It is easier for a pure one to fall into defilement..."; cf. Mark 2:9 par.; 10:25 par.; and Luke 16:17—all without "Amen"); and with a context-bound saying on the forgiveness of sins (12.9). The *Book of Thomas the Contender* has its Amen sayings within the same pronouncement (142.27–31).

This variety, in the NT and in the dialogues, is matched by the variety of formal types introduced by this traditional preface in the *Epistula*. There are seventeen Amen sayings (16.3; 19.4, 5, 6, 14; 21.1, 9; 24.1; 25.3; 26.1; 28.4; 32.4, 5; 35.3; 41.6; 42.2; and 47.7.);[71] in only one case does the formula introduce a saying identified as dominical in other early Christian literature. In addition, the presence of a number of clearly editorial themes in the Amen sayings alerts us to the discernible work of an author who, as has been

---

[67] Cf. also Mark 14:25 and Matt 26:29; Mark 11:23 and Luke 17:6.

[68] E.g., Mark 14:18 = Matt 26:21 = John 13:21; Mark 14:30 par.

[69] E.g., Matt 10:24 and Luke 6:40 (both without "Amen") = John 13:16: "Truly, truly I say to you, a servant is not greater than his master" (but cf. John 15:20).

[70] The insistence of Joachim Jeremias (*The Prayers of Jesus* [Philadelphia: Fortress, 1967] 115) that "we have here without question an incontestable linguistic characteristic of the *ipsissima vox Jesu*" does not affect the question of the authenticity of sayings introduced with the Amen formula. John D. Turner (*The Book of Thomas the Contender* [SBLDS 23; Missoula, MT: Scholars Press, 1975] 221) speaks of the "truly I tell you" introduction as a "Jesuanic formula."

[71] Berger (*Die Amen-Wörter*, 143) catalogues and briefly comments on the Amen sayings in the *Epistula*.

intimated already, favors the repeated expression of a certain fixed range of ideas.

Two of the Amen sayings can be quickly assessed form-critically. The first, "I am <glad>, and my Father who is in me, that <you> question me" (*Ep. apost.* 25.3), belongs with the "rhetoric of the revealer" already discussed. The significance of the Amen preface is the importance the author attaches to the process of dialogue.[72] The second, in *Ep. apost.* 16.3 – 5, is a complex saying concerning the parousia, widely attested (in whole and in part) elsewhere in contemporary literature.

Two pairs of Amen sayings appear to be a doublet:

> Truly I say to you, . . . I am well pleased to be with you, that you may become joint heirs with me of the kingdom of heaven of him who sent me.

> Truly I say to you, you will be my brothers and companions, for my Father has delighted in you and in those who will believe in me through you. (19.4 – 5)

> Truly I say to you, you are my brothers, companions in the kingdom of heaven with my Father, for so it has pleased him.

> Truly I say to you, also to those whom you shall have taught and who have become believers in me will I give this hope. (32.4 – 5)

A second doublet of Amen sayings concerns the resurrection:

> The resurrection of the flesh will happen while the soul and the spirit are in it. (24.1)

> The flesh will rise alive with the soul. (26.1)

A third doublet, only one of whose members is introduced with the Amen formula, is found in *Ep. apost.* 26 and 47:

> My son, on the day of judgment <you will neither fear> the rich nor will you <have pity on> the poor. (26.4)

> Truly I say <to you, in> that day I will neither fear <the> rich nor have sympathy with the <poor>. (47.7)

Here the same tradition is clearly at hand, given the strongest possible attestation: the direct speech of the Father to the Son and the authoritative "Amen" of the Son to the disciples.

In adopting the literary device of the Amen, the author of the *Epistula* was not indiscriminate in appealing to its authority. In every case the introduction prefaces a saying traditional in content or in form. Further, in employing the

---

[72] See *Pistis Sophia* 2.83: "Truly, truly I say to you: rejoice with great joy, and be exceedingly glad. If you question everything with assurance, I will be exceedingly glad because you question with assurance."

Amen formula the author again betrays an indebtedness to dialogical convention. For it is characteristic of the Amen, in noncanonical as in canonical writings, to place sayings within a verbal exchange: it establishes a "you" for the speaker's "I."

The Rhetoric of the Recipients of Revelation

The rhetoric of the revealer in the *Epistula* shows already that the writing is a dialogue not merely by virtue of the fact that there is more than one speaker: the speeches conform in specific ways to contemporary conventions of dialogue composition. The speeches of the disciples illustrate this conformity to an even greater extent.

With few exceptions the disciples' speeches begin with the simple vocative, "O Lord."[73] Like the *Epistula*'s narrative structure, this address is remarkable in its consistency when compared with other dialogues. In the *Apocryphon of James* the vocative is reserved for the four speeches of James (Peter and the other disciples merely begin speaking); the *Book of Thomas the Contender* has eleven speeches of Thomas, three of which begin with the vocative (a further four include it). Nearer to the *Epistula* is the *Apocryphon of John*. John has ten speeches, all of them questions, of which nine begin, "O Lord."[74] This recurring address, then, belongs with the stylistic features collected above.

The disciples make repeated *apology* for their questions. In doing so they express both their respect for the revealer and the necessity of their conversation:

There is a necessity upon us to inquire through you, for you command us to preach. . . . Therefore we question you frequently. (23.1)

Not as unbelieving do we ask you. . . . Rather we really believe that what you say will happen. (24.3)

Already we are ashamed that we repeatedly question and trouble <you>. (25.1)

Numerous parallel expressions are to be found, for example:

I said to him, "For this reason I inquire accurately from you as to all things." (*Herm. Man.* 4.2.3)

When I hear from you about the hidden things, then I can speak about them. (*Thom. Cont.* 138.24–26)

My Lord, be not angry with me, that I question thee, for we question all things with assurance and certainty. (*Pistis Sophia* 2.83)

---

[73] The exceptions are in 19.16; 21.6; 25.7; 32.1 ("O Teacher"); 36.3; 41.2 (Coptic; the Ethiopic has "O Lord"); and 50.7, 9.

[74] Cf. the *Sophia of Jesus Christ*, where "Lord," "Savior," and "Holy Lord" are found.

The disciples' *approval* of what they hear is repeatedly stated:

> What you have revealed to us beforehand is great. (16.1)
> It is great, how you cause to hope, and how you speak. (21.6)
> Such meaningful things you have spoken and preached to us. (34.1)

Again, these expressions are typical:

> I said to him, "Sir, all is great and wonderful and all is glorious." (*Herm. Sim.* 5.5.4; cf. 9.18.4)
> You have certainly persuaded us, Lord. (*Thom. Cont.* 142.19)
> Again his disciples wondered at all the things which he told them. (*Dial. Sav.* 136.1 – 3)
> What you have said is very good.[75] (Bardesanes *Dialogue of Destiny* 14, 19)

The Dialogue as Revelation

It is in connection with the "rhetoric of the recipients of revelation" that the author of the *Epistula* demonstrates the intended equation of dialogue and revelation. The features of its literary structure already reviewed show that the author has done more than simply impose a "He said" and "We said" scheme upon previously coherent (or incoherent) discourse. The dialogue has become the vehicle for an unrelenting rhetorical exploration of the relationship between the revealer and the recipients of the revelation. This of course has hermeneutical implications for an understanding of the *Epistula*'s author and community. It can now be seen that the *Epistula* shares specific hallmarks of the genre not only with *Hermas* but with a range of other writings. Documentation of stylistic consistency and of generic characteristics now permits a measure of confidence in the detection of the author's compositional method.

To this point, however, no instance has been noted where the author's own theological program has unmistakably shown through the conventions of the genre. Under closer scrutiny the last of the dialogical conventions reviewed, the approval of the Lord's words, begins to indicate how the author intended the work to be received and understood. Especially important in this regard is the use of the verb "to reveal" in the speeches of the disciples:[76]

> What he *revealed* is this. . . . (13.1 [V 5, 56/7])
> What you have *revealed* to us beforehand is *great*. (16.1 [IX 2, 59/4])

---

[75] Reference to Bardesanes is by page and line number in Drijvers, *Bardaiṣan of Edessa*.

[76] Already Schmidt (*Gespräche Jesu*, 202 n. 1) brought together a number of these passages.

In all things you have shown yourself *merciful* to us and have *saved* us; you have *revealed all* to us. (20.1 [XIII 15, 64/12])

Such meaningful things you have spoken and preached to us and have *revealed* to us *great* things never yet spoken, and *in every respect you have comforted us and have shown yourself gracious* to us. For after your resurrection you *revealed all this* to us that we might be really saved. (34.1 – 2 [--, 75/13])

You have *revealed everything* <to us> well. (45.1 [XXXVII 9, 87/6])

Each of these references to revelation, though placed within the normal exchange of the dialogue, is in a stereotypical and inherently contextless remark of the disciples. Any of these statements might be replaced with another without loss of sense. Here the author, through the disciples' persistent acclamation, states the nature of the dialogue: it is revelation. Its content presents a comprehensive ideal, "all things [necessary for salvation]"; its goal is "that we might be really saved."

When these "revelation" passages are pursued still further, a series of accompanying terms emerges, principally used by the disciples in reference to the revealer and the revelation—and in the most general and inclusive way. The words emphasized in the passages quoted above are seen to be part of the special vocabulary of the author, as further examples of their use demonstrates:

In *all* <*things*> you have become to us <*salvation* and> life, proclaiming to us such a <*hope*>. (19.12 [XI 6, 62/8])

It is *great*, how you cause to *hope*, and how you speak. (21.6 [XV, fragmentary, 65/11])

<In> *all things* you make us alive and *pity* <us>. (25.5 [XIX 11, 68/5])

In *every respect* you have made us rejoice and have given us rest. (28.3 [XXIII, fragmentary, 70/7])

In *all things* you have *taught* us [...] and *pitied* us and *saved* us. (40.5 [XXXI 3, 83/7])

You have *taught* and exhorted us in *everything*. (49.3 [--, 90/3])

On the basis of the identification of these recurring themes a secure connection can be established between *Ep. apost.* 1 – 12 and the dialogue in 13 – 51. In 6.3, after the miracles reported in chap. 5, the disciples exhort their audience to "be firm . . . in the knowledge and investigation of our Lord Jesus Christ"; they continue: "And he will *teach*[77] and *be merciful* and *save* always and in all never ending eternity" (--, 53/1).

The process of dialogue thus fulfills the disciples' promise in *Ep. apost.*

---

[77] The verb "he will teach" is absent from fam. 2 MS L, and hence from Duensing's translation.

6.3. The expressions noted here, together with those to be identified in the exegesis of later chapters, constitute a recurring reprise to blocks of dialogue of unequal length and diverse subject matter. They lend stability to the whole and offer evidence for the author's soteriological frame of reference: the Lord's primary task after the resurrection (34.1–2) is that of revelation through teaching. The salvation of the disciples is made possible by the revealer's condescension or pity; by extension, the salvation of all whom they teach is also made possible.

The Central Themes of the Revelation

It has already been pointed out that the *Epistula* as a revelation dialogue follows no clear agenda. Thirty-two of the disciples' speeches are, or include, questions. Presumably these questions are the most accessible measure of the author's intention; yet they are difficult to classify according to distinct formal types, and they differ widely in the topics they raise. However, six of the questions, including one in the introductory chapters, share a formal resemblance and a priority of subject matter for this writer. In form, they share the opening phrase: "How/In what way...?" or "How is it possible...?" In content they form three pairs, their subject matter being respectively (a) the resurrection of the flesh; (b) the presence of the Lord on earth and in heaven; and (c) the mission of the disciples:

a) He who has died is buried, and could it be possible (ⲛⲉ ⲟⲩⲛϭⲁⲙ, *yekel-nu*) for him to live? (10.4 [II 13, 54/8])

b) Is it possible (*yetkahhal-nu*) that you should be both here [on earth] and there [in heaven]? (17.7 [--, 60/3])

c) It is possible for you to do what you have told us [i.e., to preach and teach], but how will we be able (*ba-'aytē nekel*) to do (it)? (19.3 [--, 61/7])

a) Is it then possible (ⲙⲏ ⲟⲩⲛϭⲁⲙ, *yetkahhal-nu*) that what is dissolved and destroyed [= the body] should be whole? (24.2 [XVII 12, 67/5])

b) In what way will one be able (ⲛⲉⲍ ⲛⲍⲉ, *'efo yetkahhal*) to believe <that you> will go and leave us? (29.8 [XXV 8, 71/9])

c) How now (is it possible) (ⲛⲉⲍ ⲛⲍⲉ, *'efo yetkahhal*) that each one of us should become these three [i.e., fathers, servants, and teachers]? (42.1 [XXXII 11, 84/6])

The studies in Chapters Two through Six will cover every passage in which these questions appear. At this point one observation will suffice. Coming at the midpoint between the questions is the most emphatic answer the author attempts: "What is impossible (*yessaʿān*) on the part of men is possible (*yetkahhal*) on the part of the Father" (21.8 [--, 66/6]).

The Appeal to Tradition

Quotations

The only sources named in *Ep. apost.* 13–51 are prophetic. In 19.18, Ps 3:1–8 is introduced as "the prophecy <of the> prophet David"; in 33.5 an oracle follows the formula, "that the word of the prophet may be fulfilled, where it says";[78] in 35.3–4 "the prophet David" is again quoted (= Ps 49:18–20 + Ps 13:3/Isa 59:7 LXX). In 43.4 there is a possible quotation of Ps 81:6 LXX when the Lord says that it is the wise virgins "with respect to whom the pro<phet said>, 'They are children of God.' " In 47.5–6 a woe is introduced with the phrase "as the prophet said." Finally, in 49.2 a community regulation is invoked with the introduction, "For it is written."

Next to these quotations may be placed several proverbs or proverb-like sayings:

> What has fallen will <arise>, and what is lost will be found and what is <weak> will recover.[79] (25.8 [Context: teaching on the resurrection of the flesh])

> Are the fingers of the hand alike or the ears of corn in the field? (32.2 [Context: teaching on the calling of the gentiles])

> As you sought you have found, and as you asked you have received. (39.8 [Context: teaching on moral choice])

> A blind man who leads a blind man, <both> fall into <a> ditch. (47.4 [Context: teaching on reproof of neighbor])

Elsewhere in the *Epistula* it is impossible to speak of conscious or deliberate quotation. Probable echoes of OT and NT language abound. Yet from the above it is clear that the dialogue has as its chief medium of exchange not an authoritative scripture but what for this author is, or becomes, an authoritative tradition: the utterances of the risen Lord in the presence of his disciples.

Traditional Forms

The *Epistula* throughout shows its debt to a wide selection of the motifs, themes, and expressions in which Christians of the early centuries held their discourse. The authority inherent in specific forms will best be illustrated in the following chapters in the context of exegesis. But one form, the list, is especially characteristic of the *Epistula*; see, for example, the "I am"

---

[78] On the "saying" itself see T. Schneider, "Das prophetische 'Agraphon' der Epistola Apostolorum," *ZNW* 24 (1925) 151–54.

[79] The history of this proverb as a proof-text for the resurrection has been traced in A. H. C. van Eijk, " 'Only that can rise which has previously fallen': the History of a Formula," *JTS* n.s. 22 (1971) 517–29.

sayings in *Ep. apost.* 21.9; the lists of virgins' names in 43.6, 16; the table of vices in 49.4; and numerous groups of commands and promises. Lists serve to bind together larger blocks of tradition and in doing so to refine and interpret specific sayings. A series of *saying + list* combinations exemplifies these functions:

> *saying*: I am wholly in the Father and the Father in me
> *list*: with regard to the resemblance of form and of power (?) and of perfection and of light and of full measure and with regard to voice. (17.8)

This list will be seen to harmonize two parousia traditions (in 16.3 – 5 and 19.8 – 9), each of which contributes two elements.

> *saying*: Your rest will be <above>,
> *list*: in the place where there is (neither) eating nor drinking, neither rejoicing nor mourning nor perishing of those who are <in it>. (19.14)

Here the final element, "perishing," may be a redactional addition to the two traditional pairs; it sits uncomfortably in the list, since the rejoicing/mourning pair would suggest the further contrast, perishing/restoration.

> *saying*: I have received all power from my Father
> *list*: that I may bring back those in darkness into light and those in corruptibility into incorruptibility and those in error into righteousness and those in death into life, and that those in captivity may be loosed. (21.8)

Here the change of construction (from active to agentless passive) in the last element may make its originality suspect.[80]

The Pre-Resurrection Sayings of Jesus

As already seen, the *Epistula* has much in common with the *erotapokriseis* dialogue tradition, in that the disciples as "students" question the Lord as "teacher." But the amount of space devoted to the disciples' speeches indicates the departure from simple interrogation. Whereas in the *Apocryphon of John*, for example, each of the ten speeches of John is a brief question, in the *Epistula*, as in a wider group of dialogues (including the *Apocryphon of James*, the *Book of Thomas the Contender*, and the *Dialogue of the Savior*), the disciples are much more than the Lord's prompters. They not only

---

[80] Cf. 37.5: "And men will follow them [the false teachers] and will submit themselves to their riches, their depravity, their mania for drinking,and their gifts of bribery; and respect of persons will rule among them."

request information; they also pursue their questions with a persistence which brings forth greater precision in the responses of the Lord. This accounts in part for the deliberate posturing, through the rhetorical conventions, on the part of both revealer and disciples. But there is more. On a number of occasions the disciples question the Lord's new revelation with an appeal to another received tradition.

Central to this dialectical atmosphere is the fact that the disciples can quote even the Lord himself:

> Here now, what have you said to us, "I will come," and how do you (now) say, "It is he who sent me who will come"? (17.3)

> In what way will one be able to believe <that you> will go and leave us, as you <said> to us, "A day will come <and an hour> when I shall go up to my Father"? (29.8)

> It is you who said, "Do not call (anyone) father upon earth, for one is your father who is in heaven and your master." Why do you now say to us, "You will be fathers of many children"? (41.4 – 5)

> But, Lord, among the believers . . . should there be dissention . . . ? For you . . . said, "They will find fault with one another, without regarding the person." (49.4 – 5)

In each case the disciples do not quote the exact words of the Lord as presented in the *Epistula*. Rather their appeal is to a tradition whose presence is generally only implied, namely the pre-resurrection sayings tradition. There is clear intimation of such a two-era scheme in *Ep. apost.* 32.3 when the disciples ask, "O Lord, are you speaking again in parables to us?" That is, "are you speaking [parabolically] as the earthly Jesus rather than [openly] as the risen Lord?" It is perhaps no accident that this question with its implied temporal demarcation[81] occurs at precisely the midpoint of the dialogue.[82]

A Test Case in Dialogue Composition:
Ep. apost. 22 – 26

The various threads of this analysis of the formal and rhetorical features of the *Epistula* may now be brought together in a single test case. *Ep. apost.* 22 – 26 ostensibly constitutes a response to the disciples' question about the resurrection in 22.1. But when these chapters are viewed speech by speech,

---

[81] Note the disciples' address, "O Teacher" in 32.2, only here in *Ep. apost.* 13 – 51.

[82] The amount of text preceding 32.3 exactly equals the amount that follows; and the number of speeches of the disciples preceding this passage exactly equals the number that follow. (Also, by editorial chance, chap. 32 is numerically midway between chap. 13 and chap. 51.)

it can be seen that there is no discourse at all; indeed, there is no answer to the question. Instead, rhetorical matter and proverbial or dogmatic maxims predominate, together with glimpses of the communal theology which is central to later chapters of the *Epistula*. It is not that the question lacks precision or profundity; the author simply eschews any discursive treatment of the topic. There is nothing here of the sustained argument such as is found in Justin's *Dialogue* or in the pre-Christian form of the *Sophia of Jesus Christ* (i.e., *Eugnostos the Blessed* [NHC 3, 3]). The discussion's only substance, outside of the disciples' opening question, is a proverb; and this serves as a proof-text for a pronouncement merely *that*, not *how*, the flesh will rise. Given the position and quantity of editorial matter, that is, the "communal theology," the doctrinal argument is entirely secondary to the ethical.

22.1	*narrative introduction*:	After he had said this to us, we said to him,
	disciples' question:	"O Lord, is it really in store for the flesh to be judged (together) with the soul and
22.2		spirit, and will (one of these) really rest in heaven and the other however be punished eternally while it is (still) alive?"
22.3	*narrative introduction*:	But he said to us,
	the Lord's rebuke:	"How long do you still ask and inquire?"
23.1	*narrative introduction*:	We again said to him,
	disciples' apology:	"O Lord, there is a necessity upon us to inquire through you, for you command us to preach, that we ourselves may learn with certainty through you and be profitable
23.2		preachers, and (that) those who will be instructed by us may believe in you. Therefore we question you frequently."
24.1	*narrative introduction*:	He answered us, saying,
	Amen formula:	"Truly I say to you,
	dogmatic statement:	the resurrection of the flesh will happen while the soul and the spirit are in it."
24.2	*narrative introduction*:	And we said to him,
	disciples' question:	"O Lord, is it then possible that what is dissolved and destroyed should be whole?
24.3	*disciples' apology*:	Not as unbelieving do we ask you—nor is it impossible for you—rather we really believe that what you say will happen."
24.4	*narrative introduction*:	And <he> was angry with us, saying to us,
	the Lord's rebuke:	"O you of little faith, until what day do you ask?
24.5	*the Lord's invitation*:	But what you wish, say to me, and I will tell it to you without grudging."

[24.6 – 8: Block of communal theology: the keeping of the commandments]

25.1	*narrative introduction*:	Again <we> said to him,
	disciples' apology:	"O Lord, already we are ashamed that we repeatedly question and trouble <you>."
25.2	*narrative introduction*:	Then <he> answered and said to us,
	the Lord's approval:	"I know that in faith and from your whole heart you question me. Therefore I am glad because of you.
25.3	*Amen formula*:	For truly I say to you,
	the Lord's approval:	I am <glad>, and my Father who is in me, that <you> question me. For your boldness <affords me> rejoicing and gives yourselves <life>."
25.4	*narrative aside*:	But when he had said this to us we were <glad that> we asked him.
25.5	*narrative introduction*:	And we said to him,
	disciples' approval:	"<O Lord, in> all things you make us alive and pity <us.
	disciples' request:	Only> now will you make known to us what we will ask <you>?"
25.6	*narrative introduction*:	Then he said to us,
	the Lord's test-question:	"<What is it> then <that pa>sses away? Is it <the flesh> or the spirit?"
25.7	*narrative introduction*:	We said to him,
	dogmatic maxim:	"The flesh is perishable."
25.8	*narrative introduction*:	<Then> he said to us,
	dominical proverb:	"What has fallen will <arise>, and what is lost will be found and what is <weak> will recover

[25.8b-9: redactional gloss]

26.1	*Amen formula*:	But truly I say to you,
	dogmatic slogan:	the flesh will rise alive with the soul,
	judgment-saying:	that their accounting may take place <on> that <day>, concerning what they have done, whether it is good or bad."

[26.2 – 8: block of communal theology: the keeping of the commandments]

Summary

1) In this chapter I have described a number of generic and formal features of *Ep. apost.* 13 – 51. In beginning with the formal elements rather than with the thematic, this study differs from previous approaches to the writing. Earlier treatment of the *Episutla* according to its themes or leading ideas has all but failed to account for its compositeness. Such unity as the *Epistula* has must be addressed if two assumptions are valid: first, that the author was aware of the thematic disjointedness, and second, that the original work has neither been later expanded nor drastically rearranged. This

unity resides in the dialogue form and, hence, in the literary conventions of dialogue.

2) Although the versions are not in complete agreement, there are clear indications of stylistic consistency in the speeches' narrative introductions.

3) The dearth of narrative is almost unparalleled in contemporary dialogues. Yet even in the few narrative asides the author's awareness of the conventions of the genre is discernible.

4) The revealer and the recipients of revelation assume roles already well defined by the genre.

5) Within the framework of their conventional speech, the disciples define the dialogue as revelation. A recurring soteriological vocabulary, editorially linked with references to revelation, can be assembled.

6) Seventeen Amen sayings give evidence both of the author's theological priorities and of the possibility of elevating specific sayings by formal means.

7) The author appeals to the authority of the risen revealer rather than to the authority of the written word of scripture. Quotations are few, from the OT alone, and only illustrative.

8) The *Epistula* is less a "letter" than it is a "book of revelation," a handbook for the successors of the apostles similar in function to the Gospel of Matthew (with which it has much material in common). As a forum for the teaching of the Lord it is also presented as salvific "good news": gospel revised in light of the post-resurrection teaching and of the disciples' questions that inspire it.

2

Epistula Apostolorum 4–5:
Gospel and Aretalogy

As in the dialogue which comprises the bulk of the writing (*Ep. apost.* 13–51), so too in *Ep. apost.* 4–5 questions arise regarding the author's sources and compositional method. But these issues seem especially clearcut in chap. 5, where most of the material is reminiscent of the NT gospels. The slight attention given to chaps. 4 and 5 of the *Epistula* has been devoted almost exclusively to the source question. Schmidt's brief review of chap. 5 leads him to the conclusion that Matthew, Luke, and John are the direct, literary sources behind the account in the *Epistula*.[1] With only minor differences Hornschuh adopts the same position:[2] the author of the *Epistula* has brought together in summary form a selection of the NT miracles of Jesus.

Even if we were to accept this verdict as an assured result, more important issues would remain: the principle of selection, the structure of these chapters, and the miracles' function within the *Epistula* as a whole. Until now these issues have been set aside in a simple recourse to the NT gospels: known sources yielding a patchwork product. But will this verdict suffice? Has the author mechanically turned from gospel to gospel in order merely to supply the reader with, as it were, some scraps from the disciples' diary? Or might it be that something of the compositional sense detected in the chapters of the dialogue is to be found also in the chapters that precede it?

The starting point for this new investigation is an observation concerning these chapters' form, namely that here we have to do with a miracle *list*,

---

[1] Schmidt, *Gespräche Jesu*, 216–17.

[2] Hornschuh, *Studien*, 12.

differing in both form and function from the canonical miracle *stories* with which its content has been compared.[3] When *Ep. apost.* 4 – 5 is viewed as a list among lists, both what is typical of lists and what is not can be identified, together with the special theological orientation of the list and and its compiler.

Miracle Lists In Early Christian Literature

Miracle lists, like other oral and written forms, have certain fixed and variable characteristics. These features are sufficient in number to warrant an account of the major categories of report, their literary settings, and their typical content.

Reports and Narratives in Miracle Lists

The literary forms in the miracle lists may be divided into two broad groups: *reports* and *narratives*. The first group may be subdivided. Miracles (usually healings) as a class, described in a single phrase, for example, "he made the blind to see," "he made the deaf to hear," may be termed *collective reports.* Examples from the NT gospels include Mark 3:10 par.; Matt 11:4 – 6 par.; 15:30. Another group of reports, formally identical but referring to only one event, constitute a second report type, the *individual report.* Again, brevity is the rule. The miraculous feedings, the raising of Lazarus, Jesus' walking on the water, and the like, are related as short, single items. The frequent intermixture of these individual reports with collective reports suggests that within any given list they were considered functionally indistinguishable.

The majority of lists consist of *reports* only. But there is a second formal type, namely extended reports or, as they may be styled, *narratives.* A miracle is presented not as a simple statement of fact, but as a short prose miniature often with circumstantial or interpretive comments. In almost every case these longer items are placed at the end of their list after the standard fare of reports has been exhausted. Narratives are especially common in the later lists, and when not merely repeating canonical details they tend to include novelistic elaboration.

The Lists' Literary Settings

The lists are found in a variety of literary settings. They appear (1) as prose reports in the mouth of a first-person "eyewitness" (e.g., Peter in *Const.*

---

[3] Lists in turn may be distinguished from "miracle catenae" (series of miracle stories) such as those which Paul J. Achtemeier has argued underlie parts of Mark's gospel ("Toward the Isolation of Pre-Markan Miracle Catenae," *JBL* 89 [1970] 265 – 91; "The Origin and Function of the Pre-Marcan Miracle Catenae," *JBL* 91 [1972] 198 – 221), and from the "Signs Source" widely held to have been used by the author of the Gospel of John.

apost. 5.7.27 – 28 and in *Ps.-Cl. Hom.* 5.10,1 – 2; Pilate in the various letters under his name); in the second person (e.g., Abgar's letter in the *Teaching of Addai*: "you give sight to the blind"); and in the standard third person; (2) as prophecy (esp. in the *Sibylline Oracles*) or as its fulfillment (e.g., Justin *1 Apol.* 48.1 – 2, which actually absorbs Matt 11:5 into the prophecy of Isa 35:5 – 7); (3) in discourse, often as part of an anti-Jewish polemic (e.g., *Acts Andr.* 10: "but still they did not believe") or as one of the stock proofs of the divinity of Jesus (e.g., Abgar in the *Teaching of Addai*: "either you are God . . . or you are the Son of God"; Tertullian *Apol.* 21: "proving that he was the Logos of God, that primordial first-begotten Word"); and finally (4) in poetic or hymnic biography, in which miracles constitute but one element in a review of the career of the Christ beginning with the incarnation (see the *Acts of Paul*, quoted below; Hippolytus *C. Noet.* 18.6 – 7; *T. Adam* 3.1) or with the creation.

The Content of Early Christian Miracle Lists

Reports and narratives are frequently identifiable with specific NT miracle stories, and the language used is often close to that of the NT gospel texts. However, collective reports, even when clearly echoing NT materials, can only rarely be assigned a precise canonical reference. Moreover, with one important exception (see below on *Ep. apost.* 5.13) no standard order or selection of miracles emerges; even closely related works (such as the three recensions of the *Acts of Andrew* or the Greek and Latin versions of the *Acts of Phileas*) show freely differing selections and arrangement.

In reports of both kinds mention is often made of the manner in which a miracle was performed, often "by a word" or the equivalent. Such remarks are found already in the NT (e.g., in Matt 8:8, 16). In addition, a wide range of circumstantial details heighten the difficulty of the cures. The statement that the disease to be cured was suffered "from birth" (cf. John 9:1) is almost ubiquitous, and it goes without saying that in the lists' narratives such ideas abound, often with lengthy demonstrations of the success of the healing.

The following is a selection of miracle lists together with their immediate context (if any).[4]

---

[4] A similar set of references is given in Walter Bauer, *Das Leben Jesu im Zeitalter der neutestamentlichen Apokryphen* (Tübingen: Mohr-Siebeck, 1909) 363 – 68, and in Achtemeier, "Origin and Function," 199 n. 2; Achtemeier speaks of such lists as "summary statements which contain no clear indication that they are drawing on the canonical gospels." Cf. also Justin *De res.* 4; Origen *C. Cels.* 2.48; Tertullian *De carn.* 4; *De res.* 20; *Pistis Sophia* 2.110; Commodian *Carm. apol.* 639 – 60.

Acts of Paul:[5] (Paul's preaching in Rome)

And he did great and wonderful works, so that he chose from the tribes twelve men whom he had with him in understanding and faith, as he raised the dead, healed diseases, cleansed lepers, healed the blind, made cripples whole, raised up paralytics, cleansed those possessed by demons.

Acts of Paul (P. Heid. frg. p. 79):[6] (Speech of Jesus)

Why are you amazed <that I raise up> the dead, or that <I make the lame> walk, or that I cleanse <the lepers>, or that I raise up the <sick, or that I have> healed the paralytic and those possessed by demons, or that I have divided a little bread and satisfied many, or that I have walked upon the sea, or that I have commanded the winds?

Ps.-Hippolytus *frg. in Pss* 2:[7]

And the divine in him ... is equally manifest, when he is worshipped by angels, and seen by shepherds, and waited for by Simeon, and testified of by Anna, and inquired after by wise men, and pointed out by a star, and at a marriage feast makes wine of water, and chides the sea when tossed by the violence of winds, and walks upon the deep, and makes one see who was blind from birth, and raises Lazarus when dead for four days, and works many wonders, and forgives sins, and grants power to his disciples.

Hippolytus *C. Noet.* 18.7:[8]

This is he who is crowned in victory against the devil; this is Jesus the Nazarene, who was invited to the wedding in Cana, and changed the water into wine; and reproves the sea which is tossed by the force of the winds. And he walks on the sea as on dry land, and makes a man born blind see, and makes Lazarus, a four-day-dead corpse, rise again, and performs all sorts of acts of power, and forgives sins and gives authority to his disciples.

Tertullian *Apol.* 21.17:[9]

... the powers which he displayed,—expelling devils from men by a word, restoring vision to the blind, cleansing the leprous, reinvigorating the paralytic, summoning the dead to life again, making the very elements of nature obey him, stilling the storms and walking on the sea; proving that he was the Logos of God.

---

[5] Greek text (*P. Mich.* 1317 and *P. Berlin* 13893) in Henry A. Sanders, "A Fragment of the Acta Pauli in the Michigan Collection," *HTR* 31 (1938) 80; ET in *NTApoc* 2. 382.

[6] Coptic text in Carl Schmidt, ed., *Acta Pauli aus der Heidelberger koptischen Papyrushandschrift Nr. 1* (2d ed.; 2 vols.; 1905; reprinted Hildesheim: Olms, 1965) 1. 55*; ET in *NTApoc* 2. 382.

[7] Text in PG 10. 609–10; ET in ANF 5. 170.

[8] Greek text and ET in Butterworth, *Hippolytus: Contra Noetum*, 90–91.

[9] Latin text in Heinrich Hoppe, ed., *Tertulliani apologeticum* (CSEL 69; 1939; reprinted New York/London: Johnson, 1964) 56–57; ET in ANF 3. 35.

Cyprian *Quod idol.* 13:[10]

So when Christ Jesus according to the former predictions of the prophets by his word and the command of his voice drove demons out of man, released paralytics, cleansed the leprous, illuminated the blind, gave the power to walk to the halt, brought life back to the dead, compelled the elements to be servants unto him, the winds to serve him, the seas to obey him, those of the lower regions to yield to him, the Jews who had believed him only a man from the humility of his flesh and body, thought him a sorcerer from the freedom of his power.

Ps.-Cyprian *De rebapt.* 8:[11]

For that our Lord was born, and that he was the Christ, appeared by many reasons to be believed, not unjustly, by his disciples ... because he cured and healed weaknesses, and vices, and diseases, with very great power; because he bestowed remission of sins, with manifest attestation; because he expelled demons at his bidding; because he purified lepers with a word; because, by converting water into wine, he enlarged the nuptial festivities with marvellous joyfulness; because he restored or granted sight to the blind; because he maintained the doctrine of the Father with all confidence; because in a desert place he satisfied five thousand men with five loaves; because the remains and the fragments filled more than twelve baskets; because he everywhere raised up the dead, according to his mercy; because he commanded the winds and the sea to be still; because he walked with his feet upon the sea; because he absolutely performed all miracles.

Acts of Phileas 6:[12]   (Speech of Phileas to the prefect Culcianus)

Culcianus said: "What did he do?" Phileas said: "He cleansed lepers, made the blind see, the deaf hear, the lame walk, the mute speak, the withered to be well again; he drove demons from his creatures at a command; he cured paralytics, raised the dead to life, and performed many other signs and wonders."

Orac. Sib. 1.351 – 59:[13]   (Prophecy)

Then indeed [God] will cure the sick and all who are blemished, as many as put faith in him. The blind will see, and the lame will walk. The deaf will hear; those who cannot speak will speak. He will drive out demons, there will be a resurrection of the dead; he will walk the waves, and in a desert place he will satisfy five thousand from five loaves and a fish of the sea, and the leftovers of these will fill twelve baskets for the hope of the peoples.

[10] Latin text in Wilhelm August Hartel, ed., *S. Thasci Caecili Cypriani opera omnia* (CSEL 3/1 – 3; 3 vols.; Vienna: Gerold, 1868) 1. 29; ET in Roy J. Deferrari, *Saint Cyprian: Treatises* (FC 36; New York: Fathers of the Church, Inc., 1958) 358.

[11] Latin text in Gerhard Rauschen, ed., *Tertulliani de baptismo et Ps.-Cypriani de rebaptismate recensio nova* (Florilegium Patristicum 11; Bonn: Hanstein, 1916) 55; ET in ANF 5. 671.

[12] Text and ET in Herbert Musurillo, ed., *The Acts of the Christian Martyrs* (Oxford Early Christian Texts; Oxford: Clarendon, 1972) 334 – 35. Cf. *Acts of Phileas* (Latin) 4.

[13] Greek text in Johannes Geffcken, ed., *Die Oracula Sibyllina* (GCS 8; Leipzig: Hinrichs, 1902) 22 – 23; ET in *OTP* 1. 343 (cf. *Orac. Sib.* 6.13 – 14 and 8.273 – 78).

Testim. Truth (NHC 9, 3) 32.22 – 33.9:[14]

For the Son of [Man] clothed himself with their first-fruits; he went down to Hades and performed many mighty works. He raised the dead therein; and the world-rulers of darkness became envious of him, for they did not find sin in him. But he also destroyed their works from among men, so that the lame, the blind, the paralytic, the dumb, (and) the demon-possessed were granted healing. And he walked upon the waters of the sea.

Const. apost. 5.7.27 – 28:[15] (Peter's narration)

He that raised him up that had the palsy whole, and healed him that had the withered hand, he that supplied a defective part to him that was born blind from clay and spittle, will raise us up; he that satisfied five thousand men with five loaves and two fishes, and caused a remainder of twelve baskets, and out of water made wine, and sent a piece of money out of a fish's mouth by me, Peter, to those that demanded tribute, will raise the dead. For we testify all these things concerning him, and the prophets testify the other.

Teaching of Addai:[16] (Abgar's letter to Jesus)

I have heard concerning you and your healing that . . . by your word . . . you give sight to the blind, cause the lame to walk, cleanse the lepers, and cause the deaf to hear; by your word you heal spirits, lunatics, and those in pain. You even raise the dead. So . . . I decided . . . either that you are God . . . or that you are the Son of God.

Acts Andr. Matt. 10:[17] (Speech of Andrew to the risen Jesus)

He made the blind see, the lame walk, the deaf hear; he cleansed lepers, he changed water into wine; and having taken five loaves and two fishes, he made a crowd recline on the grass, and having blessed, he gave them to eat; and those that ate were five thousand men, and they were filled: and they took up what was over to them twelve baskets of fragments. And after all these things [the Jews] did not believe him.

Justin *1 Apol.* 48.1 – 2:[18]

And that it was predicted that our Christ should heal all diseases and raise the dead, hear what was said. There are these words: "At his coming the lame

---

[14] Coptic text and ET in Birger A. Pearson, ed., *Nag Hammadi Codices IX and X* (NHS 15; Leiden: Brill, 1981) 130 – 31.

[15] Greek text in Francis Xavier Funk, ed., *Didascalia et constitutiones apostolorum* (2 vols.; Paderborn: Schoeningh, 1905) 1. 261 – 63; ET in ANF 7. 442.

[16] Syriac text and ET in George Howard, *The Teaching of Addai* (SBLTT 16; Chico, CA: Scholars Press, 1981) 6 – 9.

[17] Greek text in Richard Adelbert Lipsius, ed., Maximilian Bonnet, rev., *Acta apostolorum apocrypha* (2 vols. in 3 parts; 1891 – 1903; reprinted Hildesheim: Olms, 1959) 2/1. 77; ET in ANF 8. 519. Cf. *Acts Andr. Matt.* (Syriac) 10.

[18] Greek text in Edgar J. Goodspeed, ed., *Die ältesten Apologeten* (1914; reprinted Göttingen: Vandenhoeck & Ruprecht, 1984) 59 – 60; ET in ANF 1. 178 – 79. Cf. *1 Apol.* 22.6; *Dial.* 69.6 – 7. In *1 Apol.* 48.3 Justin remarks: "And that he did those things, you can learn from the Acts of Pontius Pilate."

shall leap as an hart, and the tongue of the stammerer shall be clear speaking: the blind shall see, and the lepers shall be cleansed; and the dead shall rise and walk about.''

Acts Pet. Paul 41:[19] (Letter of Pilate to Claudius)

He [Jesus], then, when I was procurator, came into Judaea. And they saw [*or* I saw] him enlightening the blind, cleansing lepers, healing paralytics, expelling demons from men, raising the dead, subduing the winds, walking upon the waves of the sea, and doing many other wonders.

Ps.-Cl. Hom. 1.6:[20] (Clement's narration)

And in order that he might be believed that he uttered these things full of the Godhead, he wrought many wonderful miracles and signs by his mere command. . . . For he made the deaf to hear, the blind to see, the lame to walk, raised up the bowed down, drove away every disease, put to flight every demon; and even scabbed lepers, by only looking on him from a distance, were sent away cured by him; and the dead being brought to him, were raised; and there was nothing which he could not do.

T. Adam 3.1:[21] (Speech of Adam to Seth)

You have heard, my son, that God is coming into the world after a long time, conceived by a virgin and putting on a body, both being born a human being, and growing up as an infant, and performing signs and wonders on the earth, walking on the waves of the sea, rebuking the winds and (they are) silenced, beckoning to the waves and (they) stand still, opening (the eyes of) the blind, cleansing the lepers, causing the deaf to hear; the mute to speak; straightening up the hunchbacked, strengthening the paralyzed, finding the lost, driving out evil spirits, casting out demons.

Anaphora Pilati A 1 – 5:[22] (Pilate's report to ''the Caesar in Rome'')

He made the blind receive their sight, the lame walk; he raised up the dead, he cleansed the lepers; he healed paralytics . . . by a single word. He raised up one that had been dead four days, summoning him by a single word. . . . And strangers that were manifestly demoniac . . . by his word he restored them to soundness of mind. . . . Again there was another having a withered hand . . . [whom] by a word he healed. And a woman that had an issue of blood for

---

[19] Greek text in Lipsius-Bonnet, *Acta apostolorum apocrypha*, 1. 196 – 97; ET in ANF 8. 480.

[20] Greek text in Bernhard Rehm, ed., *Die Pseudoklementinen I: Homilien* (GCS 42; Berlin: Akademie-Verlag; Leipzig: Hinrichs, 1953) 25 – 26; ET in ANF 8. 224. Cf. *Ps.-Cl. Hom.* 2.34,2 – 3; *Ps.-Cl. Recog.* 3.60,2; 5.10,1 – 2.

[21] Syriac text and ET in Stephen Edward Robinson, *The Testament of Adam: An Examination of the Syriac and Greek Traditions* (SBLDS 52; Chico, CA: Scholars Press, 1982) 58 – 61. Cf. *Apoc. Elij.* 3.8 – 10, which Robinson judges to be a later adaptation of the same ''traditional list of messianic signs and wonders'' (p. 151).

[22] Greek text in Constantin Tischendorf, ed., *Evangelia apocrypha* (2d ed.; 1876; reprinted Hildesheim: Olms, 1966) 436 – 39; ET in ANF 8. 460. This and the following item, though probably the latest of the lists presented here, merit inclusion as evidence for the continuing vitality of the genre. Cf. *Anaphora Pilati B* (Latin) 1 – 5.

many years . . . mysteriously received strength through his overshadowing her. . . . And other signs greater than these he did, so that I have perceived that the wonderful works done by him are greater than can be done by the gods whom we worship.

Vindicta Salvatoris 6:[23] (Nathan, a physician, speaking to Titus)

As his first miracle in Cana of Galilee, he made wine from water; and by his word he cleansed lepers, he enlightened the eyes of one born blind, he healed paralytics, he made demons flee, he raised up three dead; a woman caught in adultery . . . he set free; and another woman, named Veronica, who suffered twelve years from an issue of blood, and came up to him behind, and touched the fringe of his garment, he healed; and with five loaves and two fishes he satisfied five thousand men, to say nothing of little ones and women, and there remained of the fragments twelve baskets. All these things, and many others, were accomplished before his passion.

The Structure and Literary Setting of *Ep. apost.* 4–5

Ep. apost. 5 has much in common with these early Christian miracle lists. As far as formal types are concerned, the *Epistula* has several representatives of the collective report, of the individual report, and of the narrative. With a single exception (the Temple Tax incident), the selection is not surprising. That the whole is reported from the point of view of the disciples is necessitated by the pretended apostolic authorship of the whole writing.

However, there are several features that separate the *Epistula*'s list of miracles from the others. To an extent which seems to have no parallel, the *Epistula* has its narratives interspersed among its reports. Secondly, statements regarding the efficacy or speed of the cure are almost entirely absent.[24] Thirdly, the length of the list is exceptional.[25] But of greater significance than these differences are two traits distinctive of the list in the *Epistula*: first, the apparent grouping of the miracles into three smaller lists, each including the temporal adverb ''then'' or ''and then'' (Ethiopic *wa-ʾemze*); and secondly, the presence of *dialogue* in the narratives.

The meaning of the adverb *ʾemze* here is not a simple translation matter. In assessing its meaning and function no help is available from the other lists since indications of time are all but absent except, of course, in the prophetic examples.[26] The Ethiopic adverb *ʾemze* (or, with the conjunction, *wa-ʾemze*)

---

[23] Latin text in Tischendorf, *Evangelia apocrypha*, 473; ET in ANF 8. 472. Cf. *Vindicta Salvatoris* 29.

[24] Only the word ''immediately'' in *Ep. apost.* 5.3 would qualify as such.

[25] An expanded list in the *History of St. John in Ephesus* has fourteen miracles. But it is highly novelistic, and its length is due in part to a run-on enumeration of cured Gadarenes. (Syriac text and ET in William Wright, ed., *Apocryphal Acts of the Apostles* [2 vols.; London: Williams & Norgate, 1871] 1. 17; 2. 17).

[26] Apart from the Sibylline predictions, the first clear example of a temporal sequence seems to

is the regular equivalent of two Greek expressions: τότε (then) and καὶ ἐγένετο (and it happened).[27] The latter is an attractive suggestion for this passage, but it will not do for all three occurrences of the word; furthermore, each of the passages cited by Dillmann where *wa-ʾemze* = καὶ ἐγένετο (1 Sam 7:2; 8:1; 2 Esdr 16:1; Jdt 12:10; Job 2:1) includes before its main clause a specific reference to time, a condition which is not met in *Ep. apost.* 5. Therefore it may safely be supposed that *wa-ʾemze* stands for an original Greek τότε,[28] and this is how all translators of the *Epistula* have taken it.[29]

The question becomes whether the author was thinking in terms of strict chronological progression. The nature of this list, as of the lists in general, would suggest that he was not. Rather, as Schmidt first observed, it seems that the *Epistula*'s τότε in chap. 5 is a compositional device.[30] The question must be asked, precisely how τότε functions compositionally.

Τότε (then), whether referring to the past or to the future, would seem to be almost unshakably temporal.[31] But in certain writers, in the NT most notably in Matthew, τότε comes to be used "as a connective particle to introduce a subsequent event, but not one taking place at a definite time."[32] With regard to the First Gospel, Alan Hugh McNeile has described the word as "a particle which carries the reader to the next event in the narrative, often with no strict historical sequence."[33] This understanding of τότε well suits *Ep. apost.* 5, and the attempt may next be made to learn the author's intention.

Only the present (i.e., modern) chapter divisions, and with them the content expected of miracle lists, separate chap. 4 (the story about Jesus at school) from chap. 5. The text at the beginning of chap. 4 is as confused in the Ethiopic manuscripts as it appears in translation. The long relative clause "who was delivered ... letters" absorbs an opening phrase which looks patently editorial into the tale about Jesus as a schoolboy: "This is what our Lord Jesus Christ did" (4.1 [--, 50/8]). In fact, in the phrase "who was delivered" three good manuscripts do not read the relative pronoun

---

be in the *History of St. John in Ephesus* referred to in the previous note. A feeding (presumably of the 4000) is reported as follows: "And then again, another time [i.e., this is not the feeding already mentioned], he satisfied thousands in the desert, after he had healed their lame and sick."

[27] Dillmann, *Lexicon, s.v. ze-* (1029).

[28] The presence of the Ethiopic conjunction *wa-* (and) before *ʾemze* does not necessarily mean that the Greek also had the conjunction, especially at the beginning of a sentence.

[29] Guerrier, "Le testament," 190; Duensing, *Epistula Apostolorum*, 6–7; Wajnberg in Schmidt, *Gespräche Jesu*, 19.

[30] Schmidt, *Gespräche Jesu*, 217 n. 1.

[31] See BAG, *s.v.* τότε (823b–24a).

[32] BDF §459.2.

[33] McNeile, *The Gospel According to St. Matthew* (1915; reprinted Grand Rapids: Baker, 1980) 16–17; see also idem, "Τότε in St Matthew" (*JTS* 12 [1910–11] 127–28); and Moulton-Milligan (639b), where papyri are cited in which τότε is "little more than a connecting particle."

("who"). If we omit the relative with these witnesses, it is then possible to see in the opening words of chap. 4 not an introduction to the school story only, but rather a *superscription* to the record of Jesus' earthly career in chaps. 4 and 5 together: καὶ ταῦτα ἐποίησεν Ἰησοῦς Χριστὸς κύριος ἡμῶν.

Hornschuh has already suggested that these chapters belong together.[34] This may be confirmed on the basis of the list's structure. Ethiopic *wa-zanta* in the phrase "This is what . . ." can represent either τοῦτο (this) or ταῦτα (these things),[35] and either Greek expression, of course, could preface a single or a multiple report. Two considerations favor the latter. First, in *Ep. apost.* 6.1 the apostolic authors resume their direct address to their readers: "These things (*zanta*) our Lord and Saviour revealed and showed to us . . .," almost certainly referring back to the miracles in chaps. 4 and 5. Secondly, if the school story is included in the catalogue of wonders, a structure for chaps. 4 – 5 emerges whose design suggests that it is not accidental:

> narrative (Jesus at school)   +   "then" + 4 reports[36]
> narrative (the woman's cure)   +   "then" + 4 reports
> narrative (the demon Legion)   +   "then" + 2 reports + 2 narratives.[37]

These three groups of five wonders each may now be viewed in their wider literary context. The *Epistula*, like a number of contemporary writings, presents its summary of the wonder-working career of Jesus as part of a longer christological affirmation which begins, in chap. 3, with the incarnation:[38]

We believe that the Word,
> which became flesh through the holy virgin Mary,
> was conceived in her womb by the Holy Spirit,
> and was born not by the lust of the flesh
> but by the will of God,
> and was wrapped (in swaddling clothes)
> and made known at Bethlehem;
> and that he was reared and grew up, as we saw.
And this is what our Lord Jesus Christ did. . . .

---

[34] Hornschuh, *Studien*, 2, 9.

[35] In the Ethiopic of Matt 13:28, for instance, *zanta gabra* = τοῦτο ἐποίησεν, but in Matt 21:23 *zanta tegabber* = ταῦτα ποιεῖς.

[36] For reasons to be given below the account of the changing of water into wine is included as a report rather than as a narrative.

[37] The last two items, narratives rather than the expected reports, are a pair with several shared characteristics, as will be described below.

[38] There are textual problems at the end of chap. 3 (see Wajnberg in Schmidt, *Gespräche Jesu*, 28), but some sort of progression is implied.

This is very close to the sequence found in the *Acts of Paul*:

> In these last times, God for our sakes
>> has sent down a spirit of power into the flesh,
>> that is, into Mary the Galilean,
>> according to the prophetic word;
>> who was conceived and borne by her as the fruit of her womb
>> until she was delivered and gave birth
>> to <Jesus> the Christ, our King,
>> at Bethlehem in Judaea,
>> brought up in Nazareth,
>> who went to Jerusalem and taught all Judaea:
>>> "The kingdom of heaven is at hand!
>>> Forsake the darkness, receive the light,
>>> you who live in the darkness of death!
>>> A light has arisen for you!"
> And he did great and wonderful works,
>> so that he chose from the tribes
>> twelve men whom he had with him in understanding and faith,
>> as he raised the dead, healed diseases,
>> cleansed lepers. . . .[39]

This pattern is also reflected in Melito *Pass. Hom.* frg. 15:

> Who was enfleshed in a virgin,
>> who was born in Bethlehem,
>> who in the manger was swathed with bandages,
>> who was recognized by shepherds,
>> who was praised by angels,
>> who was worshipped by magi,
>> who was preached beforehand by John, . . .
>> who gathered the apostles,
>> who preached the kingdom,
>> who cured the lame, . . .
>> who gave light to the blind,
>> who raised the dead. . . .[40]

---

[39] Greek text in Sanders, "Fragment," 80; ET in *NTApoc* 2. 382. Cf. also Justin *1 Apol.* 31.7; Ps.-Cyprian *De rebapt.* 8.

[40] ET in Stuart George Hall, ed., *Melito of Sardis: On Pascha and Fragments* (Oxford Early Christian Texts; Oxford: Clarendon, 1979) 83–84. With only slight variation this hymnic material circulated widely, and with various attributions; cf. Ps.-Hippolytus *frg. in Pss* 2, quoted above; *C. Noet.* 18.6; Irenaeus *Epideixis* (Armenian frg. 1) (in Karapet ter Mekerttschian, S. G. Wilson, and J. Barthoulot, eds. and trans., "Saint Irénée: ΕΙΣ ΕΠΙΔΕΙΞΙΝ ΤΟΥ ΑΠΟΣΤΟΛΙΚΟΥ ΚΗΡΥΓΜΑΤΟΣ," PO 12/5 [1919] 80–81).

The accommodation of a miracle list into a larger biographical scheme is taken still further in the *Epistula*: reports are developed into *narratives* and narratives into *dialogues*. In addition, the author looks back to the creation (at the start of chap. 3) for the beginning of his christological hymn. The reason for this will be suggested below in connection with *Ep. apost.* 5.3 – 8.

Ep. apost. 4.1 – 5.22

The Miracle Reports in Ep. apost. 4 – 5

Ten of the miracles in these chapters are of the report type, five individual and five collective. These may be addressed in three groups (four, four, and two wonders respectively).

Ep. apost. 5.1 – 2 (--, 50/12)

1 Then there was a marriage in Cana of Galilee. And he was invited with his mother and his brothers. 2 And he made water into wine and awakened the dead and made the lame to walk; and[41] for him whose hand was withered, he stretched it out again.

Differing only in its initial temporal reference ("then"; "On the third day" [John 2:1]), the opening clause might have been copied verbatim from the Fourth Gospel. But in three points the rest diverges from John: Jesus' mother is "invited" (in John 2:1 she is "there"); Jesus is with "his brothers" (in John they are "disciples"); and in the *Epistula* the changing of water into wine is actually reported, whereas in John only its anticipation and consequence are found.

The position of Mary, whether "invited" or "there," will hardly affect an assessment of the relation between the *Epistula* and John; as it happens, the best of the new Ethiopic manuscripts (MS O) lacks the words "his mother and." In relating the presence of "his brothers," however, either the author is drawing on material independent of John, or he is making a conscious change; or, finally, a later hand has been at work. It has long been noted that Jesus' brothers, perhaps understood by John to be the disciples, appear in John 2:12, and it was even affirmed by Bultmann that John's source at 2:2, and therefore possibly the *Epistula*'s source, read "and his brothers."[42]

But there is a much more important issue, one to which the reader is alerted by the statement "And he made water into wine." This terse

---

[41] "And" is omitted from the translation in *NTApoc* 1. 193, though read by all manuscripts.

[42] Rudolf Bultmann, *The Gospel of John: A Commentary* (Philadelphia: Westminster, 1971) 114 and n. 6. For a discussion of the manuscript evidence at John 2:12, see Robert T. Fortna, *The Gospel of Signs* (SNTSMS 11; Cambridge: Cambridge University Press, 1970) 102.

announcement marks something of a stylistic about-face. The two phrases already reviewed prepare us not for a brief report but for a story; in fact, for John's story, or something like it. Rather than unfold, as does John's narrative, the account in the *Epistula* is quickly telescoped into a simple report to which the circumstantial details contribute nothing, because the story to which they belong (including servants, jugs, etc.) does not appear. As it stands, this account in the *Epistula* is neither a report nor a narrative. The details do not even function, as in the other lists, to make a theological point.

The possibility must therefore be considered that what precedes the summary statement is a later addition to a text which originally read: "Then he made water into wine." Arguments in support of this suggestion cannot be made from the structure proposed for the list; this would be to invite circularity. But in favor of an original shorter reading is the fact that in three other cases where the list deviates from the strict catalogue format, the disciples are present as first-person narrators. Therefore if by "his brothers" is meant "his disciples," one would expect to find "we" or "us," as in the Temple Tax incident in 5.14 – 16. Three times elsewhere in the *Epistula* the disciples are referred to as "brothers" (10.2; 19.5; 32.4).

The list continues in the style characteristic of the lists. The raising of the dead, though occasionally the climax of a list, is regularly, as here, an item with no special emphasis. The healing of a paralytic is similarly recorded quite plainly.[43] This first group of reports concludes with the healing of a man with a withered hand: a simple sentence joined to what precedes it by the conjunction. The description of the afflicted man agrees with the identification both in the canonical texts (Mark 3:1 par.) and, verbatim, with the title of the story in the Ethiopic NT. The restoration of the limb, "he stretched it out," matches the command and fulfillment in Mark 3:5 par., except that in the *Epistula* the Lord is the subject of the (transitive) verb.

Ep. apost. 5.9 (--, 51/7)

Then he made the deaf to hear and the blind to see, and he exorcized those who were possessed, and he cleansed the lepers.

This second group of reports, all of the collective type, is so standard that it might have been gleaned from any contemporary list, oral or written. The collection of NT parallels can offer no reliable key to the author's sources or method; despite verbal coincidences between this list and the canonical gospels, there is no reason to conclude that random selection was the basis for

---

[43] The manuscripts are divided as to whether one or more paralytics were healed (Eth. 51/1). But that the word *madāgʷeʿ* is to be translated "paralytic" rather than "lame" is virtually certain: in the Ethiopic NT, *ḥankās* normally = χωλός whereas *madāgʷeʿ* = παραλυτικός.

this author's collection. It is at least as plausible that a source of some sort stood behind the *Epistula*'s list.

Ep. apost. 5.13 (--, 51/12)

Then he walked on the sea, and the winds blew, and he rebuked them, and the waves of the sea became calm.

The text is uncertain at one point. The final phrase is either "and the waves of the sea *became calm (ḥasʾa)*" or "and *he calmed (ʾaḥseʾa)* the waves of the sea." The best manuscripts support the second reading; it is preferable as an item in a list of the works of Jesus and as the more difficult reading (cf. Mark 4:39 par.). In either case, the report looks like an abridgement of Matt 14:22–33 par. and Mark 4:35–41 par. But the phrase, "and the winds blew," is not part of the NT accounts,[44] and this serves to emphasize that there are unresolved differences between the *two* separate NT stories and the *Epistula*'s report.

In none of the NT gospels are the accounts of Jesus' walking on the sea and his stilling of the waters found together. Yet the close connection between these two nature miracles in the tradition has long been recognized,[45] and it is therefore interesting to find that in the miracle lists, with few exceptions, the walking on the sea occurs precisely where the stilling of the waves is found (cf. Tertullian *Apol.* 21; Hippolytus *C. Noet.* 18.7; *Acts of Paul*).[46] That in each case this was a fresh combination is improbable. Rather it must be the case that these sea miracles became companion pieces, quite independent of their NT counterparts though likely derived from them.

Aside from the introductory "then" a list-source may therefore be proposed for *Ep. apost.* 5.13, as for the reports in 5.1–2 and 5.9. The presence of these wonders as the last of the reports permits another observation. Not only are these miracles often combined in the lists; in a number of other cases they are also found at the end of the collections. As for the *Epistula*'s concluding wonders, concerning the Temple Tax and the feeding, it will be seen that they are a special pair with clear editorial features. Thus with the two sea miracles it may be conjectured that the author's borrowing from a list-source is complete.

---

[44] The exact phrase is found (in a different context) in Matt 7:25, 27; cf. John 6:18 "because a strong wind was blowing."

[45] Bultmann (*History,* 216) sees the walking on the sea as a development of the original motif of the stilling of the storm, and traces this development from Mark 4:37–41 par. (the stilling) to Mark 6:45–52 par. (the walking), "until finally in Jn. 6[16–26] the stilling of the storm was entirely dropped."

[46] An especially influential literary witness to this pairing is *Orac. Sib.* 8.273–74; cf. Lactantius *Div. inst.* 4.15 and *Epit.* 40 [45].3.

The Miracle Narratives in Ep. apost. 4 – 5

Ep. apost. 4.1 – 4 (--, 50/8)

1 He was delivered by Joseph and Mary his mother to where he might learn letters. 2 And he who taught him said to him as he taught him, "Say Alpha." 3 He answered and said to him, "First you tell me what Beta is." 4 And . . . true . . . a real thing which was done.

The story of Jesus and the schoolmaster, suggested above to be the first item in a collection of fifteen events, is found with varying degrees of elaboration in the several recensions and translations of the *Infancy Gospel of Thomas*.[47] Helmut Koester has claimed that "a reference to Jesus' childhood in *Epistula Apostolorum* 4 shows that . . . an infancy gospel has been used."[48] But Hornschuh insists that *Ep. apost.* 4 is independent of at least the extant forms of the story,[49] and this judgment is compatible with Cameron's characterization of the history of the *Infancy Gospel* as a document: "the fixing in writing of a cycle of oral tradition."[50]

For inclusion in the *Epistula* the tradition has received minimal editing: the phrase with which Jesus' response to the teacher is introduced, "He answered and said to him," exactly matches the introductory formula that usually prefaces Jesus' speeches in the body of the dialogue. As to the meaning of the story, in the *Epistula* it is that Jesus is superior to all other teachers.[51] Thus in Jesus' example the author anticipates an emphasis in later

---

[47] Cf. *Inf. Thom.* 6.1 – 4 (Greek text in Tischendorf, *Evangelia apocrypha*, 145 – 46; ET in *NTApoc* 1. 394). The manuscript tradition is highly complex (see Oscar Cullmann, "The Infancy Story of Thomas," *NTApoc* 1. 388 – 92); among other issues yet to be resolved is whether the original composition was in Greek or Syriac. Irenaeus condemned the story, which he reports was used by the Marcosians: "Among other things they bring forward that false and wicked story which relates that our Lord, when he was a boy learning his letters, on the teacher saying to him, as is usual, 'Pronounce Alpha,' replied (as he was bid), 'Alpha.' But when, again, the teacher bade him say, 'Beta,' the Lord replied, 'Do thou first tell me what Alpha is, and then I will tell thee what Beta is'" (*Adv. haer.* 1.20.1; ET in ANF 1. 344 – 45). The story is further developed in the 8th- or 9th-century *Gospel of Pseudo-Matthew* 31.1 – 2 (Greek text in Tischendorf, *Evangelia apocrypha*, 100 – 102; ET in ANF 8. 379 – 80).

[48] Koester, "One Jesus and Four Primitive Gospels," in idem and Robinson, *Trajectories*, 202 n. 150.

[49] Hornschuh, *Studien*, 10: "By no means is the Ep. Ap. literarily dependent on the Infancy Gospel [of Thomas]."

[50] Cameron, *Other Gospels*, 123.

[51] Brian McNeil ("Jesus and the Alphabet," *JTS* n.s. 27 [1976] 126 – 28), who finds the genesis of the tradition in one of the proverbs in the Syriac, Arabic, and Armenian recensions of Ahiqar, summarizes its meaning thus: "Instead of needing to be taught, Jesus himself is the one who teaches" (p. 128).

chapters of the *Epistula*: the disciples (and their successors) are the teachers of their communities.

Ep. apost. 5.3 – 8 (--, 51/2)

3 And the woman who suffered twelve years from a haemorrhage touched the edge of his garment and was immediately whole; 4 and while we reflected and wondered concerning the miracle he performed, he said to us, "Who touched me?" 5 And we said to him, "O Lord, the crowd of people touched you." 6 And he answered and said to us, "I noticed that a power went out from me." 7 Immediately that woman came before him, answered him and said to him, "Lord, I touched you." 8 And he answered and said to her, "Go, your faith has made you whole."

This second narrative has two parts. The first, consisting of 5.3 alone, is concise, complete in itself, and presupposes nothing.[52] With the exception of the duration of the ailment[53] and the immediacy of the cure[54] what is said is at a minimum. There is no verbatim agreement with the NT parallels, though conceivably an alternative translation of the Synoptics' Greek could lie behind the present text. But it is entirely more probable, given the evidence from a wide range of lists, that this short form, likely the product of one or more of the Synoptic accounts, has taken on a life of its own in this abbreviated state.[55]

In 5.4, however, the hand of the author is immediately evident in the first-person-plural narration. The construction suggests an original Greek genitive absolute; the meaning of the first verb (*nehḗlli*) is not certain here,[56] but the translation "we wondered" (for *nānakker*) is secure.[57] Of greater importance than this is the noun translated "miracle." Ethiopic *sebḥat*, which regularly stands for Greek δόξα or αἴνεσις,[58] in the plural translates ἀρεταί, as for

---

[52] In translating the beginning of 5.3 "And *the* woman . . . ," Duensing (*NTApoc* 1. 193) fosters the impression that the reader's familiarity with the NT gospel accounts is presupposed by the *Epistula*'s author. There is nothing in *Ep. apost.* 4 – 5 to support this assumption, and the Ethiopic of 5.3 may equally well be translated "And *a* woman. . . ."

[53] Bultmann (*History*, 214) states: "The record of the time the sickness had lasted in [Mark 5] v.25 is typical"; see also p. 221.

[54] Bultmann (ibid., 224) points out that "the success seldom comes by degrees."

[55] Such verbal similarity as there is would put the *Epistula* nearer to Mark and Luke than to Matthew. The *Epistula* concludes the event in one sentence, as do Mark and Luke.

[56] Dillmann (*Lexicon, s.v. xallaya* [577 – 78]) gives numerous Greek equivalents for this verb. In *Ep. apost.* 11.5 (III 14, 55/7) the word here translated "we reflected" is the first of a pair of verbs rendered "thinking and doubting" (Copt. has only "doubting"); in 6.2 (--, 52/14) it is found in the phrase "reflecting upon eternal life."

[57] Dillmann, *Lexicon, s.v.* ʾankara (666). Cf. Luke 24:12, where ʾenza yānakker za-kona translates θαυμάζων τὸ γεγονός.

[58] Dillmann, *Lexicon, s.v. sabbeḥa* (357 – 58).

example in Isa 42:8, 12 and 43:21.[59] Elsewhere in the *Epistula* the noun is used with the sense "glory" (6.2; 13.8; 16.3, 4; 33.6; 36.11; 51.3); but the meaning here cannot be "glory" or "praise" in the abstract sense. What is required of the context is "mighty or glorious deed." Hence *sebḥat* must here = δόξα in this concrete sense; more probably, θαυμάσιον[60] or ἀρετή.[61] The likely presence of one of these Greek words prompts the suggestion that in *Ep. apost.* 5.4 the disciples identify themselves as the "aretologoi" of the Lord.[62]

That *Ep. apost.* 4–5 may be described as aretalogical is scarcely open to question. Yet the term "aretalogy" must be used with caution. It has been argued repeatedly by Helmut Koester and others that collections of Jesus' miracles are "closely related to the genre of the aretalogy,"[63] and the real methodological problems lie only in the too ready equation of the *gospel* genre with the aretalogy.[64] What makes the term aretalogy an appropriate one for these chapters in the *Epistula* is not just that mighty deeds are related in the form of a catalogue; more persuasive than this is the fact that like the paradigmatic "Kore Kosmou" (3d c. CE),[65] the "Aretalogy of Karpokrates"

---

[59] It also translates θαυμάσια (wonders, marvels; e.g., in Sir 18:6; 42:17) and ἔνδοξα (glorious [things]; e.g., in Isa 12:4).

[60] Cf. the Ethiopic translation of *Herm. Vis.* 4.1.3: "he had thought me worthy to show me his wonders," where τὰ θαυμάσια αὐτοῦ = *sebḥatihu* (Antoine d'Abbadie, ed. and [Latin] trans., *Hermae Pastor* [Abhandlungen für die Kunde des Morgenlandes 2/1; Leipzig: Brockhaus, 1860] 20); but for τὰ θαυμάσια in Matt 21:15 the Ethiopic has *manker* (miracles).

[61] Adolf Deissmann (*Bible Studies* [1923; reprinted Winona Lake, IN: Alpha, 1979] 96) supported the claim that "ἀρετή, even in pre-Christian usage, could mean *miracle, effet supernaturel.*" LSJ (*s.v.* ἀρετή, I.b [238b]) gives two references for the singular of the noun used of a glorious deed. Erik Peterson (Εἷς Θεός [Göttingen: Hubert, 1920] 39–40) cites the title of a Zeus-Helios-Serapis aretalogy: Διὸς Ἡλίου μεγάλου Σεράπιδος ἀρετή. For discussion of similar material see Otto Weinreich, *Antike Heilungswunder* (Giessen: Töpelmann, 1909) 119; and idem, *Neue Urkunden zur Serapis-Religion* (Tübingen: Mohr-Siebeck, 1919). In the latter study Weinreich compares the paratactic style of Serapis aretalogies with early Christian miracle lists; he also notes the status of ἀρετή as a cultic quasitechnical term (pp. 14–15). The most substantial recent discussion is in Yves Grandjean, *Une nouvelle arétalogie d'Isis à Maronée* (EPRO 49; Leiden: Brill, 1975), esp. pp. 1–5 on the word ἀρετή. Presenting evidence for ἀρετή as a synonym of θαῦμα (marvel), of δύναμις (power, might), of ἐνέργεια ([supernatural] activity), and of πρᾶξις (deed), Grandjean confirms Weinreich's claim that from the fourth century BCE ἀρετή can bear the sense "miracle." Cf. C. Spicq, "Note de lexicographie: APETH," *RB* 89 (1982) 161–76, esp. pp. 168–69.

[62] A. D. Nock (*Conversion* [London: Oxford University Press, 1972] 89) refers to "aretologoi" or "tellers of the god's wonder" attached to the cult of Serapis and Isis. For a discussion of this role see David Lenz Tiede, *The Charismatic Figure as Miracle Worker* (SBLDS 1; Missoula, MT: Scholars Press, 1972) 1–13.

[63] Koester, *Introduction*, 2. 4; cf. 1. 132–36; also 2. 166, where Koester states: "It can be assumed that the earliest collections of miracle stories of Jesus were produced as missionary manuals"; they were the missionaries' "letters of recommendation."

[64] See Howard C. Kee, "Aretalogy and Gospel," *JBL* 92 (1973) 402–22.

[65] Greek text in A. D. Nock and A. J. Festugière, *Corpus Hermeticum* (4 vols.; Paris: Les

(3d–4th c. CE),[66] and the complete Isis aretalogy *I. Kume* 41 (1st or 2d c. CE),[67] the *Epistula*'s aretalogy begins (in chap. 3) with the *creation*. The whole composition is prefaced with the disciples' declaratory "We know this" (3.1 [--, 49/5]):[68]

> Our Lord and Saviour Jesus Christ (is) God, Son of God
> who was sent from God, the ruler of the entire world, the maker and creator of what is named with every name,
> who is over all authority (as) Lord of lords and King of kings, the ruler of the rulers, the heavenly one
> who is over the Cherubim and Seraphim and sits at the right hand of the throne of the Father,
> who by his word commanded the heavens and built the earth and all that is in it and bounded the sea that it should not go beyond its boundaries, and (caused) deeps and springs to bubble up and flow over the earth day and night;
> who established the sun, moon, and stars in heaven and separated light from darkness;
> who commanded hell, and in the twinkling of an eye summons the rain for the wintertime, and fog, frost, and hail, and the days (?) in their time;
> who shakes and makes firm;
> who has created man according to his image and likeness;
> who spoke in parables through the patriarchs and prophets and in truth through him whom the apostles declared and the disciples touched.
> And God, the Lord, the Son of God—We believe that the word, which became flesh through the holy virgin Mary, was carried (conceived) in her womb by the Holy Spirit, and was born not by the lust of the flesh but by the will of

---

Belles Lettres, 1945–54) 4. 21–22 (= frg. 23.64–68); ET in Frederick C. Grant, ed., *Hellenistic Religions: The Age of Syncretism* (Library of Liberal Arts; Indianapolis: Bobbs-Merrill, 1977) 134–36.

[66] Greek text in Richard Harder, "Karpokrates von Chalkis und die memphitische Isis-propaganda," *Abhandlungen der preussischen Akademie der Wissenschaften, Berlin* 14 (1943) 7–18; ET in Grant, *Hellenistic Religions*, 133–34.

[67] Greek text first published in A. Salač, "Inscriptions de Kymé d'Éolide, de Phocée, de Tralles et de quelques autres villes d'Asie Mineure," *BCH* 51 (1927) 378–83; revised text and ET now accessible in G. H. R. Horsley, ed., *New Documents Illustrating Early Christianity, 1* (North Ryde, N. S. W.: The Ancient History Documentary Research Centre, Macquarie University, 1981) 18–20. Horsley (p. 18) remarks that "there is some kind of credal quality to be observed in these aretalogies."

[68] Guerrier ("Le testament," 49) supplies a title for *Ep. apost.* 3: "The profession of faith of the apostles." It is possible to detect fifteen relative clauses (each beginning "who . . .") in chap. 3, matching the fifteen deeds of Jesus in chaps. 4–5. Also comparable with *Ep. apost.* 3 are several of the Jewish and Christian prayers assembled from Christian sources in Erwin R. Goodenough, *By Light, Light: The Mystic Gospel of Hellenistic Judaism* (New Haven: Yale University Press, 1935) 306–58; see esp. 'Fragment VII' (= *Const. apost.* 8.12.6–27; ibid., 320–24) where the description of creation (in the hymnic second person) almost exactly parallels *Ep. apost.* 3.

God, and was wrapped (in swaddling clothes) and made known at Bethlehem; and that he was reared and grew up, as we saw.

The author has united this hymnic or poetic piece[69] with the miracle list in *Ep. apost.* 4 – 5. The result is an aretalogy whose function will be to authenticate, as exclusively saving, the baptismal "faith."

The miracle narrative in *Ep. apost.* 5.3 – 8 continues with a brief dialogue. Chaps. 4 and 5 have already been distinguished from the miracle lists in contemporary writings by the presence of dialogue. Elsewhere in the lists, even in the narratives there is no dialogue. Bultmann has suggested that in the history of Synoptic narrative there is a tendency towards the use of direct speech, and he cites the sick woman's cry in the *Epistula*, "O Lord, I touched you," as a later example of this tendency.[70]

On closer inspection, this narrative is seen to be characteristic of the *Epistula* in both form and content. First, in form the narrative introductions to the speeches follow the conventions already outlined above (Chapter One) for the body of the dialogue (*Ep. apost.* 13 – 51): the verb "to answer, reply," is reserved for prefaces to speeches of the Lord,[71] and here, as in the later chapters, both speeches addressed to Jesus begin with the vocative, "O Lord." Secondly, in content the interests of this brief dialogue coincide with those of chaps. 9 – 12 (the post-resurrection appearance account). In 5.3 the description of the healing employs as its verb of touching *lakafa* (= ἅπτεσθαι) a verb which is repeated in the disciples' words about the crowd in 5.5; but both the Lord's question (5.4) and the woman's reply (5.7) have the verb *gasasa* (= ψηλαφᾶν), as is found in *Ep. apost.* 12.1 (IV 10, 56/2):

Ethiopic	Coptic
But now we *felt* him (*gasasnāhu*),	But we <*touched*> him (ⲁ[ⲛⲋⲁⲙ]ⲋⲙⲉ ⲁⲣⲁ̄ϥ)
that	that we might truly know whether
he had truly risen in the flesh.	he <had risen> in the flesh.

This antidocetic emphasis, absent from the Synoptic accounts of the woman's cure, is here made plain by the equation of touching and faith: "Lord, I touched you"; "Go, your faith has made you whole."[72]

---

[69] Note the retention of the phrase, "whom the apostles declared and the disciples touched," incongruous now that the apostles and disciples are themselves "we."

[70] Bultmann, *History*, 313.

[71] *NTApoc* 1. 193 has "answered him and" before "[she] said," but a strong combination of fam. 1 and fam. 2 MSS lacks the phrase.

[72] Cf. Tertullian *Adv. Marc.* 3.8 and 4.20 for the same argument.

Ep. apost. 5.10 – 12 (--, 51/9)

10 And the demon Legion, that a man had, met with Jesus, cried and said, "Before the day of our destruction has come You have come to turn us out." 11 But the Lord Jesus rebuked him and said to him, "Go out of this man without doing anything to him." 12 And he went into the swine and drowned them in the sea, and they were choked.

In formal terms this narrative is close to the one preceding it. Both include dialogue, both end with the dismissal by Jesus of the person healed, and in both the action begins not with Jesus but with the object of his power. As in the previous case, a number of verbal parallels with the Synoptic Gospels can be collected. Up to 5.11b, the closest resemblance is not to the canonical Legion story (Mark 5:1 – 20 par.) but to the exorcism in the Capernaum synagogue (Mark 1:21 – 28 par.). A combination of the two stories seems to have arisen. Thus in *Ep. apost.* 5:10 "You have come to turn us out" approximates to Mark 1:24b par.[73] (but with "Before the day of our destruction" cf. Matt 8:29c); in *Ep. apost.* 5.11 "Jesus rebuked him and said to him" = Mark 1:25a and Luke 4:35a *verbatim*; and the command "Go out of this man" in *Ep. apost.* 5.11 matches Mark 1:25a and Luke 4:35a ("Be silent, and come out of him!").

Other parallels are inexact, but most striking is the correspondence of the Lord's command, "Go out of this man *without doing anything to him*," to Luke's description of the exit of the demon: "he came out of him, *having done him no harm*" (μηδὲν βλάψαν αὐτόν) (Luke 4:35b). This phrase is a detail which is found, detached from any specific canonical context, in *Acts Pet.* 11, where Peter exorcizes a youth with the command: "You too, then, whatever demon you may be, in the name of our Lord Jesus Christ, come out of the young man *and do him no harm*!"[74] What appears in both the *Epistula* and the *Acts of Peter* as a command seems therefore to be what Hornschuh, though missing the Lukan reference, took it to be: "a free, extracanonical Synoptic tradition."[75]

In two ways this narrative is uncharacteristic of the *Epistula*. First, the dialogue lacks the formulas of introduction and address which are found with all dialogue elsewhere in the *Epistula*. Secondly, the Lord is here, and only

---

[73] For "to turn us out" two MSS have "to destroy us" in agreement with Mark and Luke. From time to time a tendency toward harmonization overshadows the Eth. text of the *Epistula*, but overall the independence of the vocabulary from that of the Ethiopic NT (our only yardstick in these chapters) is more remarkable.

[74] Latin text in Lipsius-Bonnet, *Acta apostolorum apocrypha*, 1. 59; ET in *NTApoc* 2. 293.

[75] Hornschuh, *Studien*, 11. An additional example of its use is in the Coptic *P. Utrecht* 1, p.14 lines 32 – 38 (part of a cycle of *Acts of Andrew*; ET in *NTApoc* 2. 407), where a demon reports to Andrew: "Truly, O man of God, . . . I shall go out from this young man, *while I have done no harm at all to his limbs*."

here, referred to simply as "Jesus" (in 5.10, 11).[76] These formal irregularities strongly suggest that the story existed in its present shape before its incorporation into chap. 5. It is necessary to ask the reason for its inclusion. The author has already mentioned the exorcism of the possessed in 5.9. Another exorcism is therefore superfluous unless some new point is to be made by this individual encounter. A clue may be found in the fact that Jesus deals throughout not with the man possessed but with the demon; in Mark 1:21–28, by contrast, first the man, then the demon, speaks. In the *Epistula* the essential encounter is between Jesus and the demon: Jesus' authority over Legion is decisively demonstrated and also, by implication, his radical difference from any docetic spirit-figure. The term "demon" will reappear in the post-resurrection appearance account, where the disciples fear Jesus is a ghost (11.3) only to be reassured that the Lord is no "ghost of a demon" (11.8).[77]

Ep. apost. 5.14–16 (--, 52/1)

14 And when we, his disciples, had no denarii, we said to him, "Master, what should we do about the tax-collector?" 15 And he answered and said to us, "One of you cast the hook, the net, into the deep and draw out a fish, and he will find a denarius in it. 16 Give that to the tax-collector for me and for you."

The last two wonders, of which this is the first, stand apart from what precedes them; and they stand apart together. Both are introduced with an expression of the disciples' need (*'enza 'albena*, corresponding to ἡμεῖς μὴ ἔχοντες or its equivalent). This feature of the Temple Tax incident at once distinguishes *Ep. apost.* 5.14–16 from its probable source, Matt 17:24–27.[78] A second feature of this account is the shape of the simple dialogue, conforming as it does to the conscious pattern seen throughout the *Epistula*. Thereafter it is clear that the real parallel is with Matt 17:27 alone, and that the strongest point of agreement is in the use of the title "teacher" (or "master") for Jesus. But many celebrated "Mattheanisms" are absent: the concession about not causing offence; the combination of a participle of πορεύεσθαι + an imperative (a construction found seven times in Matthew);

---

[76] The MSS are in agreement in 5.10. Some MSS, notably that represented in the *NTApoc* translation, have "the Lord Jesus" in 5.11.

[77] Coincidentally the noun δαίμων occurs in the NT only in the (Matthean) Legion story (Matt 8:31).

[78] Where the texts have parallel content, the *Epistula* differs from Matthew in only one significant item of vocabulary: for Matthew's οἱ τὰ δίδραχμα λαμβάνοντες, which in the Eth. NT is found as *'ella ṣabbāhta dināra yenašše'u*, the *Epistula* has *maṣabbehān* (= οἱ τελῶναι). There are similar variations in terminology in other second- and third-century allusions to Matthew's account, e.g., in *Const. apost.* 5.7.28; Melito *Pass. Hom.* 632–33; Origen *Comm. in Matt.* 13.11, on Matt 17:24–27.

the "coming up" of the fish; "the sea"; and the opening of the fish's mouth.[79]

Bultmann was the first to suggest that "it is possible that an older tradition than Matt. 17[24ff] is showing through" in *Ep. apost.* 5 when not Peter but a nameless "one of you," is instructed to fish.[80] But Bultmann also recognized that since the whole body of disciples is narrating the incident, it would not have suited the author's purpose to have a named individual. At least it may be assumed that Peter's name has not been suppressed on polemical grounds; his name is also absent from *Ep. apost.* 15.1 – 7, a prediction apparently built on Peter's imprisonment in Acts 12. To be noted instead is the typical flexibility with which a nonexegetical writing from the early period adapts traditions about Jesus, regardless of their origin.[81]

The tax story is not known elsewhere beginning as it does in the *Epistula*, but the feeding account follows a traditional model (judging by the NT parallels) in beginning, "When we had no bread. . . ." The miraculous catch of the denarius seems therefore to be a back-formation, possibly to bring the third group of wonders up to five. It also emphasizes the disciples' solidarity and shows that the risen Lord, who will provide "all things" for salvation (34.2), was also the earthly teacher who provided for his disciples. What for Matthew is a "miraculous self-aid"[82] is in the *Epistula* an almost casually related provision for those who are now teachers and preachers.

Ep. apost. 5.17 – 20 (--, 52/5)

17 Then when we had no bread except five loaves and two fish, he commanded the people to lie down, 18 and their number amounted to 5000 besides children and women, whom we served with pieces of bread; 19 and they were filled, and there was (some) left over, and we carried away twelve baskets full of pieces.

---

[79] This is only a selection of the stylistic features cited in Robert H. Gundry, *Matthew: A Commentary on His Literary and Theological Art* (Grand Rapids: Eerdmans, 1982) 355 – 56; and in Neil J. McEleney, "Mt 17:24 – 27—Who paid the Temple Tax? A Lesson in Avoidance of Scandal," *CBQ* 38 (1976) 183 – 84. To the list of "omissions" may be added two lexical peculiarities in the *Epistula*: "the hook, the net," and the use of the word *legg[w]at*, "the deep," where "the sea" is expected.

[80] Bultmann, *History*, 310 n. 3.

[81] Elsewhere we read, for instance, that the tax was paid not only for Jesus and Peter (as in Matt 17:27) but for the Lord and the twelve (as in *Ep. apost.* 5.16), e.g., in *Acts Thom.* 143, where Thomas hymns his Lord as "he who is truth that does not lie, and paid tribute (and [Syr.]) poll-tax for himself and his disciples" (*NTApoc* 2. 518). In Melito *Pass. Hom.* 632 – 33, however, the tax is for the Lord alone: "It is he from whom you extorted money, demanding from him his two-drachma poll-tax" (Hall, *Melito of Sardis*, 48 – 49).

[82] The phrase is from Martin Dibelius, quoted by Bultmann, *History*, 218 n. 2.

This narrative consists of six short phrases, each of which suggests some familiarity with the canonical gospels' accounts of miraculous feedings (Mark 6:32–44 par.; 8:1–10 par.; John 6:1–13). What sets this narrative apart from them is its *in medias res* setting, shared with the previous narrative: "when we had no denarius/bread. . . ." But the reason for the inclusion of the feeding in the *Epistula* is not immediately clear. Although the only NT account whose sequence is closely echoed is John's, verbal similarities with the other feeding accounts are numerous; especially obvious is the Matthean "besides children and women" (Matt 14:21; 15:38).[83] But it is most improbable that the author has selectively turned from gospel to gospel to compose so brief a narrative.[84] If a clear editorial motif were present, the selection might have been explained; but there is none. In this respect the feeding differs from the previous narratives, in each of which a specific theological orientation was visible. The further difference from them, the lack of dialogue, perhaps supplies the interpretive key to this two-dimensional presentation: the miracle is reported solely for the sake of what follows it, the only prerequisite for which is the mention of five loaves. This explains the *inclusio* formed by the references to bread. Exploiting in this way the traditional mystery of the loaves (cf. Mark 6:52; 8:14), the author has set the stage for the question and answer with which chaps. 4–5 reach their climax. In 5.20 the disciples ask: "What meaning is there in these five loaves?" Thus the Lord's only action in *Ep. apost.* 5.17–20 has been to seat the crowds. He now retires as the disciples address their church.

The Baptismal Faith: Ep. apost. 5.21–22

The answer to the disciples' question has two parts. The first ("They are a picture of our faith concerning the great Christianity" [*NTApoc* 1. 194]) raises problems of translation and interpretation which are best considered after the second part, a five-clause credal statement. This is given here according to the best manuscript evidence (--, 52/10):[85]

---

[83] Matt 14:21 has "women and children," the reading of the best Eth. MSS in *Ep. apost.* 5.18; Matt 15:38 has a well supported variant, "children and women."

[84] Cf. Ernst Haenchen's comment on John's version of the feeding: "It is simply not conceivable that the Evangelist had the Synoptics before him and selected a word from this, a usage from that, and a feature of the other in composing his account" (*John* [2 vols.; Hermeneia; Philadelphia: Fortress, 1984] 1. 274). A comparable case is the feeding account in *Acts Andr.* 10. But such eclectic composition is evident in Tatian's *Diatessaron*, a second-century gospel harmony "combining distinctive phrases preserved by only one Evangelist with those preserved by another" (Bruce M. Metzger, *The Text of the New Testament: Its Transmission, Corruption, and Restoration* [2d ed.; New York/Oxford: Oxford University Press, 1968] 89).

[85] In line 1, MSS ATV om. "in"; line 2: OQR om. "and"; line 3: LOPQRV om. "in"; S om. "Holy"; B¹LMPQRSTV add "our Savior" after "Jesus Christ"; line 3: LOPQRV om. "in"; S om. "Holy"; B¹LMPQRSTV add "our Savior" after "Jesus Christ"; line 3: LOPQRV om. "in"; S om. "Holy"; line 4: LPQRSV add "the Paraclete"; line 5: CN om. "and"; QRS om. "in." Unfortunately Wajnberg (in Schmidt, *Gespräche Jesu*, 32) misrepresents Guerrier's apparatus to the first article, and he has been fol-

> . . . in the Father, the ruler of the entire world,
> and in Jesus Christ,
> and in the Holy Spirit,
> and in the holy Church
> and in the forgiveness of sins.

Among historians of the creeds, J. N. D. Kelly speaks for the consensus in describing this formula as a prototype of the *Symbolum Romanum*, the fivefold form being an expansion of an earlier threefold baptismal formula (as in Matt 28:20).[86] The most important parallels are in Hippolytus *Apostolic Tradition*:

> And when he who is to be baptised goes down to the water, let him who baptises lay hand on him saying thus: "Dost thou believe *in God the Father Almighty (in deum patrem omnipotentem)*? . . . Dost thou believe *in Christ Jesus (in Chr͞m I͞em)*, the Son of God, who was born of Holy Spirit and the Virgin Mary, who was crucified in the days of Pontius Pilate, and died, [and was buried] and rose the third day living from the dead and ascended into the heavens, and sat down at the right hand of the Father, and will come to judge the living and the dead? . . . Dost thou believe *in <the> Holy Spirit (in s͞pu s͞co)* in the Holy Church *(et sanctam ecclesiam)*, and the resurrection of the flesh *(et carnis resurrectionem)*?"[87] (21.12–17)

> And they who partake [of the eucharist] shall taste of each <cup>, he who gives <it> saying thrice: "*In God the Father Almighty (In D͞o patre omnipotenti)*; . . . *and in the Lord Jesus Christ (Et d͞no I͞eu Chr͞o)*; . . . *and in <the> Holy Spirit (et s͞pu s͞co) [and] in the Holy Church ([et] sancta ecclesia).*"[88] (23.8–10)

In addition, the Sahidic Coptic, Arabic, and Ethiopic versions of Hippolytus together insert a preliminary creed at *Apost. Trad.* 21.11:

> "Dost thou believe *in one God the Father Almighty? And in* his only-begotten Son *Jesus Christ* our Lord and our Saviour? *And in* His *Holy Spirit*, Giver of life to all creatures, the Trinity of One Substance, one Godhead, one Lordship,

---

lowed by others. See, e.g., Hans Lietzmann, "Symbolstudien VIII-XII," *ZNW* 22 (1923) 272; J. N. D. Kelly, *Early Christian Creeds* (3d ed.; London: Longman, 1972) 82; and J. Stevenson, ed., *A New Eusebius: Documents Illustrative of the History of the Church to A.D. 337* (London: S. P. C. K., 1970) 131.

[86] Kelly, *Creeds*, 122–23; cf. Hornschuh, *Studien*, 106–7.

[87] Latin text and ET in Gregory Dix, ed., ΑΠΟΣΤΟΛΙΚΗ ΠΑΡΑΔΟΣΙΣ: *The Treatise on the Apostolic Tradition of St Hippolytus of Rome* (rev. Henry Chadwick; London: S. P. C. K., 1968) 36–37. Latin text of vs 12 restored from the oriental versions in Bernard Botte, ed. and trans., *Hippolyte de Rome: La Tradition apostolique* (SC 11; 2d ed.; Paris: Cerf, 1968) 84. Emphasis added in this and following quotations highlights verbal agreements with *Ep. apost.* 5.22.

[88] Dix, *Apostolic Tradition*, 42. Dix (pp. lx–lxi) prints a Greek retroversion accepted (with only slight differences) by R. H. Connolly, B. Capelle, and Hans Lietzmann.

one Kingdom, one Faith, one Baptism *in the Holy* Catholic Apostolic
Church?'' And he who is baptized shall say <each time> thus: "Verily, I
believe."[89]

Concerning this preliminary creed Gregory Dix remarks:

> Some of this phraseology is evidently later than the Council of Constantinople I
> (A.D. 381). But this type of three-clause creed is very ancient and actually pre-
> ceded that developed Roman baptismal creed of which Hippolytus gives us the
> late-second-century text, and which we are accustomed to call the 'Apostles'
> Creed.' This ancient type of creed lasted longer in Egypt than elsewhere as is
> proved by the baptismal creed of a papyrus from Deir Balizeh, which seems to
> be a seventh-eighth century copy of a fourth-(?) century rite:
>
> "I believe *in God the Father Almighty*
> *And in* His only-begotten Son our Lord *Jesus Christ*
> *And in the Holy Ghost*
> and in the resurrection of the flesh
> *and the Holy* Catholic *Church.*"[90]

In light of these examples, it is curious that the *Epistula*, one of whose
central themes is the resurrection, should lack a reference to resurrection in
its communal confession. The reason would seem to be that the formula,
though differing from other extant early creeds, is presented in the form in
which the author received it.[91] More curious is the literary context of the confession. Comparable statements are preserved in church orders (with
catechetical questions) or within discussions of baptism (e.g., in Tertullian
De bapt. 11),[92] and this suggests that the confession now in *Ep. apost.* 5 has
been lifted from a baptismal context and stripped of its specific baptismal
reference, so that the author might resolve the mystery of the loaves.[93]

---

[89] Dix, *Apostolic Tradition*, lxii.

[90] Ibid., lxii-lxiii. Dix notes that "traces of the shorter form of creed are found in Irenaeus,
e.g. *Epideixis*, iii, and also (among the Marcosians) *Adv. Haer.* i.21.3. So also the Creed of the
Epistula Apostolorum. . . ." (p. lxii n.*).

[91] So Hornschuh, *Studien*, 106. Local forms of baptismal creeds almost certainly prevailed
until the third century: "No writer down to and including Tertullian can be quoted as showing
exclusive attachment to one structural form of summary; much less to one exact formula" (H. J.
Carpenter, "Creeds and Baptismal Rites in the First Four Centuries," *JTS* 44 [1943] 11).

[92] Tertullian comments on John 4:2 ("although Jesus himself did not baptize, but only his disciples"): "Let not (the fact) that 'he himself baptized not' trouble any. For into whom should he
baptize? Into repentance? Of what use, then, do you make his forerunner? *Into remission of
sins*, which he used to give by a word? *Into himself*, whom by humility he was concealing? *Into
the Holy Spirit*, who had not yet descended from the Father? *Into the Church*, which his apostles
had not yet founded? . . . Let none think it was some other . . ." (*De bapt.* 11, emphasis added;
ET in ANF 3. 674). Kelly (*Creeds*, 88) identifies additional passages: "Perhaps what [Tertul-
lian] had in mind in *De praescr.* 36 and *De virg. vel.* 1 was the baptismal questionnaire; several
features in those passages would harmonize with such an assumption."

[93] Cf. David Larrimore Holland, "The Third Article of the Creed: A Study in Second- and

The creed's preface, previously set aside, may now be found to supply the missing baptismal context (5.21 [--, 52/9]): "They [the loaves] are a picture of our faith *concerning the great Christianity*" (*baʾenta ʿabiy kerestennā*). This reading and translation present no insuperable logical or grammatical problems, and Schmidt accepted it as it stands.[94] Its correctness must be questioned, however, because the united witness of fam. 1 MSS reads not *ʿabiy kerestennā* but *ʿabiy kerestiyān*. The latter is admittedly difficult; according to Wajnberg it yields "no satisfactory sense."[95] Schmidt's colleague therefore suggested that the adjective, "great," be read in its construct form, *ʿabiya*, and understood as a substantive: "the Great One" or "Lord" of the Christians. This proposal was adopted by Montague Rhodes James, who translated the entire phrase "our faith in the Lord of the Christians."[96] But this translation too is open to objection, not least because in the summary of faith which follows "the Lord" is but one of five articles, each of which is the object of the faith symbolized by the loaves.

Complete and appropriate sense is accessible, however, and with no

---

Third-Century Theology," *StPatr* 13 [TU 116; Berlin: Akademie-Verlag, 1975] 193 n. 3): "That this passage is a creed seems to me highly dubious." Holland correctly observes that the word translated "picture" (in 5.21, = Eth. *ʾamsāl*) is not likely to connote "symbol in the technical sense of symbolum or creed." He therefore concludes: "There is nothing in the text itself to cause one to suppose that this passage were a creed. The five loaves demand and control the five articles of this interpretation of the Christian faith" (ibid.).

[94] Schmidt, *Gespräche Jesu*, 400; so Guerrier ("Le testament," 13) who quotes "foi au grand christianisme" without comment; Wajnberg in Schmidt, *Gespräche Jesu*, 32; Hornschuh, *Studien*, 106; and Vanovermeir, "Livre que Jésus-Christ a révélé," 135. General acceptance of this translation may be due in part to its similarity to the expression "Great Church," a term which in extant texts is apparently first found, attributed to Celsus, in Origen *C. Cels.* 5.59 (reference in Walter Bauer, *Orthodoxy and Heresy in Earliest Christianity* [2d ed.; Philadelphia: Fortress, 1979] 148). Cf. Ignatius *Rom.* 3.3: οὐ πεισμονῆς τὸ ἔργον, ἀλλὰ μεγέθους ἐστὶν ὁ Χριστιανισμός ("Christianity is not the work of persuasiveness, but of greatness"), a statement whose latter part is translated "Christianity is (truly) great" in BAG, *s.v.* μέγεθος, 2 (498b).

[95] Wajnberg in Schmidt, *Gespräche Jesu*, 32 n. 3.

[96] James, *The Apocryphal New Testament* (Oxford: Clarendon, 1924) 487. James retained the fam. 2 reading, "in the great christendom," in parentheses. The translation "the Great One [Lord] of the Christians" gains some plausibility from analogous titles in hellenistic Jewish literature. In *T. Sim.* 6.5 the patriarch prophesies that "Shem shall be glorified; because God the Lord, the Great One of Israel (κύριος ὁ Θεὸς μέγας τοῦ Ἰσραήλ) will be manifest" (Greek text in M. de Jonge, ed., *The Testaments of the Twelve Patriarchs* [PVTG 1/2; Leiden: Brill, 1978] 21; ET by H. C. Kee in *OTP* 1. 787, except that Kee's principal manuscript, and hence his translation, reads "in" for "of"); cf. *1 Enoch* 14.2: "I saw in my dream what I am now telling with a tongue of flesh, ... which the Great One has given" (*za-wahaba ʿabiy*; ὃ ἔδωκεν ὁ μέγας) (Ethiopic text and Greek fragments in R. H. Charles, ed., *The Ethiopic Version of the Book of Enoch* [Anecdota Oxoniensia; Oxford: Clarendon, 1906] 34–35; ET in Matthew Black, ed., *The Book of Enoch or 1 Enoch* [SVTP 7; Leiden: Brill, 1985] 32); and the phrase "the glory of the Great One" in *1 Enoch* 9.3; 14.20; 104.1. Cf. also *Orac. Sib.* 2.243: "[Christ] will sit on the right of the Great One" (καθίσει Μεγάλῳ ἐπὶ δεξιᾷ) (Greek text in Geffcken, *Oracula Sibyllina*, 39; ET in *OTP* 1. 351).

emendation. The phrase ʿ*abiy kerestiyān* (lit. "great" [sing.] + "Christians" [pl.]) is an Ethiopic idiom for *baptized* (or "full") Christians, in contrast to *neʾus kerestiyān* (lit. "little" or "young [among the] Christians"), who are *catechumens*.[97] Either expression can refer to one or more members of its class. The second is found in the Ethiopic NT, translating ὁ κατηχούμενος in Gal 6:6 ("Let *him who is taught the word* share . . ."). These idioms for the baptized and for the catechumens are found regularly only in church orders, and "great" or "full Christians" only where a sharp distinction is being made between catechumens and those already baptized. In the Ethiopic version of the *Statutes of the Apostles* 40, for example, there is a prayer for the oil of chrism with which catechumens are to be anointed, ". . . and for full Christians who are sick" (ʿ*abiy kerestiyān deweyān*).[98] In the same church order there is the following postbaptismal regulation (*Statute* 35):

> When everything has been finished, let them [the newly baptized] pray with all the people: and they shall not before pray with the full Christians (*mesla ʿabiy kerestiyān*), but only after they have done the thing which we say.[99]

[97] The phrase is not a common one. Dillmann (*Lexicon, s.v.* ʿ*abya* [988]) defines the expression simply as "Christians (adult or mature opp. *neʾus kerestiyān*, catechumens or neophytes)," and cites only three references: "Const. Ap. [= the Ethiopic *Statutes of the Apostles*] 34; Kid. [= the Ethiopic version of the *Testamentum Domini*] f. 10; I Pet. 3.21 rom. [= the Rome edition of the Ethiopic NT, 1548 – 49]."

In his report on the Ethiopic text of Acts, James A. Montgomery ("The Ethiopic Text of Acts of the Apostles," *HTR* 27 [1934] 169 – 205) notes in one manuscript a "doublet translation" of Acts 26:28. Agrippa's response to Paul ("In a short time you think to make me a Christian!" *RSV*) is expanded with a phrase translated by Montgomery, "and almost as if you had brought me (plus an unintelligible ʿ*abiya* 'great') among the Christians" (p. 175). The addition clearly means: "It is as if you would already have me be *a baptized Christian*."

[98] Ethiopic text and ET in George Horner, ed., *The Statutes of the Apostles or Canones Ecclesiastici* (London: Williams & Norgate, 1904) 33, 168.

[99] Ibid., 23, 155. Hugo Duensing's critical text of the Ethiopic *Statutes* (*Der aethiopische Text der Kirchenordnung des Hippolyt* [AAWG 3/32; Göttingen: Vandenhoeck & Ruprecht, 1946] 60) gives a variant reading not dissimilar to that of the fam. 2 MSS at *Ep. apost.* 5.21. For ʿ*abiy kerestiyān* in *Statute* 35 one manuscript reads ʾ*abyāta kerestiyānāt*, "the churches."

A further example of the idiom is in the Ethiopic version of the *Testamentum Domini* 16, where the congregation is divided into groups for receiving the eucharistic bread:

> Let the priests receive first thus: the bishops, presbyters, deacons; then the widows, readers, and subdeacons; after these those that have gifts; the *new full Christians* (*haddisān ʿabiy kerestiyān*); and then the children.

(Text and French translation in Robert Beylot, ed., *Testamentum Domini éthiopien: Édition et traduction* [Louvain: Peeters, 1984] 41 – 42, 172). A control is supplied by the Syriac version (= *Testamentum Domini* 1.23), which gives the literal sense: "those newly baptized" (text and Latin translation in Ignatius Ephraem II Rahmani, ed., *Testamentum Domini Nostri Jesu Christi* [Mainz: Kirchheim, 1899] 46 – 47; ET in James Cooper and Arthur John MacLean, *The Testament of Our Lord* [Edinburgh: T. & T. Clark, 1902] 76).

It is now clear that we are dealing with an Ethiopic ecclesiastical technical term, or rather, with the less common of a pair of technical terms. What separates the ʿ*abiy kerestiyān* from the *neʾus kerestiyān* is baptism.[100] The full phrase in *Ep. apost.* 5.21 must therefore be: "a picture of our faith for baptized Christians."[101]

If this is so, then "faith" here means, not "trust," "confidence," or the like, but "that which is believed," approximating to a "rule of faith" or "canon of truth."[102] This is consistent with what the disciples affirm that the loaves mean. They do not represent the believers' trust or assurance; they symbolize the *objects of belief*, collectively designated "our faith."

The list of miracles in the *Epistula*, now seen to conclude with a statement of baptismal faith, follows no other list in this. The one ending common to many of the lists is an assertion about the countless other wonders performed by the Lord (see also John 20:31; 21:25). Instead, at the list's climax the miracles are almost forgotten. Two reasons for this may be suggested. First, a summary declaration about the Lord's work would be premature, because the saving revelation—that is, the post-resurrection discourse—has yet to

---

[100] Even if the fam. 2 reading (ʿ*abiy kerestennā*)were correct, the word *kerestennā* (Christianity) would have to bear its rare secondary meaning, analogous to the English word "christening": "baptism (by which people are received into the assembly of Christians and communion of Christ)" (Dillmann, *Lexicon*, s.v. *kerestos* [836]). But this leaves ʿ*abiy* (great) unaccounted for. The regular Ethiopic word for baptism, *ṭemqat*, is found in *Ep. apost.* 27.2 and 42.3.

[101] The Ethiopic word *baʾenta*, here translated "for," usually has the meaning "about" or "concerning" (= Greek περί + genitive). But it is a flexible preposition, and raises no greater problem in this translation than in the reading translated in *NTApoc* 1. 194.

The original Greek underlying the idiom "full Christians" in 5.21 cannot of course be determined with certainty. The three strongest candidates are: (1) τέλειοι, "mature, i.e., baptized [Christians]" (in contrast with νήπιοι, "babes, infants, i.e., not yet baptized [Christians]"; cf. *LPGL*, s.v. τέλειος C.3 [1380b], νήπιος B.1 [908a]); (2) a passive participle of βαπτίζω (cf. the Eth. *Test. Dom.* 16 and Syr. 1.23 in note 99 above); (3) πιστοί, "faithful, i.e., professed, baptized [Christians]" (cf. *LPGL*, s.v. πιστός E.2 [1088a]).

With reference to option (3), it is worth noting that Hippolytus *Apostolic Tradition*, from which the church orders cited above are more or less directly derived, regularly contrasts the status of "catechumens" with that of the "faithful." As Dix's edition indicates, the Latin has "catecuminus" (e.g., in 26.5) and "fidelis" (e.g., in 32.1); the Coptic version retains the Greek κατηχούμενος and πιστός. The post-baptismal regulation from Eth. *Statutes* 35 quoted above comes (via Coptic and Arabic intermediaries) from *Apost. Trad.* 22.5: "Thenceforward they [the newly baptized] shall pray together with all the people. But they shall not previously pray with *the faithful* (Lat. *cum fidelibus*) before they have undergone all these things" (Dix, *Apostolic Tradition*, 39).

[102] For this sense in the NT, see 1 Tim 1:19; 4:1; Jude 3; cf. Hippolytus *Apost. Trad.* 16.2; 38.1. Kelly (*Creeds*, 53) notes that in the East the customary description of the creed was "the faith" (cf. *LPGL*, s.v. πίστις II and III [1086b–87b]). On the term "faith" in the later NT and post-apostolic writings Rudolf Bultmann observes: "*pistis* . . . is becoming a historical term, so to speak, for Christianity in the sense of the content of its belief" (*Theology of the New Testament* (2 vols.; London: SCM, 1952–55) 2. 211.

begin. It is not until *Ep. apost.* 29.5 (XXIV 13, 71/4) that a description of the disciples as blessed eyewitnesses becomes explicit because not until then, for the *Epistula*, have the risen Lord's *words* complemented the earthly Jesus' *deeds*: "O Lord, blessed are we, <for we see> you and hear you as you <preach> such things, for our eyes have seen these great wonders that you have done" (cf. Matt 11:4−6 par.; 13:16−17 par.). Secondly, the credal conclusion of *Ep. apost.* 4−5 is connected with the writing's claim to authority. The list testifies to the eyewitness status of the apostles (chap. 3: "as we saw"), and it is *through baptism* that the community to whom the writing is addressed are to be "associates in the grace of the Lord," in the apostles' "service and glory" (6.2). In declaring this baptismal "faith" the *Epistula* defines both its orthodoxy and its audience.

These suggestions would support the hypothesis of a catechetical life-setting for the *Epistula*. The readers, perhaps both the instructors and the instructed in the author's circle, may read with those who are "firm, without wavering, in the knowledge and investigation of our Lord Jesus Christ" (6.3), those who have received forgiveness of sins but not yet that resurrection which is the true salvation (34.1−2) now to be offered by the risen Lord.

Summary

1) *Ep. apost.* 4−5 is a summary of the earthly wonderworking career of Jesus. It is also the continuation of the christological hymn which begins in chap. 3. Chaps. 3−5 together constitute the disciples' aretalogy of the pre-existent Word and the earthly Jesus.

2) *Ep. apost.* 4−5 is composed according to a conscious pattern, in which miracle "reports" and miracle "narratives" are presented in three groups of five wonders.

3) The reports are indistinguishable from those in other early Christian miracle lists, and observations concerning the final pair of reports suggests the possibility that a source list, written or oral, was taken over by the author of the *Epistula*.

4) The narratives, five in number, differ from those in other lists in that they include dialogue. In three cases this dialogue conforms to the literary conventions adopted in the dialogue of chaps. 13−51.

5) The narratives' relation to their NT counterparts is of a kind which makes direct borrowing from texts almost impossible to demonstrate. Random quotation is also an improbable compositional theory; the Legion story, for example, reflects two distinct traditions, now inextricably interwoven.

6) The narratives display specific theological interests:
The school story: Jesus is the teacher *par excellence*.
The sick woman: The earthly Jesus, like the risen Lord, is no phantom.

The Legion story: Jesus, himself no demon, has authority over demons.
The denarius and the feeding: The Lord supplies the needs of his disciples,
who are now the Lord's representatives in ministering to the community.

7) The list ends, not with the customary reference to a host of unrecorded
miracles, but with a baptismal confession now seen to be so designated by
the *Epistula*'s author. The list and the confession define the authority of
the writer and the status of the recipients of the revelation. *Ep. apost.*
3 – 5 is the first of two prefaces to the revelatory dialogue in chaps.
13 – 51. The second preface is the post-resurrection appearance account in
Ep. apost. 9 – 12.

3

Epistula Apostolorum 9 – 12:
The Post-Resurrection Appearance

It was seen in Chapter One that it is not possible to recover a single thematic thread in the earlier chapters of the *Epistula*, although a sequence of credal topics is covered. It was also noted that the question of the author's use of sources, though a necessary one, can yield results that are both inconclusive and, in themselves, incapable of responding to a more important issue: the intention of the author and the compositional method by which it has been carried out. Thus in *Ep. apost.* 9 – 12, the last section before the revelation dialogue begins, the search for the author's traditional resources must again be complemented with the detection of compositional method and unifying redactional theology. My principal intention in this chapter is twofold: first, to show how *Ep. apost.* 9 – 12 serves as an introduction to the revelation dialogue in 13 – 51, and secondly, to identify the traditional background and the function of the proof-text in 11.8.

The narrative in chaps. 9 – 12 moves from the disciples' self-identification ("he concerning whom we bear witness," 9.1) to the inauguration of the Lord's discourse ("Rise up, and I will reveal to you . . . ," 12.3). This movement is brought about by a brief summary of the events surrounding the Lord's death and burial, and by an account, without precise analogy in other early Christian literature, of the appearance of the risen Lord to the women at the tomb and to the disciples. These chapters serve to authenticate both the message and the messenger, the former through the demonstrated power of the resurrection ("the power to take you up," 12.4), the latter through the identification of the resurrected one as the disciples' teacher (10.2).

The relation of *Ep. apost.* 9 – 12 to the canonical accounts has seemed to the writing's few commentators to be clear. John E. Alsup's conclusion, based in part upon the *Epistula*'s failure to retain a "family resemblance" with the form of the accounts in the NT gospels, is that "the writer seems to have gathered themes at will from [the canonical gospels'] accounts in order to create a composite picture for his dialogue/revelational goals."[1] In this view Alsup follows Adolf Harnack[2] and Schmidt.[3] Indeed, Schmidt tersely refers to the author's mechanical method of composition, and with Harnack sees the whole section as a thoroughly literary construction with a single theological tendency, namely an antidocetic polemic. Yet Schmidt rightly strives to uncover a unifying compositional scheme, based on the recurring threes: the three women, the threefold mission to the twelve, and the three named disciples.[4]

With reference to Alsup's critique, it must be asked what constitutes the "family resemblance" of the canonical appearance accounts. C. H. Dodd, building on the work of Martin Albertz[5] and Lyder Brun,[6] identified two classes of post-resurrection appearance account: the "concise" type (Class I) and the "circumstantial" type (Class II).[7] For the concise type (Matt

---

[1] Alsup, *The Post-Resurrection Appearance Stories of the Gospel Tradition* (CTM A/5; Stuttgart: Calwer, 1975) 128–30.

[2] "Ein jüngst entdeckter Auferstehungsbericht," in *Theologische Studien Bernhard Weiss zu seinem 70. Geburtstage dargebracht* (Göttingen: Vandenhoeck & Ruprecht, 1897) 1–8. Harnack found three traditional elements combined in *Ep. apost.* 9–12: (1) the visit of several women to the tomb; (2) the unbelief of the disciples; and (3) the assurance that the resurrected Jesus is not incorporeal (pp. 3, 8). Harnack, of course, reported on the basis of only those few portions of the text accessible by 1908, i.e., in Schmidt, "Eine bisher unbekannte altchristliche Schrift," 706–11.

[3] Schmidt, *Gespräche Jesu*, 222–23. Cf. Bultmann, *History*, 314.

[4] Schmidt, ibid.

[5] "Zur Formengeschichte der Auferstehungsberichte," *ZNW* 21 (1922) 259–69. Albertz distinguished seven groups of post-resurrection reports: (1) "catechism-style" enumerations of events (e.g., Luke 24:34; 1 Cor 15:3–8); (2) christophanies and angelophanies (e.g., Matt 28:16–20; John 20:19–23; Mark 16:14–18); (3) narratives from the life of Jesus placed after his death (e.g., John 21:1–14; *Gos. Pet.* 14.58–60 [cf. Luke 5:1–11]); (4) reports as evidence for the resurrection, including such motifs as proof from scripture (e.g. John 20:9), the empty tomb (Mark 16:4; John 20:5–8), evidence for the reality of the resurrected one, esp. through the inspection of his wounds, and the former unbelief of the disciples; (5) "realistic" reports, e.g., with additional characters (as in Matt 27:62–66; 28:11–15); (6) reports of the lengthy presence of the resurrected one (e.g., Acts 1:3); and (7) reports establishing the inception of Jesus' divinity, such as the baptism and the transfiguration. Albertz (p. 264) notes that "a firm ordering of the traditions is not ascertainable."

[6] *Die Auferstehung Christi in der urchristlichen Überlieferung* (Oslo: Aschenhoug-Nygaard; Giessen: Töpelmann, 1925). Under three section headings ("Tomb Narrative"; "Appearance of the Resurrected One"; "Ascension") Brun catalogues the traditions, literary themes, and compositional devices in the canonical gospels and in the *Gospel of Peter*, the *Gospel to the Hebrews*, the *Kerygmata Petri*, the *Epistula* and the Syriac *Didascalia*. See also Maurice Goguel, *La foi à la résurrection de Jésus dans le christianisme primitif* (Paris: Leroux, 1933), esp. pp. 195 (the empty tomb), 341–43 and 352–53 (the appearance), and 380 (the ascension).

[7] Dodd, "The Appearances of the Risen Christ: An Essay in Form-Criticism of the Gospels," in D. E. Nineham, ed., *Studies in the Gospels: Essays in Memory of R. H. Lightfoot* (Oxford:

28:8 – 10; 28:16 – 20; John 20:19 – 21) Dodd proposed the following "common pattern":[8]

a) the situation: Christ's followers bereft of their Lord;
b) the appearance of the Lord;
c) the Greeting;
d) the Recognition;
e) the Word of Command.

Dodd suggested that Mark 16:14 – 15 and Luke 24:36 – 49 fit this pattern sufficiently to warrant inclusion under this heading, though apologetic motives are apparent in both.[9]

In the second of these formal types, as their title suggests, the author provides circumstantial or apologetic details, as in the Walk to Emmaus in Luke 24:13 – 35 or the Appearance by the Sea in John 21:1 – 14. John 20:11 – 17 (the appearance to Mary Magdalene) and John 20:26 – 29 (the appearance to Thomas) are identified by Dodd as special cases, strictly neither Class I nor Class II.[10]

There is enough formal correspondence to bring *Ep. apost.* 9 – 12 within the Class II scheme. But on methodological grounds it must be noted that with the exception of the motif of "recognition" (ἀναγνώρισις),[11] Dodd offers no external criteria (e.g., formal analogies outside of the gospel tradition) to describe the particular shape of each narrative.[12] There is a danger, therefore, that the description of the form will be made on the basis of a prior

Blackwell, 1957) 9 – 35; reprinted in idem, *More New Testament Studies* (Manchester: Manchester University Press, 1968) 102 – 33.

[8] Dodd, "Appearances," 11.

[9] Ibid., 16 – 17.

[10] Ibid., 13, 18 – 20.

[11] Dodd (ibid., 14) asserts that "it seems proper . . . to use the technical term applied by ancient literary critics to the recognition-scene which was so often the crucial point of a Greek drama." A description of the dramatic "recognition" device is given by Aristotle in the *Poetica* 11.4 – 8; 16.1 – 5. He points out that the fundamental change is from ignorance to knowledge. The discovery of one character by another can be by "tokens" (διὰ τῶν σημείων), and "these may be congenital . . . or they may be acquired, and these may be on the body, for instance, wounds (οὐλαί)" (16.1).

[12] Dodd concludes with the observation that "in certain respects the more circumstantial narratives recall accounts of theophanies in the Old Testament and in profane literature," but he judges that "the points of difference are more numerous and striking than the points of resemblance" ("Appearances," 34). He also suggests that "*formally*, there is nothing to distinguish the narratives we have been examining from the 'Paradigms' and other concise narratives on the one hand, and the 'Novellen,' or 'Tales,' on the other, which occur in other parts of the Gospels"; but for Dodd this is less a heuristic appeal to form-critical parallels than it is a summons to see the post-resurrection accounts "not only in their aspect as witnesses to the faith of the early Church, but also as ostensible records of things that happened" (p. 35).

decision, namely that only certain texts are legitimate resources for the recon-struction of a formal type. Even Bultmann's analysis, based on the more modest twofold scheme of (1) the motif of proving the resurrection by the appearance of the risen Lord and (2) the motif of the missionary charge of the Lord,[13] does not equip us to deal with representatives of the appearance tradition which are outside the canonical family circle. *Ep. apost.* 9 – 12 has no mission charge, and it is not concerned exclusively with proof of the resurrection.

Hence the collection of parallels, here as elsewhere in the *Epistula*, will only take us so far. Once it is established that there is no single canonical model behind these chapters and that there is no discernible pattern of selec-tion from known sources, the task has only begun. The critical area, as Alsup notes, is that of "compositional structure and thought-world."[14] *Ep. apost.* 9 – 12, whatever else it may be, is no slavish rehash of canonical materials. But this judgment can be instructive only when the new shape and purpose have been accounted for.

The Structure of *Ep. apost.* 9 – 12

A cursory reading of these chapters is sufficient to indicate that several dif-ferent intentions are at work in the material taken over by this writer. In par-ticular we have to contend with at least two types of "proof" that the account is claiming to offer: proof of the identify of the risen one, and proof of his resurrection. But these proofs, together with the threefold mission to the twelve already referred to, do not yet provide a secure picture of the structure of the narrative. However, two distinct themes seem to hold the whole account together: first, the *appearance* of the risen Lord (and with it the issues of identity and of resurrection as a theoretical possibility); and second, the *demonstration* of the resurrected body to the disciples. The former concern dominates *Ep. apost.* 10.3 – 11.6 and 12.2 – 4; the latter occupies 11.7 – 12.1.

This distinction, made on the basis of dominant themes, can be supported on the basis of the literary structure of the narrative. Just as it was seen that the temporal adverb τότε (then) serves as a compositional device in *Ep. apost.* 4 – 5, so too in *Ep. apost.* 9 – 12 this adverb, found five times, serves as one of four elements in a recurring pattern in 10.3 – 11.6 and 12.1 – 4:

   a) movement towards the disciples, or of the disciples to the Lord;
   b) an expression of disbelief;

---

[13] Bultmann, *History*, 288 – 90.
[14] Alsup, *Appearance Stories*, 128.

c) the temporal adverb, τότε;

d) a speech of the Lord.

The first cycle of these elements is not as clear as those that follow, but thereafter four times the rhythm has a deliberateness about it which makes it a useful analytical tool. Filled out with the narrative and dialogue, the pattern appears as follows:

1) *Ep. apost.* 10.3 – 7:

   a) Martha *came and told it to us.* We said to her, "What do you want with us, O woman? He who has died is buried, and could it be possible for him to live?"

   b) *We did not believe her*, that the Saviour had risen from the dead.

   c) *Then* she went back to the Lord and said to him, "None of them believed me that you are alive."

   d) *He said*, "Let another one of you go to them saying this again to them."

2) *Ep. apost.* 10.8 – 11.1:

   a) *Mary came and told us again,*

   b) and *we did not believe her.* She returned to the Lord and she also told it to him.

   c) *Then*

   d) *the Lord said to Mary and also to her sisters*, "Let us go to them."

3) *Ep. apost.* 11.2 – 4:

   a) *And he came and found us* inside. He called us out.

   b) But we thought it was a ghost, and *we did not believe it was the Lord.*

   c) *Then*

   d) *<he said> to us*, "Come, do not be afraid. I am your <master> whom you, Peter, denied three times; and now do you deny again?"

4) *Ep. apost.* 11.5 – 6:

   a) But *we went to him*

   b) *doubting in <our> hearts* whether it was possibly he.

   c) *Then*

   d) *he said to <us>*, "Why do you still doubt and are you not believing? I am he who spoke to you concerning my flesh, my death, and my resurrection."

   [*Ep. apost.* 11.7 – 8: Demonstration of the Resurrected Body]

5) *Ep. apost.* 12.1 – 4:

   a) But *now we <touched> him* that we might truly know whether he <had risen> in the flesh,

b) and we fell on our <faces> confessing our sin, that *we had been* <un>*believing*.

c) *Then*

d) *the Lord our redeemer said,* "Rise up, and I will reveal to you what is above heaven and what is in heaven, and your rest that is in the kingdom of heaven. For my <Father> has given me the power to take up you and those who believe in me."

Therefore in terms both of its theme and of its structure the account of the *demonstration* of the resurrected body is separable from the *appearance* account. The question becomes whether there are formal grounds, in terms of the prior history of these post-resurrection traditions, on which this separation may be explained. A clue may be had in the last section, *Ep. apost.* 12.2 – 4. Whereas in the NT texts the goal of the appearance, according to Dodd's concise pattern, is the commissioning of the disciples (Matt 28:20; Luke 24:47; John 20:21), in the *Epistula* the command to preach is not at all connected with the appearance account, but rather with a discourse on the return of the Lord and the giving of a new commandment (chap. 19). The goal of *Ep. apost.* 9 – 12 is the revelation discourse itself.

The appropriate literary analogue, as Helmut Koester has indicated, is the Gnostic gospel or "revelation discourse."[15] Yet three features typical of the Gnostic revealer's appearing, namely cosmic signs, polymorphous shape, and luminosity,[16] are absent from the post-resurrection appearance account in the *Epistula,* and Koester therefore proposes that the original features of the revelation gospels' introduction have been suppressed.[17] But if we look back to what may be the OT models on which the revelation gospels' appearance form was probably based, the suggestion is prompted that in the *Epistula* it is the wish to preserve continuity between the earthly Jesus and the risen Lord that has led to the exclusion of traditional theophanic matter: the vision offered the disciples in *Ep. apost.* 9 – 12 is a vision of the risen revealer himself. As this *vision* (11.2 – 3; 12.1 – 2) gives way to *audition* (12.3 – 4), the parallels between the *Epistula* and both OT epiphanies and NT post-resurrection accounts become more numerous. In the *Epistula* the cosmic signs of the epiphany tradition now have a secure place in the context of the *parousia* (see *Ep. apost.* 16.3 – 5).

Thus in Ezek 1:4 – 28a the vision dominates, but the summary and audition which follow bring us close to the form of *Ep. apost.* 12.2 – 4.

[15] Koester, "One Jesus and Four Primitive Gospels," in idem and Robinson, *Trajectories,* 202.

[16] See Perkins, *Gnostic Dialogue,* 49 – 52.

[17] Koester, "One Jesus," 202 – 3.

Such was the appearance of the likeness of the glory of the Lord. And when I saw it, I fell upon my face, and I heard the voice of one speaking. And he said to me, "Son of man, stand upon your feet, and I will speak with you." And when he spoke to me, the Spirit entered into me and set me upon my feet; and I heard him speaking to me. (Ezek 1:28b-2:2)

Dan 8:15 – 19 repeats the pattern:[18]

When I, Daniel, had seen the vision, I sought to understand it; and behold, there stood before me one having the appearance of a man. And I heard a man's voice between the banks of the Ulai, and it called, "Gabriel, make this man understand the vision." So he came near where I stood; and when he came, I was frightened and fell upon my face. But he said to me, "Understand, O son of man, that the vision is for the time of the end." As he was speaking to me, I fell into a deep sleep with my face to the ground; but he touched me, and set me on my feet. He said, "Behold, I will make known to you what shall be the latter end of the indignation."

Matthew's account of the transfiguration (Matt 17:1 – 9) incorporates the same pattern of prostration and elevation:

When the disciples heard [the voice from heaven], they fell on their faces, and were filled with awe. But Jesus came and touched them, saying, "Rise, and have no fear." (Matt 17:6 – 7)

Text and Translation of Ep. apost. 11.2a

The form-critical connection between *Ep. apost.* 9 – 12 and the OT epiphanies can be shown further through a consideration of the translation of 11.2a: "He came and found us inside, veiled" (III 8, 55/4; *NTApoc* 1. 196). The two versions do not, in fact, both read ". . . inside, veiled." The Coptic has only ". . . inside" (Ⲛ̄ⳅⲞⲨⲚ).[19] The Ethiopic manuscripts, in agreement regarding the first part of the sentence ("and he came and found us"), are thereafter divided between three readings:

a) 'enza negēlleb	MSS ABCKNOQRT	"while we were fishing"
b) 'enza netgellabab	MSS B(corr.)LMP	"we being veiled"
c) 'enza negalleb	MSS S	"while we were fishing"

---

[18] See also Dan 10:8 – 12; *1 Enoch* 14:24 – 15:2; 60:4 – 6; and *2 Enoch* 22:5 – 23:7. For the various OT prophetic "call" patterns from which the form in the *Epistula* is likely derived, see W. Eugene Marsh, "Prophecy," in John H. Hayes, ed., *Old Testament Form Criticism* (San Antonio: Trinity University Press, 1974) 170 – 72, and the literature cited there; and Perkins, *Gnostic Dialogue*, 49 – 52.

[19] This is correctly reflected in the translations of James (*Apocryphal New Testament*, 488) and Duensing (*Epistula Apostolorum*, 10). It should be added that the Coptic rendered "he called us out" (11.2b) need mean no more than "he called (out) to us."

The consonantal similarity between the readings is obvious, but in no case is a correspondence between the Ethiopic and Coptic easy to recover. Wajnberg pointed to John 21:3 (Jesus' appearance by the Sea of Tiberias) for the theme of fishing, but nevertheless opted with Schmidt for the reading "veiled."[20] Schmidt suggested that the Ethiopic translator did not understand the original Greek ἔσω (or its Coptic or Arabic intermediary), and that the reference is to the grief of the disciples (note the women's grief in 9.5; 10.1).[21] But is it conceivable that Greek ἔσω, or even Coptic ⲚⲌⲞⲨⲚ, was misunderstood? The single recurrence of ⲚⲌⲞⲨⲚ in the extant Coptic text (in 43.11; XXXV 15 = "within," *NTApoc* 1. 222) has as its Ethiopic parallel the expected *westa*.

Support for reading "while we were fishing" may be claimed from *Gos. Pet.* 14.60,[22] which seems to be preparing for a dominical appearance like that in John 21:1 – 14. But it is not likely that a later hand would deliberately contradict the canonical location of the demonstration account; and more problematical still is the fact that the normal Ethiopic verb for fishing is not *galaba* but *ʾašgara* (as in John 21:3).[23]

More promising possibilities, in terms of helpful literary parallels, derive from the minority reading. A passage that is close to *Ep. apost.* 11 both in structure and in vocabulary is *1 Enoch* 13 – 14. Indeed, given the recognition accorded the Enochian corpus in the Ethiopian Church it is not improbable that *1 Enoch* exerted some influence on the Ethiopic translation of the *Epistula*. In *1 Enoch* 13 Enoch is commanded to report his vision by way of reproof to the sons of heaven. On hearing Enoch's words the Watchers recognize their guilt. Enoch continues:

> And I woke up and went to them, and they were all sitting gathered together as they mourned, . . . with their faces covered [Eth.: *ʾenza gelbubān gaṣṣomu* = Gk.: περικεκαλυμμένοι τὴν ὄψιν].[24] (*1 Enoch* 13.9)

More striking is the formal resemblance between *1 Enoch* 14 and *Ep. apost.* 11 – 12:

---

[20] Wajnberg, in Schmidt, *Gespräche Jesu*, 40. For veiling in grief in the OT, see, e.g., 2 Sam 19:4; 1 Chr 21:16.

[21] Schmidt, *Gespräche Jesu*, 41.

[22] References to the *Gospel of Peter* are from M. G. Mara, ed., *Évangile de Pierre* (SC 201; Paris: Cerf, 1973); ET in *NTApoc* 1. 183 – 87.

[23] Dillmann (*Lexicon*, *s.v. galaba* [1138]) cites only this passage for *galaba* = "to fish," and he does so solely on the basis of a cognate Arabic verb.

[24] Charles, *Book of Enoch*, 34 – 35.

1 Enoch 14:24 – 15:1	Ep. apost. 11.1 – 12.3
Until then *I had a covering on my face* (Eth. *diba gaṣṣeya galbābē*) as I trembled.	He came and found us inside/*veiled*. (Eth. *'enza netgellabab*)
And *the Lord called me . . .* and *said to me,*	*He called us* [out]. . . . Then *he said to us,*
"*Come near* to me, Enoch . . . *Do not be afraid . . .*	"*Come, do not be afraid. . . .*
Come near to me and *hear my voice*. . . ."	*Rise up,* and *I will reveal to you. . . .*"

Fragments of the same epiphany form are detectable in other post-resurrection accounts. In *Gos. Pet.* 7.26 Peter reports: "I mourned with my fellows, and being wounded in heart we hid ourselves (ἐκρυβόμεθα)." The stated motivation here is fear of the Jews who seek the disciples, as in John 20:19.[25] In a different context Origen quotes Celsus on the distinction between the pre- and post-resurrection manifestations of Jesus:

> While he was in the body, and no one believed upon him, he preached to all without intermission; but when he might have produced a powerful belief in himself after rising from the dead, he showed himself secretly (κρύβδην) only to one woman and to his companions.[26]

This motif of the hiddenness of the disciples is taken up, probably from the *Gospel of Peter*,[27] by Cyril of Jerusalem (d. 386) in his *Catechetical Lectures*:

> For the day of Azumes and at the time of the feast the women mourned and wept, and the Apostles who had hidden themselves (ἀποκρυβέντες οἱ ἀπόστολοι) were overwhelmed with anguish.[28]

[25] Cf. *Ep. Pet. Phil.* (NHC 8, 2) 133.17 – 134.9: "Then, when the apostles had come together [on the Mount of Olives] and thrown themselves upon their knees, they prayed . . . saying, 'Son of Life, . . . give us power, for they seek to kill us.'"

[26] Origen, *C. Celsum* 2.70 (ANF 4.460).

[27] So H. B. Swete, *The Akhmîm Fragment of the Apocryphal Gospel of St Peter* (London/New York: Macmillan, 1893) 13.

[28] *Catech.* 13.25 (Greek text in PG 33. 804; ET in L. P. Macauley and A. A. Stephenson, *The Works of Saint Cyril of Jerusalem* [2 vols.; ACW 64; Washington, DC: Catholic University of America Press, 1970] 2. 21). A further occurrence of this motif, in a somewhat later source, is in Ps.-Athanasius *Fragmenta in Cant.* In chaps. 2 and 3 there is a fourfold refrain: "Then the disciples, for fear of the Jews, were gathered together in the room *hidden*" (κρυπτόμενοι = veiled?); "Let Judas not laugh, when the disciples are *hidden* and the slain one is crucified"; "Then let the disciples of the Lord, *hidden within* the room (ἔσω ἐν τῷ κελλίῳ κρυπτόμενοι), say..."; "On this account, therefore, let the disciples *hidden within* the room say..." (Greek text in PG 27. 1353 – 56).

The Coptic and Ethiopic readings of *Ep. apost.* 11.2 may therefore be tentatively reconciled in that they represent respectively a minimal (Coptic: "within") and a maximal (Ethiopic: "veiled") rendering of the idea found in the *Gospel of Peter's* ἐκρυβόμεθα. In either case, the notion of concealment and fear before the revealer is present, as in the OT epiphanic models.

In summary, those portions of *Ep. apost.* 9–12 which follow a conscious compositional pattern, that is, elements (a)–(d) outlined above, appear to have as their literary inspiration certain well-established features of the epiphany tradition. The traditional antecedents of the *demonstration*, on the other hand, must be sought outside the context both of the epiphany tradition and of Jewish and Christian revelatory literature. How, and to what ends, has the author refashioned and combined these traditional materials?

Ep. apost. 9.1 – 11.6:
The Lord Announced as Risen Teacher

Ep. apost. 9.1 – 3 (I 11, 53/10)

Ethiopic	Coptic
1 He of whom we are witnesses we know as the one crucified in the days of Pontius Pilate and of the prince Archelaus, who was crucified between two thieves	1 . . . he concerning whom <we>bear witness that the Lord is he who was crucified by Pontius Pilate and Archelaus between the two thieves,
2 and was taken down from the wood of the cross together with them,	
3 and was buried in the place called *qarānejō*.	3 <and> who was buried in a place called the <place of the skull>.

Compared with the narrative that follows, these verses are brief and economical. The repeated pronoun, "*he* concerning whom," "*he who*," "*who*," suggest that we have to do with a confessional declaration of some sort, although the clauses relating to the manner of death ("under Pontius Pilate and Archelaus between two thieves") and burial ("in a place called the place of a skull") are found in no extant creed. A passage similar in form to this summary is found in the Nag Hammadi *Ep. Pet. Phil.* (NHC 8, 2) 139.15 – 21:

> Our illuminator Jesus [came] down and was crucified.
> And he [wore] a crown of thorns.
> And he put [on] a purple robe;
> and he was [crucified] upon a cross;
> and he was buried in a tomb;
> and he rose from the dead.[29]

---

[29] Coptic text and ET in Marvin W. Meyer, *The Letter of Peter to Philip: Text, Translation*

Marvin W. Meyer, who describes the passage as a "traditional credo" and a "christological credo," notes that

> such items as these were combined very early in Christian circles to form ker-
> ygmatic formulae testifying to the passion of Christ. Already in the NT we can
> see such credos in 1 Cor 15:3–5, a pre-Pauline formulation which Paul has
> received from the church tradition and passes on to his readers, and in several
> passages in Acts (for example 2:22–24; 3:13–15; 5:30–31; 10:36–42),
> where Luke has Peter and the apostles bear witness to the passion and resurrec-
> tion of Christ.[30]

As in *Ep. Pet. Phil.* 139.16, so in *Ep. apost.* 9.1 "the initial reference to [Christ's] crucifixion . . . seems to be of an introductory sort, intended to provide, in a word, a comprehensive reference to the passion of Christ."[31]

"By Pontius Pilate" is of course a credal commonplace. The Ethiopic text, with "*in the days of . . .* ," presumably reflects a more idiomatic understanding of an original ἐπί + genitive.[32] But the addition of a second synchronistic point of reference (Archelaus) is the exception rather than the rule in early summaries of the passion. Ignatius *Smyrn.* 1.2 speaks of Jesus "nailed to a tree . . . under Pontius Pilate and Herod the Tetrarch," but twice elsewhere Ignatius contents himself with the name of Pilate;[33] Justin once (*1 Apol.*13.3) glosses Pilate's name with the comment, "who was procurator in Judaea in the days of Tiberius Caesar." The *Epistula*'s reference to Archelaus, however, cannot be explained by reference to contemporary accounts, nor by an appeal to the NT gospels, although Schmidt rightly looks to the possibility that this may be a confused reference to Archelaus, the son of Herod I, referred to in Matt 2:2.[34]

---

and Commentary (SBLDS 53: Chico, CA: Scholars Press, 1981) 28–29.

[30] Ibid., 152–53. See also G. P. Luttikhuizen, "The Letter of Peter to Philip and the New Testament," in R. McL. Wilson, ed., *Nag Hammadi and Gnosis: Papers Read at the First International Congress of Coptology (Cairo, December 1976)* (NHS 14; Leiden: Brill, 1978) 101. Further parallels are to be found in the hymnic materials discussed in connection with *Ep. apost.* 3–4 above (Chapter Two).

[31] Meyer, *Letter of Peter to Philip*, 153.

[32] Cf. BAG, *s.v.* ἐπί I.2 (286b): "of time: *in the time of, under*"; the Coptic (I 13) has ϩⲓⲧⲛ̄, cf. Crum, 429a. In the Ethiopic NT, a third (spatial) rendering of ἐπί + genitive is found in 1 Tim 6:13: Christ's "good confession ἐπὶ Ποντίου Πιλάτου" (Eth. *ba-qedma Pilātos Pantēnāwi*) is to be imitated by the readers' confession ἐνώπιον πολλῶν μαρτύρων (*ba-qedma bezuxān samāʿt*, 6:12; cf. BAG, *s.v.* ἐπί I.1.a. [286a]).

[33] Ignatius *Magn.* 11.1; *Trall.* 9.1; so also Justin *1 Apol.* 61.13; *Dial.* 30.3; 76.6; 85.2; and Irenaeus *Adv. haer.* 2.32.4.

[34] Schmidt, *Gespräche Jesu*, 218. Edgar J. Goodspeed (*A History of Early Christian Literature* [rev. Robert M. Grant; Chicago: University of Chicago Press/Phoenix, 1966] 23), holding this to be an example of the author's "historical weakness," suggests that Antipas was the name intended.

J. de Zwaan has pointed out, however, that there is no need to suppose that the Synoptic chronology was the only one available to the author; another plausible Archelaus is Julius Archelaus, son of Helcias. According to Josephus (*Ant.* 19.354–55; 20.140, 147; *Ap.* 1.51) this Archelaus married Marianne, daughter of Agrippa I, in 41 CE. In this way to place the death of Jesus in the fifth decade of the first century is not as idiosyncratic as it appears.[35] Exegesis of John 8:57 ("You are not yet fifty years old . . .") led Irenaeus, for instance, to state clearly that Jesus "did not want much of being fifty years old."[36] The evidence is insufficient to claim the chronological issue as settled for the *Epistula*, and the further question may be posed, whether or not the addition of Archelaus's name is intended to root these events more firmly in contemporary history. It has been noted that Ignatius's references to Pontius Pilate are always in contexts where the reality of the death and resurrection is being stressed.[37] But again there are no adequate criteria for making a determination, and it may be best to assign Archelaus's name here to independent tradition.[38]

The crucifixion of the two criminals with Jesus is familiar from all four NT gospels and from the *Gospel of Peter* (Matt 27:38; Mark 15:27; Luke 23:33; John 19:18; *Gos. Pet.* 4.10). Yet the *Epistula*, or perhaps its source, seems to have absorbed this element of the passion narrative into the credal or confessional form, in which each clause has the Lord as its subject: "who was crucified . . . who was buried. . . ." It is therefore strange that there is no clause specifically relating Jesus' death.

At this point the Ethiopic continues, "and was taken down from the wood of the cross together with them." Schmidt assumed this phrase to be a later addition,[39] but Hornschuh rightly asks what an interpolator would have achieved by adding this material. He goes on to propose that the Ethiopic reading may be taken seriously in light of Paul's words in Acts 13:29: "And when [those who live in Jerusalem and their rulers] had fulfilled all that was written of him, they took him down from the tree, and laid him in a tomb."[40]

---

[35] De Zwaan ("Date and Origin," 349) notes: "Our author does not follow the Synoptic chronology, but an early and widespread one of a wholly different character."

[36] Irenaeus *Adv. haer.* 2.22.6 (ANF 1. 392). According to de Zwaan ("Date and Origin," 349–50), this tradition was also known (presumably through Irenaeus) to Hippolytus, Chrysostom, Augustine, and Jerome. Regarding John 8:57, it may be noted that (Λ*) *pc* and Chrysostom read τεσσεράκοντα (forty) for John's πεντήκοντα (fifty).

[37] Kelly, *Creeds*, 149–50. Kelly denies any deliberate antidocetic emphasis in the use of proper names.

[38] A further, and remote, possibility is that "Archelaus" is not a proper name at all, but rather the rare Greek adjective meaning "leading the people, chief" (LSJ, *s.v.* ἀρχέλαος [251b]), used for the title or office held by Pilate. In this case the Ethiopic addition, "prince" (*mak^wannen*, better translated "judge" or "ruler"), could be explained as a gloss on this unfamiliar title.

[39] Schmidt, *Gespräche Jesu*, 218.

[40] Hornschuh, *Studien*, 12–13. Ernst Haenchen (cited by Hornschuh) disagrees: "In reality Luke has only shortened the account as much as possible" (*The Acts of the Apostles* [Philadel-

This summary statement clearly indicates that those who crucified Jesus took him down from the cross *and* buried him. It is precisely this latter possibility that the NT gospels and the *Gospel of Peter* seem intent on denying. Mark 15:45 expressly states that Joseph of Arimathea took the body; in John 19:38 – 40, Joseph takes the body away (from the site of the crucifixion?), and is joined by Nicodemus for the burial preparation. *Gos. Pet.* 2.5 even has Herod say that "even if no one had begged him [i.e., someone did], we should bury him, since the Sabbath is drawing on." And in *Gos. Pet.* 6.21 the role of the Jews is again pointedly delimited: "the Jews drew the nails from the hands of the Lord and laid him on the earth." As far as the primitive kerygma is concerned, Paul, of course, simply relates that "he was buried" (1 Cor 15:4; cf. *Ep. Pet. Phil.* 139.19 – 21, quoted above). In any case, inasmuch as it is the more difficult reading, the Ethiopic "addition" cannot be lightly dismissed.[41] Finally, the clause relating to Jesus' burial calls for comment only in that here the place of *burial* rather than of crucifixion bears the title "the skull" (in its Greek form only, as in Luke 23:33; in John 19:41 the place of crucifixion has in it the garden of burial).

Ep. apost. 9.4 – 11.1 (II 1, 54/1)

Ethiopic	Coptic
4 to which three women came, Sarah, Martha, and Mary Magdalene.	4 There went to that place <three> women: Mary, she who belonged to Martha, and Mary <Magd>alene.
5 They carried ointment to pour out upon his body, weeping and mourning over what had happened.	5 They took ointment to pour upon his body, weeping and mourning over what had happened.
6 And they approached the tomb and found the stone where it had been rolled away from the tomb, and they opened the door and did not find his body.	6 But when they had approached the tomb they looked inside and did not find the body.

---

phia: Fortress, 1971] 410). But as late as the fourth century the Romans are credited with the burial of Jesus. Lactantius writes: "Since he had foretold that on the third day he should rise again from the dead, fearing . . . lest there should be a much greater disturbance among the people, they [the Romans] took him down from the cross, and having shut him up in a tomb, they secured it with a guard of soldiers" (*Div. inst.* 4.19; ANF 7. 122). The Ethiopic additions in 11.6 (referring to the "door" of the tomb), however, are of a different sort, and stem from a desire to harmonize the text with the Synoptic Gospels.

[41] See now John Dominic Crossan (*Four Other Gospels: Shadows on the Contours of Canon* [New York: Seabury/Winston, 1985] 149 – 64) who argues that there was an original Passion-Resurrection gospel, in which Jesus was buried by his enemies (so the *Gospel of Peter*'s source), and that this tradition was revised by stages until in John's gospel Jesus is buried with great ceremony by his disciples.

1	And as they were mourning and weeping, the Lord appeared to them and said to them, "Do not weep; I am he whom you seek.	1	But as they were mourning and weeping, the Lord appeared to them and said to them, "For whom are you weeping? Now do not weep; I am he whom you seek.
2	But let one of you go to your brothers and say to them, 'Come, our Master has risen from the dead.'"	2	But let one of you go to your brothers and say, 'Come, the Master has risen from the dead.'"
3	And Mary came to us and told us.	3	Martha came and told it to us.
4	And we said to her, "What have we to do with you, O woman? He that is dead and buried, can he then live?" 5 And we did not believe her, that our Saviour had risen from the dead. 6 Then she went back to our[42] Lord and said to him, "None of them believed me concerning your resurrection."	4	We said to her, "What do you want with us, O woman? He who has died is buried, and could it be possible for him to live?" 5 We did not believe her, that the Saviour had risen from the dead. 6 Then she went back to the Lord and said to him, "None of them believed me that you are alive."
7	And he said to her,[43] "Let another one of you go saying this again to them." 8 And Sarah came and gave us the same news, and we accused her of lying. 9 And she returned to our[44] Lord and spoke to him as Mary had.	7	He said, "Let another one of you go to them saying this again to them." 8 Mary came and told us again, and we did not believe her. 9 She returned to the Lord and she also told it to him.
1	And then the Lord said to Mary and to her sisters, "Let us go to them."	1	Then the Lord said to Mary and also to her sisters, "Let us go to them."

To this point we have been dealing with material whose compactness has suggested that the author is simply setting the scene for the narrative proper. *Ep. apost.* 9.4 – 10.2 is also introductory, since only in 10.3 does the four-part literary pattern begin; yet with these verses *Ep. apost.* 9 – 12 joins the mainstream of post-resurrection tradition, and points of contact with other gospels are numerous. Whatever the author's intention in the verses already reviewed (9.1 – 3), it now becomes clear that a narrative plan is unfolding. It is parallel to a great extent with the canonical reports, but it has something other than the canonical pattern as its foundation. The sequence of events in the *Epistula* is closest, in fact, to that in Mark 16:9 – 14 in that in both accounts there is a pair of disbelieved reports before the final appearance to the eleven.[45]

---

[42] For "our Lord" fam. 1 MSS BKO read "the Lord" (cf. Coptic).

[43] Fam. 1 MSS BKNOR omit "to her" (cf. Coptic).

[44] For "our Lord" fam. 1 MSS BCKNO read "the Lord" (cf. Coptic).

[45] So Hornschuh, *Studien*, 14.

The report of the visit to the tomb has little to distinguish it from its NT counterparts. No satisfactory reason has been offered for the fact that the names of the women (Copt.: Mary, Martha [by conjecture], Mary Magdalene; Eth.: Sarah, Martha, Mary Magdalene) do not agree with those of the visitors enumerated in the NT accounts (to which may be added *Gos.Pet.* 12.50–51, where Mary Magdalene is accompanied by "her women friends"). Perhaps this feature of *Ep. apost.* 9–12, like the mention of Archelaus, is to be attributed to independent, albeit late, tradition.[46]

The women approach the tomb "weeping and mourning." This expression of grief is certainly not classically biblical,[47] and it would be no special cause for comment were it not that its repetition in *Ep. apost.* 10.1 alerts us to the author's interest in it. The phrase, or some similar expression, is found in the NT (e.g., in Matt 5:4; 9:15; Luke 6:25; and esp. Rev 18:11, 15, 19), but as a distinct motif it is absent from the passion narratives except in the longer ending of Mark; it is also present in the *Gospel of Peter*. In the NT accounts of the passion, among various expressions of fear and amazement the theme of mourning and/or weeping is found only in Mark 14:34 par., where Jesus is in sorrow in Gethsemane (cf. Matt 26:22); in Mark 14:72 par., where Peter grieves after his denial of Jesus; in Luke 23:38, where the "daughters of Jerusalem" are charged, "Do not weep for me";[48] and in John 20:11–13,

---

[46] In Luke 24:10 (where the first-named woman [Mary Magdalene] is common to Mark 16:1 and to Luke 8:2, and the second [Joanna] and third [Mary, mother of James] are the second named in Luke 8:2–3 and Mark 16:2 respectively), Richard J. Dillon finds evidence that "the ternary number was required throughout the different stages of the tradition" (*From Eye-Witnesses to Ministers of the Word: Tradition and Composition in Luke 24* [AnBib 82; Rome: Biblical Institute Press, 1978] 56).

The differences among the gospels concerning the names of the women and the reasons for their visit to the tomb were early noted, for example in Origen's gospel commentaries and in Dionysius of Alexandria (d. 264 CE) *Epistula canonica* 1 (ANF 6. 94–96). For a discussion of the confusion of the Marys at the tomb in post-NT tradition, see Robert Murray, *Symbols of Church and Kingdom* (Cambridge: Cambridge University Press, 1975) 329–35.

The Coptic *Book of the Resurrection of Jesus Christ by Bartholomew the Apostle* has no fewer than nine women visit the tomb: the three mentioned in Mark, together with "Mary who ministered [unto him], and Martha [her] sister, and Susannah . . . and Berenice . . . and Leah . . . and the woman unto whom the Saviour said, 'Thy sins . . . are remitted unto thee'" (Coptic text and ET in E. A. Wallis Budge, *Coptic Apocrypha in the Dialect of Upper Egypt* [London: Longmans, 1913] 10, 187–88). Cf. *Gos. Phil.* (NHC 2, 3) 59.6–11: "There were three who always walked with the Lord: Mary his mother and her sister and Magdalene, the one who was called his companion. His sister and his mother and his companion were each a Mary"; and *1 Apoc. Jas.* (NHC 5, 3) 40.24–26: "Encourage these [four]: Salome and Mariam [and Martha and Arsinoe . . .]."

On the possible significance of Martha, as a named visitor to the tomb, for the provenance of the *Ep. apost.*, see Hornschuh, *Studien*, 104–5, and the literature cited there.

[47] The closest OT analogy is probably 1 Sam 19:2, where David mourns over Absalom; cf. Gen 23:2; Isa 22:12.

[48] See also Luke 24:33 D c e sa: λυπούμενοι for ἠθροισμένοι.

where Mary weeps outside the tomb. The fourth evangelist neglects to take up the prediction in John 16:20, "You will weep and lament."

In the *Gospel of Peter*, however, the disciples' grief has a secure place: "But I [Peter] mourned (ἐλυπούμην) with my fellows" (7.26); "Because of all these things we were fasting and sat mourning and weeping (πενθοῦντες καὶ κλαίοντες) night and day" (7.27); and "But we, the twelve disciples of the Lord, wept and mourned" (ἐκλαίομεν καὶ ἐλυπούμεθα, 14.59). The mourning of the disciples is complemented by the lamentation of the women. The reason for their visit to the tomb, they state in *Gos. Pet.* 12.52, is their obligation to bewail and lament him. Mark 16:10 has the disciples weeping and mourning.

The *Epistula* refers both to the women's lamenting and to their anointing of the body. As with the grief of the disciples, so with these new themes in the *Epistula* the accounts in the canonical gospels and in the *Gospel of Peter* must be compared. Mark 16:1 (with Luke 24:1) has the anointing of the body as the only motive for the journey. Matthew does not have the anointing at all; the two Marys go "to see the sepulchre" (28:1). In John, Mary, whose role as anointer has been usurped by Joseph of Arimathea and Nicodemus (19:38–40), is left going to the tomb for no given reason. Mary's arrival is necessary to John, however, for the dramatic encounter which John wishes to present in 20:11–18: Mary stands weeping at the tomb (20:11), and as she weeps she looks inside—but for this evangelist the point is not mourning but belief or unbelief. Lamentation, which presumably characterizes Mary's crying in the traditional material reworked by John, is no longer an issue for him. The question addressed to Mary twice, by an angel (20:13) and by Jesus (20:15), goes beyond mourning to the present resurrection: "Woman, why are you weeping?" The resurrection, already quietly announced by John in 20:8 ("the other disciple . . . saw and believed"), is here presupposed. Otherwise a question such as this ("*Why* . . . ?"), addressed to a woman visiting a tomb, would have little point. The further question "Whom do you seek?" confirms the author's intention, and raises the question of identity (John 20:15–16).

The lamentation motif in *Ep. apost.* 10.1 leads to the appropriate question "*For whom* are you weeping?" Here at last the question of identity emerges in the *Epistula*: "I am he whom you seek." The correlation between question and answer may be contrasted with the NT accounts and with the *Gospel of Peter*, in none of which is the identity question comfortably accommodated. Not one of the narratives mentions seeking as a motive for the visit to the tomb; and properly so, for according to them there can be no reason for a search since the women, having closely observed what has happened, are in no doubt as to where the tomb is and, in consequence, where the body will be found. Indeed, at its origin the motif of seeking may presuppose the empty-tomb tradition. The young man's statement in Mark 16:6, "You seek Jesus of Nazareth, who was crucified,"[49] has an *informative* ring about it that is scarcely softened by Matthew, whose angel says, "I know that you seek Jesus who was crucified" (Matt 28:5). John's question, "Whom do you seek?" (John 20:15) is asked but not answered. Luke reformulates with the proverb-like question, "Why do you seek the living among the dead?" (Luke 24:5). And *Gos. Pet.* 13.56, again apparently obliged by the tradition to incorporate the question on seeking, lessens its incongruity by adding, "Why have you come?"

The *Epistula*'s account has no intermediary figure. The Lord announces himself as the one whom the women are seeking, and the believing response of these seekers is only implied, as the writer hastens on to the Lord's commission. The message that is to be delivered is essential for *Ep. apost.* 9–12 and for the writing as a whole: "*the Teacher* (Copt.: пслг; Eth.: *liq*) has risen from the dead."[50]

The title διδάσκαλος (teacher) for Jesus, though common in the Synoptic tradition (in Mark, 12 times; Matthew, 12; Luke, 16) and in John (8 times), fades away at the start of the passion narratives.[51] Only John retains the designation within the passion narrative, in his translation of Mary's "Rabboni" in 20:16.[52] For the *Epistula*, however, great importance is attached to Jesus in his role as the exemplary teacher of the disciples. In 17.5 the disciples ask, "Will you really leave us until your coming? Where will we find a teacher?" The disciples themselves are to be, and to be called, teachers (chaps. 41–42). Indeed, beginning in chap. 13 a transference of attributes from the Lord to the disciples, and thence to all who believe, is carefully described, just as the Lord's resurrection is made the type of that of the believers in its physical reality (chap. 21). It is hardly going too far to speak of a *communicatio idiomatum* between the risen one and the disciples, effected, incidentally, with no hint at a doctrine of the Holy Spirit.[53]

Finally, in *Ep. apost.* 10.3–11.1, the author takes complete charge of the literary structure of the section. In this verse begins the pattern, described above, that shapes all of 10.3–12.4 except 11.7–8. The source here, if not

---

[49] The Greek could be translated "Do you seek . . . ?" but the speech is not marked as a question in the Nestle-Aland (26th ed.) or the United Bible Societies (3d ed.) Greek Testament.

[50] Compare the names and titles used elsewhere for the resurrected one: "Jesus" (Matt 28:5); "Jesus of Nazareth" (Mark 16:6; Luke 24:19); "the Son of man" (Luke 24:7); "the Christ" (Luke 24:26); "the Lord" (John 20:2, 13, 18).

[51] The last occurrence of the title "teacher" in the Synoptic Gospels is in Mark 14:14 par., where the disciples are to find a room for the teacher's celebration of the Passover.

[52] This passage shares something of its formal shape with John 1:38: "Jesus turned, and saw [the two disciples] following, and said to them, 'What do you seek?' And they said to him, 'Rabbi' (which means Teacher). . . ."

[53] Cf. John 14:26, where it is the Paraclete "who will teach you all things."

Mark 16:9 – 11, shares its mission/disbelief structure. Significant here is the issue of *resurrection* rather than of *identity*:

"He who has died is buried, and *could it be possible for him to live?*" (10.4)

We did not believe her, that the Saviour *had risen from the dead.* (10.5)

"None of them believed me *that you are alive* [Eth.: *concerning your resurrection*]." (10.6)

There are many indications that this material has been reworked to suit the overall scheme of chaps. 9 – 12, and the author's vocabulary and interests are present everywhere. For example, the form of the question in 10.4 ("Could it be possible . . . ?") is shared by five other fundamental questions in the *Epistula* (see Chapter One); the designation "Saviour" in 10.5 appears in editorial contexts at the beginning of chap. 6 ("These things our Lord and Saviour revealed . . .") and in 12.3 ("Then the Lord and Saviour said . . ."); and the brevity of the account of the second visit to the disciples in 10.8 – 9 suggests that it is a compositional makeweight. At this point the narrative is entirely two-dimensional, and the section concludes with the last mention of the women as the Lord charges in 11.1: "Let us go to them." A break is signalled between this and what follows, for 11.2 reports only that "*he* came. . . ."

Ep. apost. 11.2 – 6 (III 8, 55/3)

Ethiopic	Coptic
2 And he came and found us, veiled. And we doubted and did not believe.	2 And he came and found us inside. He called us out.
3 He came before us like a ghost and we did not believe that it was he. But it was he. 4 And thus he said to us, "Come, and do not be afraid. I am your teacher whom you, Peter, denied three times before the cock crowed; and now do you deny again?"	3 But we thought it was a ghost, and we did not believe it was the Lord. 4 Then <he said> to us, "Come, do not be afraid. I am your <master> whom you, Peter, denied three times; and now do you deny again?"
5 And we went to him, thinking and doubting whether it was he. 6 And he said to us, "Why do you doubt and why are you not believing that I am he who spoke to you concerning my flesh, my death and my resurrection?"	5 But we went to him, doubting in <our> hearts whether it was possibly he. 6 Then he said to <us>, "Why do you still doubt and are you not believing? I am he who spoke to you concerning my flesh, my death, and my resurrection."

Since *Ep. apost.* 10.1, when the Lord announced that "I am he whom you seek," the visits of the women and the disbelief of the disciples have centered on the issue of *resurrection*: Is it possible that one who has died has been raised? In 11.2 the disappearance of the women from the scene also marks a move away from the question of resurrection to that of the *identity* of the risen one:

We did not believe *it was the Lord*. (11.3)

I am your teacher. (11.4)

We went to him, doubting in <our> hearts *whether it was possibly he*. (11.5)

I am he who spoke to you. . . . (11.6)

That you may know that *it is I, . . .* (11.7)

The peculiar tension in *Ep. apost.* 11 between a concern with *resurrection* and a concern with *identity* is felt most acutely in the words following the call of the Lord: "But we thought it was a ghost, and we did not believe it was the Lord."[54]

Mention of a "ghost" (φαντασία) looks forward to the demonstration account, where the word is found in the prophetic saying quoted by Jesus. But at once the writer's principal concern, belief, resurfaces. A second communal concern, that of denial of the Lord, is here raised in Peter's denial, knowledge of which is assumed (cf. Mark 14:29 – 30, 66 – 72 par.). Its special appropriateness in this context is that Peter's denial, at least according to the canonical witnesses, is not of belief in the resurrection but of recognition and knowledge of the Lord (see Mark 14:71), that is, it conforms to the question of identity.

Again in 11.6 the Lord chastises the disciples, here entirely in the words of the author: "Why do you still doubt and are you not believing?[55] I am he who spoke to you concerning my flesh, my death and my resurrection." The combination "my death and my resurrection" is found again in 19.17, as an introduction to the quotation from Ps 3:1 – 8: ". . . that the prophecy <of the> prophet David might be fulfilled concerning what he <foretold> about me and <*my*> *death and my resurrection*. . . ." The addition of "my flesh" to the recollection in 11.6 anticipates the resolution of the demonstration account.

Ep. apost. 11.7 – 8:
Demonstration and Prophetic Proof-text

The appearance of the risen Christ to his disciples is described or alluded to many times in early Christian writings. As in the canonical gospels, so in the

---

[54] There is a (possibly intended) parallel here between the disciples' mistaking the identity of the Lord ("we thought it was a ghost") and that of the angels, at the descent of the Lord through the heavens in chap. 13, "thinking in their hearts that I was one of them" (13.5).

[55] Cf. 10.5, 6, 8; 11.3, 5.

later literature it is clear that reference to the post-resurrection appearance could and did serve more than one theological purpose. Therefore it is not possible to speak of a single development of the appearance tradition. Instead, several broad lines of development may be detected, amounting to several distinct appropriations (e.g., devotional, apologetic, polemical) of traditional material. Most fruitful for the present discussion are those texts in which fragments of the appearance tradition are supplied as evidence for the physical nature of the resurrection.[56] In many cases, perhaps in most, these brief narratives have been harmonized with the canonical accounts.[57] But occasionally the parallel is so inexact as to suggest an independent tradition, as in Ignatius *Smyrnaeans* 3, to be dealt with shortly.

The methodological consequence of this variety of applications of the post-resurrection tradition is a twofold caution: first, against an assumption as to the tradition's function, and secondly, against the presupposition that all development is necessarily from the simple to the complex, from the innocent to the sophisticated, and here, from the "reserve and modesty" of the canonical models to the "bizarre" and "disproportionate" account of the *Epistula*, as Alsup characterizes it.[58]

Therefore the immediate impression of *Ep. apost.* 11.7–8 as an extravagant paraphrase of the doubting Thomas story in John 20 must be resisted. Closer inspection shows that there is more at stake in terms of source material, of editorial intention, and of history-of-religions background.

Ep. apost. 11.7–8 (IV 3, 55/10)

Ethiopic	Coptic
7 And that you may know that it is I, lay your hand,[59] Peter, (and your finger) in the nailprint of my hands; and you, Thomas, in my side; and you also, Andrew, see whether my foot steps on the ground and leaves a footprint.	7 That you may know that it is I, put your finger, Peter, in the nailprints of my hands; and you, Thomas, put your finger in the spear-wounds of my side; but you, Andrew, look at my feet and see if they do not touch the ground.
8 For it is written in the prophet, "But a ghost, a demon, leaves no print on the ground.'"	8 For it is written in the prophet, "The foot of a ghost or a demon does not join to the ground.'"

---

[56] Cf. Albertz, "Zur Formengeschichte," 261–62.

[57] See Alfred Resch, *Außerkanonische Paralleltexte zu den Evangelien* (TU 10/1–4; Leipzig: Hinrichs, 1895–96) 2. 785; 4. 188–94.

[58] Alsup, *Appearance Stories*, 128.

[59] For "your hand" MSS CNO read "your fingers"; the addition in parentheses, "(and your finger)," should be plural, "(and your fingers)," as is read by MSS BCKQR.

It has been seen already that the questions of resurrection (10.2 – 11.1) and identity (10.1; 11.2 – 6) have in turn dominated the *Epistula*'s account to this point. These twin poles of the narrative together embrace the account of the demonstration in 11.7 – 8. The disciples touch and see by invitation ". . . that you may know that it is I" (11.7); but they touch, according to their own testimony: ". . . that we might truly know whether he <had risen> in the flesh" (12.1).

The close parallels in Luke and John show that this confusion of intention is typical. Luke's report is as follows:

> As they were saying this, Jesus himself stood among them. But they were startled and frightened, and supposed that they saw a spirit. And he said to them, "Why are you troubled, and why do questionings rise in your hearts? See my hands and my feet, *that it is I myself*; handle me and see; for a spirit has not flesh and bones as you see that I have." (Luke 24:36 – 40)

But this account, while it has a clearly stated goal in the words, "it is I myself," makes no explicit reference to the wounds in Jesus' hands and feet.

John's story about Thomas, possibly standing on an older tradition[60] but more probably the construction of the evangelist based on the motif of doubt,[61] pointedly avoids a deduction from the showing of the Lord's hands and feet:

> Unless I see in his hands the print of the nails, and place my finger in the mark of the nails, and place my hand in his side, I will not believe. (John 20:25)

> Put your finger here, and see my hands; and put out your hand, and place it in my side; do not be faithless, but believing. (vs 27)

The fourth evangelist does not give away just what theological purpose the demonstration account must serve in his gospel until vs 29.

The *Epistula*, however, has three disciples. As for the Lord's appearance to Peter, this of course stands at the fountainhead of the appearance tradition, 1 Cor 15:5: "He appeared to Cephas, then to the twelve"; and evidence from Ignatius *Smyrn.* 3.2 also specifies Peter as one of those invited to examine the Lord's body: "And when he came to those with Peter he said to them, 'Take, handle me and see that I am not a phantom without a body.' "[62] But even if

---

[60] So Reginald H. Fuller, *The Formation of the Resurrection Narratives* (rev. ed.; London: S. P. C. K., 1980) 142 – 43.

[61] See Dodd, "Appearances," 20. Dillon (*Eye-Witnesses*, 162) collects evidence favoring the view that "the Thomas-story is Jn's own construction, deliberately tailored to correspond structurally to the preceding episode (20,19 – 23) and composed of elements from the latter" (n. 16).

[62] Jerome, paraphrasing Ignatius, removes any doubt that Peter was invited to touch: "When he came *to Peter* and to those with Peter . . ." (*De vir. ill.* 16; Latin text in Ernest Cushing Richardson, ed., *Hieronymus Liber de viris inlustribus* [TU 14/1a; Leipzig: Hinrichs, 1896] 17). Epiphanius, on the other hand, makes Thomas the focus in reporting that he appeared "to those

we were to explain the presence of Peter on the basis of the tradition handed on by Paul, and of Thomas on the basis of the account in John 20,[63] in terms of known antecedents to this narrative Andrew would have no necessary place. The question arises, whether an "Andrew tradition" lies behind this third charge, or whether the author of the *Epistula* has himself created a role for Andrew here.[64]

In light of the new manuscript evidence it seems certain that the reason for Andrew's presence as the third named disciple lies within the *Epistula* itself. *Ep. apost.* 2 begins with a list of the apostles.[65] John is the first named, perhaps because he is considered to be the amanuensis, or even the chief tradition-bearer, of the eleven. Peter, Thomas, and Andrew are now seen to be the next named, *and in the same order* as that in which they are found in *Ep. apost.* 11.7.[66] The theological point, anticipated in the order of apostles in chap. 2, is secured in chap. 11: to participate in this recognition of the resurrection is the privilege not of the weakest of the apostles but of these mighty three. As for what Andrew is charged to do, it is hard to find in this place evidence of a tradition developing "in ever more explicit terms."[67] Instead we must extend the range of comparative materials beyond the canonical borders.

The starting point for such an extension is the observation that the command to Andrew does not continue the pattern established with Peter and Thomas. Less surprising would have been a command to examine the *nail-prints* in the Lord's feet; but Andrew is requested to inspect the Lord's feet as they touch the ground and make footprints.[68] This suggests that the author

---

with Thomas" (*Ancoratus* 62); cf. 91: ". . . to Thomas and to his disciples" (reference in Resch, *Paralleltexte*, 4. 193).

[63] But note that the saying of Jesus in John 20:29 is found in a different setting in the *Epistula*; see *Ep. apost.* 29.6.

[64] It is surely inadequate (as well as inaccurate with respect to Andrew's commission) to suggest that "it is characteristic that in the Apocryphal tradition [of] *Epist. Apost.* 11 . . . Peter should put his hand into the nail-prints of Jesus' hand, Thomas into his side and Andrew into his foot-print" (Bultmann, *History*, 309), though doubtless this account in the *Epistula* does witness to "a tendency to differentiation and individualization" (ibid.).

[65] For the relation between this list and other early lists of apostles, see Schmidt, *Gespräche Jesu*, 229–32.

[66] This is the order given in five strong fam. 1 MSS: BKOQR. There are other, minor differences in the Ethiopic MSS: MS M omits Matthew (by homoeoteleuton: "Matthew" = *Māttēwos*; "Bartholomew" [the preceding name] = *Bartalomēwos*), and replaces "Zelotes and Cephas" with "and James"; N adds "and James and Matthias" after "Zelotes"; S places "Zelotes before "and Judas." Note that the Ethiopic reading in *Ep. apost.* 19.11, "and *we twelve* said to him," does not represent the best MSS; fam. 1 omits "and we" and has the conjunction before "we said." The number "twelve" is a scribal intrusion, possibly influenced by the Ethiopic text of *Herm. Man.* 12.3.2.

[67] So Dillon, *Eye-Witnesses*, 159 n. 8.

[68] In Greek drama, recognition of a relative or friend is occasionally achieved by the identification of his or her footprints. E.g., Electra in Aeschylus *Choephori* 197–202 is called

first decided to include the prophetic proof-text about footprints and then worked to incorporate it into the scene despite the conflict with what is soon to be reported by the apostles: "But then we *touched* him . . ." (*Ep. apost.* 12.1). The alternative, that the author composed this saying on the basis of Luke 24:39,[69] is more difficult to sustain; but in rejecting it we are bound to ask whence the saying may have originated and what intention its inclusion displays.

Several proposals have been made as to the saying's source. Harnack, following Schmidt,[70] believed it to be an adaptation of Wis 18:17a: "Then at once apparitions (φαντασίαι) in dreadful dreams greatly troubled them."[71] Guerrier cited Dan 14 (= Bel):19–20, where Daniel asks Cyrus, "Look at the floor, and notice whose footsteps these are" (τίνος τὰ ἴχνη ταῦτα).[72] Nearer in thought would seem to be Job 11:7a LXX: "Can you find the footprint of the Lord?" (ἴχνος κυρίου εὑρήσεις;). But here too we are a long way from establishing a source, and in the absence of a closer parallel it is more appropriate to take the author at his word, that it is "written in the prophet,"[73] and to ask what precisely the "agraphon," or unwritten saying, means.[74]

The text of *Ep. apost.* 11.8 (IV 9, 56/1) is as follows:[75]

---

upon to recognize Orestes, her brother, by the likeness of his footprints to hers. A different but equally poignant use of the motif is to be found in *Orac. Sib.* 2.25–26, when it is said of the time of eschatological crisis that "there will be a scarcity of men throughout the whole world so that if one were to see a man's footprint (ἴχνος) on the ground, one would wonder."

The Greek word ἴχνος (footprint) can be used for the mark of a wound, as in Plato *Gorgias* 524c, a passage of particular interest in connection with *Ep. apost.* 11.7–8: "If anyone had been a sturdy rogue, *and bore traces of his stripes in scars on his body* (ἴχνος πληγῶν), either from the whip or from other wounds, while yet alive, then after death too his body has these marks visible upon it." It is conceivable that one or both of the commands to Peter and to Thomas included the word ἴχνος, and that the ambiguity of the word was exploited by the *Epistula*'s author for the inclusion of the prophetic saying.

[69] Cf. Schmidt, *Gespräche Jesu*, 211.

[70] Schmidt, "Eine bisher unbekkante altchristliche Schrift," 708 n. 1.

[71] Harnack, "Ein jüngst entdeckter Auferstehungsbericht," 8. This biblical reference is also cited in Erwin Preuschen, ed., *Antilegomena: Die Reste der Außerkanonischen Evangelien und urchristlichen Überlieferung* (2d ed.; Giessen: Töpelmann, 1905) 84.

[72] Guerrier, "Le testament," 56 n. 1; accepted by Jakob Delazer, "De tempore compositionis Epistolae Apostolorum," *Anton* 4 (1929) 273.

[73] So Hornschuh, *Studien*, 78–79, and n. 39.

[74] A. A. T. Ehrhardt's hypothesis, that the saying originated in a midrash on 1 Sam 28:7–25 (the witch of Endor), is worthy of mention but must remain unproven for want of evidence ("Judaeo-Christians in Egypt, the Epistula Apostolorum and the Gospel to the Hebrews," *StEv* III [TU 88; Berlin: Akademie-Verlag, 1964] 362).

[75] The Ethiopic reading is that of MSS CON, which have the construct, "the ghost *of . . .*"; other manuscripts read two nominatives, with which the contemporary designation of tomb-spirits as δαιμόνιον πνεῦμα may be compared (see Deissmann, *Bible Studies*, 273–74).

Copt.: ογϕαντасιа ⲛⲁⲁⲓⲙⲱⲛ ⲙⲁ[ⲣⲉ]ⲣⲉⲧ̅ϥ̅ ⲧⲟⲩⲙⲉ ⲍⲓⲭⲛ̅ ⲡⲕⲁⲍ

Eth.: *methata gānēn-sa 'albo 'asar westa medr*

The demands of English grammar obscure to some extent the verbal closeness of the two versions: in their first and their last two words they exactly correspond with each other. But the middle two words are probably incompatible with any single, hypothetical Greek original, and the modern translator is left wondering which version has conceded the most to its native idiom. The Coptic has "foot" but not "print"; the Ethiopic has "footprint" but no verb "to join." Nevertheless, if the two middle elements must remain uncertain, a beginning can still be made with a definition of the being referred to.

It will be seen at once that the translation of the Coptic in *NTApoc* 1. 197 has suffered a misprint, since it has "or" where "of" should be read.[76] The Coptic probably reflects φαντασία δαίμονος or two nominatives. Both φαντασία and δαίμων are capable of a wide range of meaning in this period. In the NT each is found only once, the former in Acts 25:23 (*RSV* "pomp"), the latter in Matt 8:31 ("demon").[77] While φαντασία can be a synonym for φάντασμα ("apparition," phantom"), its basic meaning is "appearance, presentation, image."[78] Similarly, δαίμων is not necessarily synonymous with δαιμόνιον. Its primary signification, the divine power, extends to the power or fortune of the individual, including the departed soul.[79] Therefore we must hesitate before exactly equating the *Epistula*'s φαντασία δαίμονος with the δαιμόνιον ἀσώματον (bodiless demon) which Ignatius has the risen Lord deny himself to be (*Smyrn.* 3.2). A literal translation therefore yields the following: "The (mere) appearance of a divine/departed spirit. . . ."[80]

This sense suits the context well. Neither a divine spirit, nor the ghost of the departed Jesus, is as real as the risen Lord has to be for the *Epistula*. That an apparition, a ghost, or a demon, leaves no imprint on the ground is of

---

[76] The original German of Duensing's translation has "Eines Dämonsgespenstes Fuß . . ." (*Epistula Apostolorum* 10).

[77] In addition, the genitive δαιμονίου in Luke 8:29 (in the Legion story) has a well-attested variant, δαίμονος. For the full range of possible meanings, see E. C. E. Owen, "Δαίμων and Cognate Words," *JTS* 32 (1931) 133–53.

[78] LSJ, *s.v.* φαντασία (1915b).

[79] LSJ, *s.v.* δαίμων II.1 (366a), citing Lucian *De Luctu* 24; also Pausanius 6.6, 8 for the meaning "ghost."

[80] I have found no other instance of the combination φαντασία δαίμονος. There are a number of similar expressions, however, which suggest that Duensing's "the ghost of a demon" overloads the Greek. Plutarch *Dion* 2 has φάντασμα δαίμονος (a spectre from heaven). L. Jalabert and R. Mouterde give an inscription with the following request: λύσατε τὴν Ἰουλιανην ἀπὸ πάσης ἐνεργίας καὶ φαντασίας δαιμονώδους (*Inscriptions grecques et latines de la Syrie* [2 vols.; Paris: Guethner, 1929] 1. 119–20). Athanasius often uses the expression φαντασία τῶν δαιμόνων, but for him δαίμων invariably means "evil demon," and φαντασία is regularly in parallel with ἀπάτη, μανία, μαγεία or the like (see, e.g., *De incarn.* 12.6; 14.3; 46.2).

course common knowledge; by definition a spiritual being has no substance.[81] Therefore the command to Andrew, and this saying that supports it, becomes the acid test of daimonhood. A similar test, in fact a potential exorcism, is undergone by the risen Lord in *Acts Pil.* 15.6. Joseph of Arimathea speaks the commandments, and the Lord, who has appeared to him in a vision, repeats them; in an aside to the reader, Joseph remarks: "Now as you well know, a phantom immediately flees if it meets anyone and hears the commandments."[82] For the *Epistula* even the ghost of Jesus will not suffice.

Two roughly contemporary writings further illustrate this "search-for-the phantom's-footprint" *topos*. In Philostratus *Heroicus* 13.2, the Vinedresser narrates his encounter with an athletic spirit:

> But as he ran you could not see a footprint, nor did his foot make any mark upon the ground.
>
> δραμόντος δὲ αὐτοῦ οὐκ ἂν εὕροις ἴχνος, οὐδ' ἂν ἐνσημήναιτό τι τῇ γῇ ὁ πούς[83]

This is strikingly similar to the more familiar passage in *Acts John* 93, where John writes of his encounters with Jesus:

> And I often wished, as I walked with him, to see his footprint in the earth, whether it appeared . . . and I never saw it.
>
> ἐβουλόμην δὲ πολλάκις σὺν αὐτῷ βαδίζων ἴχνος αὐτοῦ ἐπὶ τῆς γῆς ἰδεῖν εἰ φαίνεται . . . καὶ οὐδέποτε εἶδον.[84]

In both cases the test is the same. It is applied to borderline cases, and its goal is the separation of physical reality from spiritual. For the *Epistula* this amounts to a separation of the powerful from the impotent.[85]

[81] Cf. Goguel, *La foi à la résurrection*, 289.

[82] ET in *NTApoc* 1. 466.

[83] Ludo de Lannoy, ed., *Flavii Philostrati heroicus* (Bibliotheca scriptorum graecorum et romanorum Teubneriana; Leipzig: Teubner, 1977) 14.

[84] Greek text in Lipsius-Bonnet, *Acta apostolorum apocrypha*, 2/1. 197; ET in *NTApoc* 2. 227.

[85] Franz Joseph Dölger (*Die Eucharistie nach Inschriften frühchristlicher Zeit* [Münster: Aschendorff, 1922] 115 n. 4), chastising Schmidt for failing to see the history-of-religions significance of the "footprint" motif, traces the evidence for speculation about footprints back to exegesis of Homer *Iliad* 13.68–72 (the departure of Poseidon from his mission of encouragement during battle). In the late 2d c. CE Clement of Alexandria (*Stromateis* 5.14; ANF 2. 471) comments on *Iliad* 22.8 that "[Homer] shows that the Divinity cannot be captured by a mortal, or apprehended either with feet, or hands, or eyes, or by the body at all"; cf. *Gos. Truth* (NHC 1, 3) 37.25–29: "His [the Father's] trace (ἴχνος) is the will, and no one will know it, nor is it possible for one to scrutinize it in order to grasp it"; and Aristotle *De mirabilia* 97 (838a): "About Pandosia in Iapygia footprints of the god (Heracles) are shown, upon which no one may walk."

In light of the *Epistula*'s concern to portray the risen Lord as Teacher, cf. *Apoc. Elij.* 5.12: "Where now is the footprint of a righteous person,/ that we should follow you?/ or where is our teacher, that we might appeal to him?" Jean.-M. Rosensthiel (*L'Apocalypse d'Élie* [Paris:

Within this broader context of contemporary speculation the saying in *Ep. apost.* 11.8 may be seen as a proof-text for determining what (or who) is not a spirit (or demon). It therefore has nothing intrinsically to do with the *Christian* post-resurrection accounts in general, nor with the demonstration of the body of the risen Jesus in particular.[86] This raises the question as to whether similar proverbial sayings are elsewhere attracted to narrative or discourse about the resurrection of Jesus. The earliest passage that might show the use of such a saying is Luke 24:39, a verse which may be punctuated as follows:

See my hands and feet, that it is I myself. Handle me, and see; for *"A spirit has not flesh and bones"* as you see that I have.[87]

Ignatius *Smyrn.* 3.2–3 seems to reflect a development of this tradition, though doubtless Ignatius reports it independently.[88] Here the formulation is thoroughly personalized: *"I am not an incorporeal demon"*; the saying in Ignatius is therefore identified with and absorbed into the account of the post-resurrection appearance of *Jesus*. But a little later Tertullian twice cites an impersonal proverbial proof to argue for the corporeality of the resurrected Jesus. Tertullian's proverb, which he borrows from Lucretius *De rerum natura* 1.304, is quoted in *De anima* 5 and (with reference to Luke 4:29) in *Adv. Marc.* 4.8: *Tangere et tangi, nisi corpus, nulla potest res* ("Nothing can touch or be touched, except body").

A third example of the use of such a saying is found in Commodian *Carm. apol.* 559–568. Here, as in the *Epistula*, the author incorporates a proverbial proof-text into an account of the demonstration of the body of the risen Lord to the disciples. In Commodian the account of the appearance is clearly a paraphrase of John 20:19–29, and this draws attention to the fact that the proverbial saying is separable from—indeed, it interferes with—the Johannine narrative:

Guethner, 1972] 111) finds here an intercessory appeal for a just man (cf. Gen 18:22–23).

[86] Philostratus *Vit. Ap.* 8.10–12 offers a further history-of-religions parallel to the post-resurrection appearance scene as portrayed in *Ep. apost.* 9–12.

[87] The emphasized phrase is described as a "non-Lukan expression" by Xavier Léon-Dufour (quoted in Dillon, *Eye-Witnesses,* 165 n. 27).

Marcion's tortuous exegesis of Luke 24:39, to the effect that Jesus said "A spirit, such as you see me to be, hath not bones" (*apud* Tertullian *Adv. Marc.* 4.43; ET in ANF 3. 422), becomes more understandable, if still tortuous, when the phrase "A spirit has not flesh and bones" is seen as a self-contained proverbial saying.

[88] This was recognized by J. B. Lightfoot, *The Apostolic Fathers* (2 parts in 5 vols.; repr. of 1889–90 ed.; Grand Rapids: Baker, 1981) 1/1. 11; 2/2. 296–97. See further Helmut Koester, *Synoptische Überlieferung bei den apostolischen Vätern* (TU 65; Berlin: Akademie-Verlag, 1957) 47–50; and now Ron Cameron, *Sayings Traditions in the Apocryphon of James* (HTS 34; Philadelphia: Fortress, 1984) 49–51.

Then on the Lord's day [Jesus] came back to them, and stood in their midst. "Peace be with you," he said. And at once he approached the unbelieving Thomas: "Come near, and touch (my) body as (it was) before. I am not a shadow, such as are the dead: *A shadow does not make a mark* (*vestigium umbra non facit*); inspect (my) wounds." He stretched out his hands; and Thomas began to touch (him), and put his hand in Jesus' side, into which the spear had been thrust. Then he prostrated himself, confessing: "Truly you are my God and my Lord."[89]

In light of this evidence it seems certain that *Ep. apost.* 11.8 functions as do the sayings in Tertullian and Commodian, and like them depends for its background on contemporary speculation about the footprints of the departed. Following as it does upon the author's concern, first with the *dogmatic* question about resurrection (10.4 "How is it possible . . . ?"), secondly with the question of *identity* (11.7 "that you may know that it is I. . . ."), *Ep. apost.* 11.8 responds to the third concern of these chapters: to affirm the *corporeal nature* of the resurrected Jesus and hence, for the author's community, the enduring power of the risen Lord.

Ep. apost. 12.1 – 4:
Inauguration of the Revelation

Ethiopic	Coptic
1 But now we felt him, that he had truly risen in the flesh.	1 But we <touched> him that we might truly know whether he <had risen> in the flesh,
2 And then we fell on our faces before him, asked him for pardon and entreated him because we had not believed him.	2 and we fell on our <faces> confessing our sin, that we had been <un>believing.

The disciples touch the Lord for the sake of their testimony, "he had risen in the flesh." Their prostration has been anticipated by the epiphanic form as outlined above, but the stated motive is not to worship but to request pardon for disbelief. For the *Epistula* the apostles therefore become models for the author's community; and the Lord and Revealer is revealed as the one who forgives. But the narrative's rapid movement towards the beginning of the revelation dialogue permits no time for the question of forgiveness to be

---

[89] Latin text and Italian translation in Antonio Salvatore, ed., *Commodiani carmen apologeticum* (Corona patrum 5; Turin: Società Editrice Internazionale, 1977) 82 – 83. James (*Apocryphal New Testament*, 488 n. 1) ventured to say that Commodian "appears to quote" the saying in *Ep. apost.* 11.8.

developed here. The time has come in *Ep. apost.* 12.3–4 for the author to set
out the program for the revelation in chaps. 13–51:

Ethiopic	Coptic
3 Then our Lord and Saviour said to us,	3 Then the Lord our redeemer said,
"Stand up and I will reveal to you	"Rise up, and I will reveal to you
what is on earth,	what is above heaven
and what is above heaven,	and what is in heaven,
and your resurrection that is	and your rest that is
in the kingdom of heaven, 4 concerning	in the kingdom of heaven.
which my Father has sent me,	4 For my <Father> has given me
that I may take up you	the power to take up you
and those who believe in me."	and those who believe in me."

Summary

1) In *Ep. apost.* 9–12 the author has combined materials from various
sources according to an overall compositional pattern. This pattern gives
formal expression to the theological content of these chapters: a movement, effected by the resurrection, from the unbelief of the disciples to the
invitation of the Lord to rise and receive revelation.
2) Three distinct and separable motifs dominate the discussion: the possibility of resurrection; the identity of the risen one; and the nature of the risen
body.
3) Although knowledge of the canonical gospels, or of other writings such as
the *Gospel of Peter*, is presupposed (e.g., in the reference to the possibility
of Peter's denying "again," in 11.4), the special interests of the author are
clearly imposed on the source material.
4) The risen Lord announces himself as the disciples' teacher. This title is
consistent with the disciples' repeated approval (in chaps. 13–51) of what
the Lord has taught, and with the role of the disciples as teachers in the
image of their Lord.
5) In narrating the demonstration of the Lord's risen body to the disciples,
the author, ignoring or unaware of the climax of the story about Thomas
(i.e., John 20:29, a saying found in a different context in *Ep. apost.* 29),
elevates Peter, Thomas, and Andrew to the task of an exemplary
verification of the resurrection. The disciples' names derive, in the same
order, from the list of apostles in *Ep. apost.* 2.
6) *Ep. apost.* 11.8, like Luke 24:39 and passages in several other early Christian writings, retains a proof-text for the physical reality of the risen one.
In doing so the writing preserves a motif distinct from that of recognition,
and thereby finds an additional argument against the opponents' docetism.

7) A promise of revelation concludes the appearance account. But no heavenly revelation follows. Thus both the revelation and the revealer are from the outset "demythologized": the Lord as the risen, fleshly teacher, and the revelation as instruction for belief in a particular community engaged in a specific struggle against opponents as yet identified only as "Simon and Cerinthus" (*Ep. apost.* 1 and 7).

4

Epistula Apostolorum 16 – 19:
The Lord's Parousia

The *Epistula*'s author by no means presents a systematic christology.[1] Diverse theological views are bound together, often unresolved in their diversity, by the exchange of the dialogue. For example, in chap. 13 the Lord is pictured as having appeared in the world via a descent through the heavens;[2] following this cosmic descent, as if a report of the second half of the same christological history, is an account of the incarnation by the agency of the Lord himself through Mary (*Ep. apost.* 14.5 – 7).[3] Nevertheless, it is clearly the author's intention to instruct the reader about the mission of Jesus Christ, and from chap. 14 until the end of chap. 19 christological issues dominate the discussion. Thereafter the example of the Lord's resurrection and ascent is the starting point for instruction about the disciples' resurrection and judgment.

The central section of this long christological dialogue consists of *Ep. apost.* 16.1 – 19.4. These chapters present for the first time in the *Epistula* several important theological concerns and literary motifs: the Amen saying (16.3); the theme of judgment (16.5); the combination of a saying and a list (17.8); the Lord's "commandment" (18.5); and the charge to preach and teach (19.1). Thus ideas and compositional devices which are central to the

---

[1] See the surveys in Schmidt, *Gespräche Jesu,* 264 – 304; and Hornschuh, *Studien,* 30 – 61.

[2] With *Ep. apost.* 13 cf. *Gos. Phil.* (NHC 2, 3) 57.28 – 58.10; *Treat. Seth.* (NHC 7, 2) 56.20 – 57.6; *Trim. Prot.* (NHC 13, 1) 49.6 – 23.

[3] Cf. *Asc. Isa.* 10.17 – 31 (cosmic descent) and 11.1 – 16 (incarnation).

author's method and message are encountered for the first time under the subject-head of the coming of the Lord.

Within the wider context of the *Epistula*, however, the parousia[4] may be considered part of a pattern of descent and ascent which conceptually is the spatial framework of the dialogue. Every christological moment in the *Epistula* involves vertical movement, expressed or implied. This vertical frame of reference shows through repeatedly:

> . . . as I was about to come down from the Father. . . . (13.2)
>
> . . . that I might . . . go to [the Father]. (13.8)
>
> . . . after I have gone to the Father. (14.8)
>
> . . . how I shall go to heaven to my Father who is in heaven. (18.4)
>
> I have descended to <the place of> Lazarus. . . . (27.1)
>
> . . . when I shall go up to my Father. (29.7)
>
> After I have gone away and remain with my Father, . . . (33.7)
>
> . . . I have come down from heaven. (39.11)

The critical task is again to determine not only the extent of the author's traditional resources but also the compositional method by which they have been incorporated into the writing as a whole. As in earlier chapters of this study, the focus here will be upon the use of specific traditions to identifiable communal ends.

Ep. apost. 15.8 – 16.5:
The Coming of the Lord with His Martyrs

The Context of Ep. apost. 16.3 – 5

Ethiopic	Coptic
15.8 And we said to him, "O Lord, have you then not completed the drinking of the passover? Must we, then, do it again?"	15.8 And we said to him, "O Lord, is it perhaps necessary again that we take the cup and drink?"
9 And he said to us, "Yes, until I come from the Father with my wounds."	9 He said to us, "Yes, it is necessary until the day when I come with those who were killed for my sake."

---

[4] The word is used in *Ep. apost.* 17.3. In early Christian writings parousia (lit. "advent, arrival," or "presence"; *LPGL, s.v.* παρουσία [1043b – 44a]) refers to the incarnation as often as it does to the second coming. Indeed, two "parousias" are often spoken of, e.g., in Justin *1 Apol.* 52.3; *Dial.* 14.8; 32.2; 49.2; Hippolytus *De antichr.* 44; Tertullian *Apol.* 21; Cyprian *Quod idol.* 12. See further Albrecht Oepke, "παρουσία, πάρειμι," *TDNT* 5 (1967) 858 – 71, esp. pp. 870 – 71.

16.1 And we said to him, "O Lord, great is this that you say and reveal to us. 2 In what kind of power and form are you about to come?"	16.1 We said to him, "O Lord, what you have revealed to us beforehand is great. 2 In a power of what sort or in an appearance of what order will you come?"

The Lord himself introduces the subject of the return. The disciples, who until chap. 15 have spoken only twice since the dialogue began, each time merely saying "Yes, O Lord" (14.2, 4), ask in 15.8 if they are again to "take the cup and drink." The Lord's reply in 15.9 appears to form an *inclusio*, almost concealed by the length of the intervening material, with the beginning of *Ep. apost.* 15 (VII 13, 58/5):[5] "And you remember my death" (15.1) . . . "until I come . . ." (15.9). These two phrases together strongly recall Paul's summary statement in 1 Cor 11:26: "As often as you eat this bread and drink this cup, you proclaim the Lord's death until he comes."[6] Since the *Epistula* has no apparent knowledge of Paul's writings (nor of Pauline theology, for all the biographical pretensions of chaps. 31–33), it is hazardous to suggest direct borrowing of the phrase. Yet it is generally held that 1 Cor 11:26 is Paul's own afterword on the verses (23b–25) that precede vs 26.[7] Quite possibly, therefore, the Pauline phrase had already been incorporated into the eucharistic liturgy. A connection between the eucharist (or *agape*) and the Lord's return is reflected in the "maranatha" of *Did.* 10.6, and at

---

[5] Note, however, that 15.1 possibly belongs with the phrase preceding it in 14.8: ". . . after I have gone to the Father, *remember my death*" (see Wajnberg in Schmidt, *Gespräche Jesu,* 52 n. 3).

[6] The phrase in the Coptic of *Ep. apost.* 15.9, "until the day when . . .," is probably an idiomatic rendering of the Gk. ἄχρις οὖ ἔλθω, as the Ethiopic here ("until . . .") and similar passages elsewhere suggest. In the *Epistula* the Coptic ⲍⲟⲟⲩⲉ (day), is found ten times (including frg. a2 [Schmidt, *Gespräche Jesu,* 25*]). Only in fixed expressions, and where "day" means specifically "day" and not "time," does the Eth. read ʿ*elat* (day):

  a) 13.7 (VI 4, 57/5): Copt. "in that *day*" = Eth. "then" [= Lat. frag.].
  b) 22.2 (XVII 1, 66/12): Copt. (lit.) "Until what *day* . . . ?" = Eth. (lit.) "Until when . . . ?"
  c) 24.4 (XVIII 2, 67/7): Copt. "Until what *day* . . . ?" = Eth. "Until when . . . ?"
  d) 26.1 (XX 9, --): Copt. "<on> that <day>" (reconstructed); no Eth. equivalent.
  e) 26.4 (XXI 1, 69/2): Copt. = Eth. "on the *day* of judgment."
  f) 29.8 (XXV 10, 71/10): Copt. "a *day* will come" = Eth. "there is coming a time."
  g) 37.2 (frag. 2a, 80/2): Copt. = Eth. "In those years and *days*."
  h) 39.3 (XXVIII 5, 81/9): Copt. = Eth. "in that *day*."
  i) 43.13 (XXXVI 6, 86/8): Copt. "on what *day* . . . ?" = Eth. "when . . . ?"
  j) 47.7 (XL 8, 89/5): Copt. = Eth. "in that *day*."

Eth. ʿ*elat* occurs an additional eight times, six times where there is no extant Coptic, and in 9.1 (53/10: "in the days of Pontius Pilate"; Copt. understands Gk. ἐπί differently).

[7] C. K. Barrett, *The First Epistle to the Corinthians* (2d ed.; BNTC; London: Black, 1973) 270; Hans Conzelmann, *1 Corinthians* (Hermeneia; Philadelphia: Fortress, 1975) 201.

least by the time of *Const. apost.* 8.12.37 the Pauline commentary was included in the words of institution, but in the first person, as in the *Epistula*: "until I come" (ἄχρις ἂν ἔλθω).[8]

The words that follow ("with those who were killed . . .") will be discussed below in connection with 16.3 – 5 as a whole. It is the simple fact of the Lord's return that is the subject of the approval of the disciples in the formulaic language of 16.1.[9] The rhetorical formula quickly gives way to a question designed by the author to correspond to the tradition to be utilized in 16.3 – 5. This question, in 16.2, concerns the "power" (Copt. ϭΑΜ; Eth. *xāyl*) and the "appearance" (Copt. ΑΙϹΘΗϹΙϹ ; Eth. 'ar'ayā) of the Lord's coming. Schmidt makes much of "power" and "appearance" as alternatives; the question, he suggests, is whether the Lord will come "in visible bodily form, i.e., ἐν αἰσθήσει," or "in divine power, i.e., ἐν δυνάμει."[10] This may be correct, but the terms are not necessarily antithetical.[11] Schmidt's suggestion is in any case weakened by the *Epistula*'s use of the Coptic word ϭΑΜ where he understands the Greek δύναμις, because δύναμις itself survives in the Coptic text four times (in 13.2 = V 9; 13.6 = VI 4; 15.5 = VIII 5; and 30.2 = XXVI 15). In addition, a good precedent for the combination of terms in 16.2 is established in *Ep. apost.* 15.5 (VIII 5, 58/8): "I will send my *power* in the <*form*> of the angel Gabriel." Indeed, in light of 15.5 the disciples' question is not unexpected. Despite the emphasis on the physical reality of the earthly Jesus (chap. 5) and of the risen Lord (chaps. 9 – 12), in *Ep. apost.* 13 – 15 the Lord appears but a little higher than the angels:

> I passed by the angels and archangels *in their form* (ΝΠΟΥΕΙΝΕ ; ba-'amsālihomu). (13.3 [V 11, 56/9])
>
> . . . when I took the *form* (ΤΜΟΡΦΗ; 'amsāl) of the angel Gabriel. (14.5 [VII 6, 58/1])
>
> . . . in an *appearance of the form* (ϨΝ ΟΥΑΙϹΘΗϹΙϹ ΝΕΙΝΕ ; ba-'ar'ayā 'amsāla) of an angel. (14.7 [VII 12, 58/4])

[8] Cf. Conzelmann, *1 Corinthians*, 201 n. 98. Text of the *Constitutiones apostolorum*. in Funk, *Didascalia et constitutiones apostolorum*, 1. 508.

[9] In 16.1 the Coptic adverb ΝϨΑΡΠ (*NTApoc* 1. 200: "beforehand") means "before it happens" (see Crum, *s.v.* ΝϢΟΡΠ [587b]). Both the context and the Ethiopic reading (59/4: the first verb is *nagara*, which can equal προαπαγγέλλω [e.g., in Ezek 33:9] or προλέγω [e.g. in Isa 41:26; 2 Cor 13:2; references in Dillmann, *Lexicon, s.v. nagara* (688)]) favor this sense. The Lord's role as foreteller is affirmed, one that is to recur often within the conventional statements of approval made by the disciples.

[10] Schmidt, *Gespräche Jesu*, 341.

[11] Cf. Irenaeus *Epideixis* 62, interpreting Amos 9:11a ("In that day I will raise up the booth of David that is fallen") as a prediction of the resurrection: "after his death he [the Son of God] would rise again, and that he would be in *figure* a man, but in *power* God"; and the references in Schmidt, *Gespräche Jesu*, 341.

Some overlapping in terminology makes precision elusive, but the overall effect is a significant compromise of the firm antidocetic stance of the earlier chapters. But the point of the disciples' question can probably be settled by the use of the term αἴσθησις, which throws the greater part of the question's weight onto the viewpoint of the questioners. For the αἴσθησις, as "sense-perception, sensation, perception," or "impression of sense,"[12] is at its reception not that of the Lord but of his disciples, who in effect ask, "How are we to perceive your coming?"

Ep. apost.16.3–5 and Contemporary Witnesses

Ep. apost. 16.3–5 is the first of the seventeen Amen sayings in the writing. In each case the formula prefaces a saying which is traditional in form or in content. The saying in chap. 16, however, is unmatched by any of the remaining sixteen in both length and complexity; and it seems that we meet here but one configuration of a cluster of images which individually and together have had a lively history.[13] As Schmidt observes,[14] there are numerous partial parallels in early Christian literature, for example:

> And then shall appear the signs of the truth. First the sign spread out in heaven, then the sign of the sound of the trumpet, and thirdly the resurrection of the dead; but not of all the dead, but as it was said, "The Lord shall come and all his saints with him." Then shall the world "see the Lord coming on the clouds of heaven." (*Did.* 16.6–8)
>
> Behold, as the Son of man he cometh in the clouds of heaven, and his angels with him. (Justin *1 Apol.* 51.9)
>
> Some [prophecies] have reference to the first advent of Christ, . . . but others had reference to his second advent, when he shall appear in glory and above the clouds; and your nation shall see him whom they have pierced. . . . (Justin *Dial.* 14.8)

The quest to distinguish between what has been received and what is editorial in *Ep. apost.* 16.3–5 is greatly aided by the presence of several close and substantial parallels. There are parallels in Matthew 24; in three writings

---

[12] LSJ, *s.v.* αἴσθησις I, II (42b); references include Plato *Phaedo* 111b: αἰσθήσεις θεῶν ("visible appearances of the gods").

[13] Cf. Isa 59:18–19, to cite just one OT passage which may have contributed something to the present shape of the tradition:

> According to their deeds, so will he repay, wrath to his adversaries, requital to his enemies; to the coastlands he will render requital. So they shall fear the name of the Lord from the west, and his glory from the rising of the sun; for he will come like a rushing stream, which the wind of the Lord drives.

[14] Schmidt, *Gespräche Jesu*, 342 n. 3; cf. *Acts Thom.* 28; Irenaeus *Adv. haer.* 5.30.4; Tertullian *Adv. Prax.* 30.

approximately contemporary with the *Epistula*: the *Apocalypse of Peter*, the *Apocalypse of Elijah*, and book 2 of the *Sibylline Oracles*; and in Ps.-Hippolytus *De consummatione mundi*. But these sources must be handled with caution. Discrepancies between the *Epistula* and even the closest witness, the *Apocalypse of Peter*, cannot be explained in terms of simple development, and so the most primitive form of the tradition is probably not recoverable at present. Nevertheless, an examination of the texts together can do much to inform an understanding of the particular elements in *Ep. apost.* 16.3–5.

Matt 24:27, 30–31[15]

Matthew's description of the coming of the Son of man is a composite of Markan, OT (see Dan 7:13; Zech 9:14; 12:10) and other eschatological materials.[16]

> As the lightening comes from the east and shines as far as the west, so will be the coming of the Son of man. . . . Then will appear the sign of the Son of man in heaven, and then all the tribes of the earth will mourn, and they will see the Son of man coming on the clouds of heaven with power and great glory; and he will send out his angels with a loud trumpet call, and they will gather his elect from the four winds, from one end of heaven to the other.

Apoc. Pet. 1.2–6

The *Apocalypse of Peter*, which probably dates from the middle of the second century,[17] presents the fullest form of this complex saying. In *Apoc. Pet.* 1 the disciples ask the Lord for the signs of his parousia and of the end of the world. The Lord replies:

> 2 Take heed that men deceive ye not and that you do not become doubters and serve other gods. 3 Many will come in my name saying "I am Christ." Believe them not and draw not near unto them. 4 For the coming of the Son of God will [not] be manifest, but like the lightning which shineth from the east to the west, so shall I come on the clouds of heaven with a great host in my glory;

[15] Cf. Luke 17:24: "As the lightning flashes and lights up the sky from one side to the other, so will the Son of man be in his day."
[16] See McNeile, *St. Matthew*, 351–53; A. Feuillet, "La synthèse eschatologique de saint Matthieu (XXIV-XXV)," *RB* 56 (1949) 349–56; and Barnabas Lindars (*Jesus Son of Man* [Grand Rapids: Eerdmans, 1983] 109) who says: "Matthew's expansion of Mark is not merely the result of his own biblical studies, but reflects the wider use of such ideas in the church of his time." Cf. 1 Cor 15:52; 1 Thess 4:16; Rev 1:7.
[17] Christian Maurer ("Apocalypse of Peter," *NTApoc* 2. 664) dates it "in the first half of the 2nd century"; cf. Adela Yarbro Collins, "Early Christian Apocalypses," *Semeia* 14 (1979) 72–73.

5 with my cross going before my face will I come in my glory, shining seven
times as bright as the sun will I come in my glory, with all my saints, my
angels, 6 when my Father will place a crown upon my head, that I may judge
the living and the dead and recompense every man according to his work.[18]

Apoc. Pet. 1.4 – 6 is so similar to *Ep. apost.* 16.3 – 5 that James claimed
the *Epistula* was "probably" on the *Apocalypse of Peter*.[19] But a comparison
of the *Apocalypse of Peter* with Matthew 24 suggests instead that what in the
Epistula is a saying virtually free of verbal agreement with the NT has been
absorbed into a Matthean context in the *Apocalypse of Peter* (cf. Matt 24:4,
5, 26, 27). The geographical setting, too, is Matthean: the Mount of Olives
(Matt 24:3 = *Apoc. Pet.* 1.1). It is even possible that the raw material of
Apoc. Pet. 1.4 – 6, with no Matthean coloring, is present in *Apoc. Pet.* 6:

And all will see how I come upon an eternal shining cloud, and the angels of
God who will sit with me on the throne of my glory at the right hand of my
heavenly Father. He will set a crown upon my head. As soon as the nations
see it, they will weep, each nation for itself. And he shall command them to go
into the river of fire, while the deeds of each individual one of them stand
before them. <Recompense shall be given> to each according to his work.[20]

Apoc. Elij. 3.2 – 4

The *Apocalypse of Elijah* as a whole is commonly judged to be either "a
Christian composition which made use of Jewish traditions" or "a Christian
edition and expanded version of one or more Jewish documents."[21] As for
Apoc. Elij. 3.2 – 4, this is obviously "a digression inserted by a Christian editor of this work":[22]

---

[18] Ethiopic text and French translation in Sylvain Grébaut, ed., "Littérature éthiopienne
pseudo-Clémentine," ROC 15 (1910) 199, 208 – 9; ET in *NTApoc* 2. 668. I have bracketed the
word "not" in vs 2 as a likely scribal error in the Ethiopic; several of the verbs preceding "will
be manifest" have the negative particle *ʾi-*. Cf. also *Apoc. Pet.* 6: "All will see. . . ."

[19] James, *Apocryphal New Testament*, 490 n. 1. Goodspeed (*Early Christian Literature*, 35)
stated that the *Apocalypse of Peter* was "evidently used" in the *Epistula*. More recently Richard
Bauckham ("The Two Fig Tree Parables in the Apocalypse of Peter," *JBL* 104 [1985] 274) has
called this judgment into question, noting that the *Epistula* "seems to show no other sign of
dependence on the *Apocalypse of Peter*." Bauckham adds: "It is at least equally likely that both
works reflect common traditional descriptions of the parousia."

[20] Grébaut, "Littérature éthiopienne pseudo-Clémentine," 203, 211; *NTApoc* 2. 671 – 72.
James (*Apocryphal New Testament*, 521) claims that *Orac. Sib.* 2.190 – 338 "is most evidently
taken from the Apocalypse of Peter."

[21] Yarbro Collins, "Early Christian Apocalypses," 99.

[22] O. S. Wintermute, "Apocalypse of Elijah," *OTP* 1. 724. Wintermute dates the *Apocalypse*
from the 1st to the 4th century CE.

When the Christ comes, he comes in the manner of a bevy of doves with his crown of doves encircling him, as he walks on the clouds of heaven, with the sign of the cross preceding him, while the whole world sees him like the sun which shines from east to west. This is the way the Christ comes, with all his angels surrounding him.[23]

This saying, like that in *Apoc. Pet.* 1, is introduced with reference to the claims of an antichrist: "In the fourth year of that king there will appear one who says, 'I am the Christ,' but he is not. Do not believe him" (3.1).

Orac. Sib. 2.238–44

According to John J. Collins, books 1 and 2 of the *Sibylline Oracles* consist of "an original Jewish oracle and an extensive Christian redaction"; the redaction "should probably be dated no later than A.D. 150."[24] *Orac. Sib.* 2.238–44, in the middle of a larger section (2.221–51) on the resurrection of the dead, presents the following prediction:

When Sabaoth Adonai, who thunders on high, dissolves fate
and raises the dead, and takes his seat
on a heavenly throne, and establishes a great pillar,
Christ, imperishable himself, will come in glory on a cloud
toward the imperishable one with the blameless angels.
He will sit on the right of the Great One, judging at the tribunal
the life of pious men and the ways of impious men.[25]

Ps.-Hippolytus De consumm. 36.2–6

The extant form of Ps.-Hippolytus is doubtless late.[26] But in chap. 36 it is the author's wish to quote a series of eschatological proof-texts, and there is no reason to suppose that the second "saying," although it lacks a canonical origin, is recorded as other than an authoritative tradition. As in *Apoc. Pet.* 1 so in Ps.-Hippolytus the Matthean context is explicit; but it is virtually certain

---

[23] Coptic text and ET in Albert Pietersma and Susan Turner Comstock, with Harold W. Attridge, eds. and trans., *The Apocalypse of Elijah based on P. Chester Beatty 2018* (SBLTT 19; Missoula, MT: Scholars Press, 1981) 42–43. In the fourth line I have substituted "clouds" for "vaults" according to the suggestion made by K. H. Kuhn in his review of Pietersma, et al., in *JSS* 27 (1982) 315. Franz Joseph Dölger (*Sol Salutis: Gebet und Gesang im christlichen Altertum* [2d ed.; Münster: Aschendorff, 1925] 216) detects a "folk tradition" in the crown of doves.

[24] Collins, "Sibylline Oracles," *OTP* 1. 330, 332.

[25] Greek text in Geffcken, *Oracula Sibyllina*, 39; ET in *OTP* 1. 351.

[26] Mention of "the honorable (and life-giving) cross" in chaps. 20, 28, 33, and 40 suggests at least a post-Constantinian date. The earliest use of this expression cited by *LPGL*, *s.v.* τίμιος 3 (1394a) is in Cyril of Alexandria (d. 444 CE); cf. also references in *LPGL*, *s.v.* σταυρός D.4.b (1254a), and *s.v.* ζωοποιός 4.g (598b); to which add *Apoc. Dan.* 2.20 (ET in *OTP* 1. 764).

that Matt 24:27–28 and the parousia tradition following it are to be considered distinct traditions (or perhaps "testimonies"):

> 2 For the Lord says, "For as the lightning cometh out of the east, and shineth even unto the west, so shall also the coming of the Son of man be; for wheresoever the carcase is, there will the eagles be gathered together" (= Matt 24:27–28). 3 *"For the sign of the cross shall arise from the east even unto the west, in brightness exceeding that of the sun, and shall announce the advent and manifestation of the Judge, to give to every one according to his works."* 4 For concerning the general resurrection and the kingdom of the saints, Daniel says: "And many of them that sleep in the dust of the earth shall awake, some to everlasting life, and some to shame and everlasting contempt" (= Dan 12:2). 5 And Isaiah says: "The dead shall rise, and those in the tombs shall awake, and those in the earth shall rejoice" (= Isa 26:19a). 6 And our Lord says: "Many in that day shall hear the voice of the Son of God, and they that hear shall live"[27] (cf. John 5:25).

Ep. apost. 16.3–5: Preliminary Observations

Ep. apost. 16.3 (IX 6, 59/5)

Ethiopic	Coptic
ꞌemaṣṣeꞌ kama ꞌenta ḍaḥay	ϯⲛⲏⲩ ⲅⲁⲣ ⲛ̄ⲧⲍⲉ ⲛ̄ⲡⲣⲓ
za-yešarreq	ⲉⲧⲡⲣ̄ⲓⲱⲟⲩ
kamāhu ꞌana mesbeꞌito	ⲁⲟⲩ ⲉⲉⲓⲉ ⲛ̄ⲟⲩⲁⲉⲓⲛⲉ
ꞌenza ꞌebarreh	ⲛ̄ⲥⲁⲍ̄ϥ ⲛ̄ⲕⲱⲃ ⲡⲁⲣⲁⲣⲁϥ
ba-sebḥat	ⲍ̄ⲛ̄ ⲡⲁⲉⲁⲩ
I will come as the sun	I will come as does the sun
which bursts forth;	that shines,
thus will I, shining	and shining
seven times times[28] brighter than it	seven times brighter than it
in glory.	in my brightness.

The sun, combining light, heat, and apparent motion, is naturally a common image in early Christian literature as in the OT. The Coptic and Ethiopic verbs here need mean nothing more than "shine,"[29] but some stronger sense, such as that of Greek ἀνατέλλω, is likely; hence Duensing's translation of the Ethiopic, "which bursts forth." Not the Lord but the sun is the subject of the relative clause. At first glance, comparison with the *Apocalypse of Peter* would suggest that the sun in the *Epistula* has displaced "the lightning." But lightning is already present in the Matthean passage which has influenced the *Apocalypse of Peter*, and further, in the *Apocalypse of*

---

[27] Greek text in PG 10. 937–40; ET in ANF 5. 251.

[28] For *mesbeꞌito* ("seven times") MSS PQRS read *ba-tesbeꞌt* ("in [my] incarnation").

[29] Crum, *s.v.* ⲡⲉⲓⲣⲉ (267a); Dillmann, *Lexicon, s.v. šaraqa* (239).

Elijah it is not the lightning, but the sun, which shines from east to west. A final observation concerns the application of the image of the sun: in the *Epistula* the Lord himself, not his coming, is likened to the sun.[30]

The combination of creation's supreme light and the number of perfection effects a pronouncement of the completeness of the Lord's coming. The image is not a conceptual novelty, nor is its goal a purely abstract one. To be sure, the metaphor of the sun's brightness is a commonplace,[31] as is the surpassing of the sun's light.[32] The *sevenfold* brightness, however, is less frequently found, and may derive from a single, biblical source, namely the eschatology of Isa 30:26: "Moreover the light of the moon will be as the light of the sun, and the light of the sun will be sevenfold, as the light of seven days."

In Isaiah 30 this imagery is part of a renewed creation, brought about on the day of the Lord (cf. Zech 14:6–9). This picture of brightness contrasts strongly with another OT model of the day of the Lord, as a the day of darkness (cf. Amos 5:18–20; Isa 13:9–10) found also in the Synoptic apocalypse (Mark 13:24 par.). Possible allusions to Isa 30:26 are found occasionally in hellenistic Jewish and early Christian literature:[33]

> As for the intensity of [the sun's] light, it is sevenfold brighter than that of the moon. (*1 Enoch* 72.37)

> All the powers of heaven shall shine forever sevenfold.[34] (*1 Enoch* 91.16)

---

[30] Dölger (*Sol Salutis*, 375) suspects that the *Epistula* reflects a widespread Christian struggle against adherents of the cult of the sun. He points to *Ep. apost.* 3, where the Son of God is explicitly described as creator of the sun (and moon).

[31] Cf. Judg 5:31 (of the Lord's friends); 2 Sam 23:4 (of a just ruler); Dan 12:3 (of the wise).

[32] Cf. *1 Enoch* 14.20: "[God's] gown, which was shining more brightly than the sun"; Sir 23:19: "the eyes of the Lord are a thousand times brighter than the sun"; Acts 26:13: "a light from heaven, brighter than the sun"; *2 Enoch* 19.1: "(the angels') faces were more radiant than the radiance of the sun"; Clement of Alexandria *Protrepticus* 12: "Christ . . . will shed on thee a light brighter than the sun" (ANF 2. 205); Ps.-Hippolytus *In sanctas theophanias* 10: "(He who is baptized) comes up from baptism brilliant as the sun" (ANF 5. 237).

[33] Isa 30:26 is not often referred to in extant early Christian discussions of eschatology. Irenaeus (*Adv. haer.* 5.34.2) and Lactantius (*Div. inst.* 7.24.7) quote the verse in connection with the end time, but both without specific reference to the return of the Lord.

The rabbis are similarly sparing in their use of Isa 30:26. In Midrash Rabbah it is quoted only nine times. In *Gen. Rab.* 3.6, "the light which was created in the six days of Creation" is "stored up for the righteous in the Messianic future" according to Isa 30:26 (cf. *Exod. Rab.* 18.11; 50.5; *Eccles. Rab.* 11.7.1); in *Exod. Rab.* 15.21 the first of the ten things which the Holy One will renew in the time to come is the sun, which (according to Isa 30:26) will then give forty-nine times as much light. (H. Freedman and Maurice Simon, trans. eds., *Midrash Rabbah* [10 vols.; London: Soncino, 1961] 1. 22, 73, 93; 3. 186, 227, 561; 6. 524, 849; and 8. 295.) The two quotations of Isa 30:26 in the Babylonian Talmud (*b. Pesaḥ.* 68a and *b. Sanh.* 91b) are a doublet; both contrast Isa 24:23 (referring to "the world to come") with Isa 30:26 (referring to "the days of the Messiah"). (Isidore Epstein, trans. ed., *The Babylonian Talmud* [18 vols.; London: Soncino, 1948–52] 3. 346–47; 12. 612–13.)

[34] Ephraim Isaac ("1 [Ethiopic Apocalypse of] Enoch," *OTP* 1. 73 n. s2) compares 4QEn

And a spirit took me and brought me into the fifth heaven. And I saw angels who are called "lords," and the diadem was set upon them in the Holy Spirit, and the throne of each of them [cf. Dan 7:9] was sevenfold more (brilliant) than the light of the rising sun.[35] (*Apoc. Zeph.* A [*apud* Clement of Alexandria *Strom.* 5.11.77])

[Then we went] up to the seventh [heaven and I saw] an old man [...] light [and whose garment] was white. [His throne], which is in the seventh heaven, [was] brighter than the sun by [seven] times. (*Apoc. Paul* [NHC 5, 2] 22.23 – 30)

In somewhat later Christian writings this metaphor is found heightening the simpler "as the sun" of canonical texts. For example, in *Acts Phil.* 20 the Lord appears to Philip with "his face seven times brighter than the sun" (cf. Matt 17:2);[36] similarly in the *Testament of our Lord in Galilee* 7 it is stated that "the righteous . . . will have a countenance seven times brighter than the sun" (cf. Matt 13:43).[37]

It is in one of the Qumran hymns that the image of a sevenfold light is first seen transferred from its exclusively heavenly referent to an individual. The psalmist declares (1QH vii 23 – 24):

Thou didst help my soul and raise my horn on high. And I have shone forth with a sevenfold li[ght] with [the light which] Thou [hast establi]shed for Thy glory.[38]

What unites this Qumran text with the *Epistula* and *Apoc. Pet.* 1 is the absence of a specified location (e.g., face, garment) for the brightness. It is the speaker, whole and entire. Just as in *Ep. apost.* 16.3a the Lord, and not his coming, is the true subject of the principal verb, so too in 16.3b any intermediary element is set aside. The image has passed completely from creation to redeemer.[39]

Aram. frg. g: "the powers of heaven shall rise for all eternity [with sevenfold] brightness."

[35] *OTP* 1. 508.

[36] James, *Apocryphal New Testament*, 441.

[37] Guerrier, "Le testament," 44. The *Testament of our Lord in Galilee* is prefixed to the *Epistula* in all Ethiopic manuscripts. Cf. also *2 Enoch* 66.7: "How happy are the righteous who shall escape the Lord's great judgment; for they will be made to shine seven times brighter than the sun" (*OTP* 1. 194).

[38] ET in Menahem Mansoor, *The Thanksgiving Hymns* (STDJ 3; Grand Rapids: Eerdmans, 1961) 151. George W. E. Nickelsburg (*Resurrection, Immortality, and Eternal Life in Intertestamental Judaism* [HTS 26; Cambridge, MA: Harvard University Press, 1972] 148) states: "The author's exaltation has already begun."

Cf. also *Asc. Isa.* 4.14: "The Lord will come with his angels and with the host of the saints from the seventh heaven, *with the glory of the seventh heaven* . . ." (*OTP* 2. 162). Michael A. Knibb ("Martyrdom and Ascension of Isaiah," *OTP* 2. 149) dates *Asc. Isa.* 3.13 – 4.22 "at about the end of the first century [CE]"

[39] The extract from Hippolytus *Capita contra Gaium* to be examined below will show a prox-

Ep. apost. 16.4 (IX 8, 59/7)

Ethiopic	Coptic
ʾenza ba-kenfa dammanā ʾeṣṣawwar	ENTⲚⲌ ⲚⲔⲖⲞⲞⲖⲈ ⲌⲒ [ⲞⲨⲤ]ⲀⲠ(?)
ba-sebḥat wa-ʾenza masqaleya	ⲌⲀⲢⲀⲒ ⲌⲚ ⲞⲨⲈⲀⲨ ⲈⲠⲤⲎⲘⲈⲒⲞⲚ
qedmēya yaḥawwer	[ⲚⲠⲤ]ⲦⲀⲨⲢⲞⲤ ⲌⲒⲦⲀⲈⲌⲒ
while I am carried on the wings	with the wings of the clouds
of the clouds in splendour	<carry>ing me in splendour
with my cross going on before[40] me.	and the sign of the cross before me.

The presence of clouds at the coming of the Lord is part of the legacy of Dan 7:13 ("there came one like a son of man ἐπὶ [LXX] or μετὰ [Theod.] τῶν νεφελῶν") to the Synoptic Gospels.[41] Apart from the fact that in the Coptic of *Ep. apost.* 16.4 the clouds appear to be involved in "carrying" the Lord, what distinguishes this phrase from Daniel 7 is the mention of the clouds' "wings,"[42] a concept not taken up in the NT. The OT base from which such language springs is wider than Daniel 7 alone:[43]

> [The Lord] rode upon a cherub, and flew; he was seen upon the wings of the wind. (2 Sam 22:11; cf. Ps 17[18]:10)

> [Thou] who makest the clouds thy chariot, who ridest on the wings of the wind. (Ps 103 [104]:3; cf. Exod 16:10; 34:5)

The language of the *Epistula* is entirely at home in such company. What, then, is to be made of the agency of the clouds?

On inspection it seems that the clouds in the *Epistula*, as in the parallel witnesses to this tradition, are the Lord's location rather than his means of locomotion. This is because (a) the Coptic of 16.4, which is corrupt here and

---

imity of the two motifs perhaps at only one stage removed from their combination in the *Epistula* and the *Apocalypse of Peter*.

[40] In place of "before me" (*qedmēya*) two fam. 1 MSS (AT) read "with me" (*mesleya*). Since all Ethiopic witnesses have "my cross" rather than "the sign of the cross" (= Coptic), it is possible that the reading of AT is a minor corruption from a more primitive Ethiopic reading, *mesleya* (my sign), from the noun *mesl* (likeness, form, image).

[41] The difference in prepositions is reflected in Mark 14:62 (= Theod.) and Matt 26:64 (= LXX) and compounded in Luke 21:27 (= ἐv). On the phrase and its probable sense in Daniel as the setting of the scene as a whole, see R. B. Y. Scott, " 'Behold He Cometh with Clouds,' " *NTS* 5 (1958–59) 127–32; and esp. A. J. B. Higgins, *Jesus and the Son of Man* (Philadelphia: Fortress, 1964) 62–64, where the textual evidence is presented in full.

[42] Crum, *s.v.* ⲦⲚⲌ (421a); Dillmann, *Lexicon, s.v. kenf* (858). Both terms signify wings of birds and angels.

[43] Cf. also Rev 10:1 ("Then I saw another mighty angel coming down from heaven, wrapped in a cloud, with a rainbow over his head, and his face was like the sun"), on which Tertullian (*De cor.* 15) comments: "In like manner, the elders sit crowned around . . . and the Son of man himself flashes out above the clouds."

only by conjecture yields "carrying me,"[44] would in any event be expected to render a passive verb by means of a periphrastic active;[45] and (b) the Ethiopic text, "while I am carried," has no expressed agent, since the preposition with "the clouds" is *ba-*, which more commonly means "in," "into," "on," or "with," than it does "by" of an agent. The simplest explanation is that the original Greek had a participle of φέρεσθαι. In the Ethiopic this is translated very literally; in the Coptic (depending upon conjecture) we read either (a) a clause whose subject is the clouds, or (b) a paraphrase involving the addition of a makeweight adverb (ⲍⲓⲟⲩⲥⲁⲡ = Greek ἅμα) together with a prepositional phrase meaning literally "under me" (ⲍⲁⲣⲁⲓ̈).[46] The Greek φερόμενος in this context need mean no more than "coming";[47] hence "coming in (on, upon) the clouds."

Only Matthew among the Synoptic Gospels reports the coming appearance of the "sign of the Son of man" (Matt 24:30). Yet Matthew's intended referent remains uncertain, despite the near consensus among patristic writers that the sign is the cross.[48] In the passage from Ps.-Hippolytus quoted above the identification of the sign with the cross is made explicit, since the tradition under discussion (*De consumm.* 36.3) follows and hence interprets Matt 24:27 – 28, as if it were a substitute for Matt 24:30.[49]

---

[44] Schmidt, *Gespräche Jesu*, 57 n. 8.

[45] See Thomas O. Lambdin, *Introduction to Sahidic Coptic* (Macon, GA: Mercer University Press, 1983) §13.4.

[46] The phrase is still difficult, but is at least logically compatible with similar early Christian parousia texts, e.g., *Did.* 16.8 and Justin *1 Apol.* 51.9, where the Lord is said to be coming "on (ἐπάνω) the clouds"; cf. Isa 19:1 "Behold, the Lord is riding on a swift cloud."

[47] Cf. Dan 9:21 LXX: ὁ ἀνὴρ . . . Γαβριηλ τάχει φερόμενος προσήγγισέ μοι ("the man Gabriel . . . came to me in swift flight"); Acts 15:29 D; and 2 Pet 1:21.

[48] Critical opinion has looked principally to three possible referents: (1) the cross, (2) an ensign or "standard," and (3) the Son of man himself. McNeile (*St. Matthew*, 352) adds the possibility that "it may have been an eschatological feature known to Mt.'s Jewish readers but not to us." See also Feuillet, "La synthèse eschatologique," 351 – 56; A. J. B. Higgins, "The Sign of the Son of Man (Matt. xxiv 30)," *NTS* 9 (1962 – 63) 380 – 82; and T. Francis Glasson, "The Ensign of the Son of Man (Matt. xxiv 30)," *JTS* n.s. 15 (1964) 299 – 300.

For the cross as the sign of the parousia in Christian sources until the time of Augustine see Erich Dinkler, *Das Apsismosaik von S. Apollinare in Classe* (Wissenschaftliche Abhandlungen der Arbeitsgemeinschaft für Forschung des Landes Nordrhein-Westfalen 29; Cologne/Opladen: Westdeutscher Verlag, 1964) 77 – 87. Dinkler dates the identification of the sign with the cross from at least the beginning of the second century (p. 80).

In *Ep. apost.* 34.7 the Lord speaks of the cosmic signs, including "a trumpet in heaven, and the sign of great stars," visible at the endtime to believers and nonbelievers. On cosmic signs of the end, see further Wilhelm Bousset, *The Antichrist Legend* (London: Hutchinson, 1896) 232 – 33.

[49] As for the cross going "before" the Lord, Dölger (*Sol Salutis*, 216) has suggested that the *Epistula* reverses the ascent to heaven in *Gos. Pet.* 10.39, where the cross follows.

Ep. apost. 16.5 (IX 10, 59/8)

Ethiopic	Coptic
'emaṣṣe' westa medr 'ekʷannen	†NHY aϩPHï aϫN̄ ΠKaϩ
ḥeyāwāna wa-mutāna	Ta†ϩeΠ aNeTaNϩ M̄N̄ NeTMaYT
I will come to the earth	I will come down to the earth
to judge the living and the dead.	to judge the living and the dead.

Within the group of witnesses to this parousia tradition, only the *Epistula* employs both a verb of descent and a stated destination, "to the earth." These two features of *Ep. apost.* 16.5 should be kept distinct. It is often observed that in Daniel 7 the son of man *ascends* to the Ancient of Days; and that "nowhere in the whole range of O.T. prophecy, pre-Christian apocalyptic, and Gospel teaching, is the word 'descend' used of the Messiah."[50] Nevertheless, the verb is used of God,[51] and by the time of the earliest extant Christian writing an equation is made of the coming of the Lord (Jesus) and his descent: "The Lord himself will descend (καταβήσεται) from heaven . . ." (1 Thess 4:16).[52]

With the exception of the *Apocalypse of Elijah*, all the representatives of the tradition are concerned with judgment. Christ as "the judge" or "he who will judge the living and the dead" is already a well-established figure by the middle to late 2d century (cf. Acts 10:42; 2 Tim 4:1; 1 Pet 4:5; Polycarp *Phil.* 2.1; *Barn.* 7:2; *Acts Thom.* 28; 30).

Synopsis of the Tradition

When the seven witnesses to the tradition are compared according to the particular motifs present in each, a checklist of features may be assembled:

1) the name or title of the coming one;
2) the natural phenomenon to which the coming is likened;
3) the direction of his coming;
4) a metaphorical description the brightness;
5) the sign or signal;
6) the mode of the heavenly journey;
7) those accompanying the Lord;
8) a statement concerning judgment; and
9) the witnesses.

---

[50] T. Francis Glasson, *The Second Advent: The Origin of the New Testament Doctrine* (2d ed.; London: Epworth, 1947) 173.

[51] Ibid.; cf. Exod 19:20; 34:5: Num 11:25; Isa 31:4; Mic 1:3.

[52] Cf. also the formulaic 1 Thess 1:9–10; and 2 Thess 1:7.

The content of the texts may thus be represented as follows. (In Ps.-Hippolytus, asterisks indicate elements in *De consumm.* 36.2–3 supplied from Matthew 24.)

Matthew 24	*Apoc. Pet.* 1	*Apoc. Pet.* 6	*Apoc. Elij.* 3
1) son of man	son of God ("I")	"I"	the Christ
2) lightning	lightning	—	the sun
3) east to west	east to west	—	east to west
4) (cf. 24:29)	7x the sun	—	—
5) sign of the son of man	my cross before my face	—	sign of the cross before him
6) on the clouds of heaven	on the clouds of heaven	on a shining cloud	on the clouds of heaven
7) angels	all my saints	angels of God	all his angels
8) (cf. 19:28)	living and dead	—	—
9) tribes of the earth	—	the nations	the whole world

Ps.-Hippolytus	*Orac. Sib.* 2.241–44	*Ep. apost.* 16.3–5
1) the judge	Christ	"I"
2) *	—	the sun
3) east to west	toward the imperishable one	down to earth
4) exceeding the sun	in glory	7x the sun's brightness
5) sign of the cross	—	sign of the cross
6) *	on a cloud	on wings of clouds
7) *	blameless angels	(cf. 15.9)
8) everyone	pious and impious	living and dead
9) —	—	(?disciples)

The Function of Ep. apost. 16.3–5 and 15.9

A comparison of the texts according to these features shows that *Ep. apost.* 16.3–5 is exceptional in two important respects. First, as noted in connection with the translation of these verses, the *Epistula* is the only witness to specify the Lord's destination, "to the earth." Although the Ethiopic lacks the adverb "down," this reading is secure. Thus, for the author of the *Epistula*, it needs to be stressed that the earth is the arena in which a decisive judgment is to take place. The significance of this, however, can become evident only in consideration of the second difference, which is that in *Ep. apost.* 16.3–5 the coming Lord lacks a heavenly entourage.

There is scarcely a feature of early parousia tradition as constant as the company of the holy ones or angels.[53] Its absence from the *Epistula* gives the immediate impression that the Lord returns alone. However, the beginning of the parousia discussion must now be recalled. To the disciples' question, whether they will have to "take the cup and drink" (15.8), the Lord replied (15.9 [VIII 15, 59/2]: "Yes, it is necessary until the day when I come with those who were killed for my sake." If "those who were killed for my sake" are the equivalent of "saints" or "holy ones" (cf. *Apoc. Pet.* 1.5),[54] it is likely that the *Epistula* reflects a widespread use of Zech 14:5 ("Then the Lord your God will come, and all the holy ones with him"); ἅγιοι in the LXX was found capable of interpretation respecting either saints or angels.[55]

The phrase in the *Epistula* certainly brings the concept of saints to mind. But it is not possible that the word "holy one" or "saint" was unfamiliar to the author. Therefore it must be asked if the ambiguous term has been avoided in a deliberate reaction to the tradition: negatively, in the removal of the angels, who in this writing would be found unworthy to share the Lord's return;[56] positively, in the elevation of a particular group. Schmidt suggested that for the prepositional phrase "with those who were killed for my sake" the Greek original read μετὰ τῶν ἀποτεθνηκότων ἕνεκεν ἐμοῦ, and he cited Rev 20:4 for comparison: "I saw the souls of those who had been beheaded (τῶν πεπελεκισμένων) for their testimony to Jesus."[57] Thematically this is a helpful comparison, and Schmidt's retroversion is a plausible one. But there is one major disadvantage in the retroversion: the two versions of *Ep. apost.* 15.9 are left irreconcilable, since the Ethiopic text here reads "with my wounds."

This Ethiopic reading can throw important light on the Coptic. Schmidt himself pointed out that the idea of the Lord's return "with his wounds" has great antiquity: Rev 19:13 speaks of the Word of God, "clad in a robe dipped in blood," upon a white horse from heaven;[58] *Barn.* 7.9 reports that "they will see him on that day with the long scarlet robe." But it is with another writing nearly contemporary with the *Epistula* that the Ethiopic reading can

---

[53] Schmidt, *Gespräche Jesu*, 342–43. In Matt 24:30 it is possible that μετὰ δυνάμεως καὶ δόξης πολλῆς (*RSV*: "with power and great glory") signifies an angelic host (McNeile, *St. Matthew*, 353); in any case, in Matt 24:31 it is the angels who are sent out to gather the elect.

[54] Cf. BAG, *s.v.* ἅγιος 2.d.α,β (10a).

[55] Cf. Bauckham ("Two Fig Tree Parables," 274 n. 22), who states: "It is not clear whether 'my saints, my angels' [in *Apoc. Pet.* 1.5] should be read to mean 'my holy angels' . . . or to mean 'my holy ones (i.e. Christians) and my angels.'" But see *Asc. Isa.* 4.14, quoted in n. 38 above.

[56] The angels are deceived (13.2–4), and they are to be denied a view of the Christians' joy (19.6).

[57] Schmidt, *Gespräche Jesu*, 57 n. 1.

[58] Ibid. It is probable, however, that the blood in Rev 19:13 is not that of the horseman but of the slain Parthians (cf. R. H. Charles, *The Revelation of St. John* [2 vols.; ICC; Edinburgh: T. & T. Clark, 1920] 2. 133).

be more precisely compared. Hippolytus *Comm. in Dan.* 4.10.4 (on Dan 7:17–18) speaks of the Lord's return in strikingly similar terms:

ἐρχόμενος ἥξει μετὰ τῶν τραυμάτων αὐτοῦ
καὶ ἀποδώσει ἑκάστῳ κατὰ τὰ ἔργα αὐτοῦ

When he comes he shall come *with his wounds*,
and will render to each according to his works.[59]

Hippolytus's words offer the possibility of accounting for the divergence of the versions in *Ep. apost.* 15.9. For if the Ethiopic text can reflect the Greek μετὰ τῶν τραυμάτων μου ("with my wounds"), the Coptic reading can equally reflect the Greek μετὰ τῶν τραυματιῶν μου ("with my slain ones").

In the LXX the word τραυματίας (lit. "wounded man") regularly translates Hebrew *ḥālāl* (pierced, fatally wounded, slain).[60] The latter meaning is clear from such passages as Deut 21:1: "If in the land which the Lord your God gives you to possess, any one is found *slain* . . . and it is not known *who killed him*. . . ."[61] The word becomes almost a technical term for a man slain in battle; the qualifying phrase, "with a sword," is common.[62] The word also attracts the genitive of a person or nation, signifying possession and, inasmuch as the slain are representatives of a nation,[63] allegiance.

That this term, apparently not common in contemporary Greek, was

---

[59] Greek text and French translation in Maurice Lefèvre, *Hippolyte: Commentaire sur Daniel* (SC 14; Paris: Cerf, 1947) 280–81. There is a variant reading, γραμματίων, probably bearing the sense "account-books" (cf. LSJ, *s.v.* γραμματεῖον [= γραμμάτιον] I.2 [358b]); in addition, Theodore Zahn proposed emending to στρατευμάτων ("armies, hosts"; see G. N. Bonwetsch and H. Achelis, eds., *Hippolytus Werke* vol. 1 [GCS 1/1; Leipzig: Hinrichs, 1916] 210). Bonwetsch and Achelis print and translate "wounds." But Hippolytus's words as quoted above are to be seen as a modest anticipation of what would later be depicted as a full-blown recapitulation, at the time of the parousia, of the post-resurrection demonstration of the wounded, risen Jesus. This tendency is already visible in the application of Zech 12:10 ("when they look on him whom they have pierced"; cf. John 19:37) to descriptions of the parousia, as in Justin *Dial.* 14.8; 32.2; and *Const. apost.* 5.20.2. It makes an explicit and lengthy reappearance in Ps.-Hippolytus *De consumm.* 40:

> For the people of the Hebrews shall see him in human form, as he appeared to them when he came by the holy virgin in the flesh, and as they crucified him. And he will show them the prints of the nails in his hands and feet, and his side pierced with the spear, and his head crowned with thorns, and his honorable cross. (Greek text in PG 10. 941–43; ET in ANF 5. 252.)

[60] BDB, *s.v. ḥālāl* 1 and 2 (319b); cf. Hatch-Redpath, *s.v.* τραυματίας (2. 1369–70). The noun occurs over sixty times in the LXX, but not once in the NT. The meaning "slain" seems to be peculiar to the LXX (cf. LSJ, *s.v.* τραυματίας II [1811a]; and F. C. Conybeare and St. George Stock, *Grammar of Septuagint Greek* [1905; reprinted Peabody, MA: Hendrickson, 1988] 215).

[61] See also 2 Sam 1:19; Jer 32(25):33; Ps 87(88):5; Ezek 28:8.

[62] Cf. Jer 14:18; Ezek 32:23.

[63] Cf. Isa 34:3; Ezek 6:4.

known to the *Epistula*'s author is not at all improbable in a community familiar with the LXX.[64] And in light of the difference now suggested to lie behind the Coptic and Ethiopic of *Ep. apost.* 15.9, it is interesting to find that in the Greek versions of Num 19:18 the word τραυματίου in Vaticanus and Sinaiticus is read as τραύματος in Alexandrinus; in this case too the secondary reading is the more common word, "wound."[65] For *Ep. apost.* 15.9 the question becomes whether or not the extant Coptic is likely to have derived from the Greek proposed for it.

First, the Coptic verb ⲍⲱⲧⲃ can translate τραυματίας, for example, in Deut 21:2.[66] Second, inasmuch as "those who were slain" is a periphrastic passive in Coptic (lit. "those whom they slew them"), the verbal form could not have taken an additional suffix (to express the possessive, "my"). Therefore the Coptic translator was obliged to choose a prepositional phrase. Many Greek prepositions can be represented by the preposition ⲉⲧⲃⲉ-: διά + accusative; ἕνεκα + genitive; περί + genitive; ὑπέρ + genitive; ἐπί + dative or accusative.[67] The prepositional form ⲉⲧⲃⲏⲧ supplied the translator with a satisfactory, if potentially interpretive, rendering of the Greek possessive pronoun.

Further, external support for this understanding of 15.9 comes from an additional early witness to the parousia tradition in *Ep. apost.* 16.3 – 5. In Hippolytus *C. Gaium* frg. 5 (on Rev 20:2 – 3) the parousia is spoken of as follows:

And the number of the years is not the number of days, but it represents the space of one day, glorious and perfect; in which, *when the King comes in glory with his slain*, the creation is to shine: according to the text, *the sun shall shine twofold* [marg. *sevenfold*; cf. Isa 30:26]: while the righteous eat with him and drink of his vine. *This is the day which the Lord hath made* [Ps 118:24], which David spoke of. Accordingly, when with the eye of the spirit John saw the glory of that day, he likened it to the space of *a thousand years* [Rev 20:2, 3];

---

[64] Josephus uses the noun nineteen times. Among ancient authors it is found with some frequency in the earlier period, e.g., in Pindar (5th c. BCE) frg. 223 (244).3; Herodotus (5th c. BCE) *Hist.* 3.79; Thucydides (5th c. BCE) 7.75.3; 8.27.4; Aeneas Tacticus (4th c. BCE) *Poliorcetica* 16.15; 26.7; but in the hellenistic era the term is less common, and almost completely confined to technical military or medical use; e.g., in Polybius (2d c. BCE) *Hist.* 3.66.9; Galen (2d c. CE) *In Hippocratis librum vi epid. comm. vi* 17; Rufus of Ephesus (2d c. CE) *Questiones medicinales* 54; 59; Lucian (2d c. CE) *Nigrinus* 37; Longus (3d c. CE) *Daphnis et Chloe* 2.19.1.

[65] Cf. Aeneas Tacticus 26.7, where the manuscripts show precisely the τραυματιῶν/τραυμάτων variation here suspected in *Ep. apost.* 15.9 (*Aeneas Tacticus, Asclepiodotus, Onasander* [LCL; London: Heinemann; Cambridge, MA: Harvard University Press, 1923] 134 – 35).

[66] "Then your elders and your judges shall come forth, and they shall measure the distance to the cities which are around *him that is slain*" (reference in Crum, *s.v.* ⲍⲱⲧⲃ [723b]).

[67] References for these and other Greek prepositions in Crum, *s.v.* ⲉⲧⲃⲉ- (61a).

according to the saying, *One day* in the world of the righteous *is as a thousand years* [cf. Ps 90:4].[68]

Who then, according to the author of the *Epistula*, are "the slain" who are to accompany the Lord at his return? Several passages in the *Epistula* suggest that they include members of the author's group who have been persecuted for their faith:

> If [the elect] suffer torment, such suffering will be a test for them, whether they have faith and whether they keep in mind these words of mine and obey my commandment. (36.4 [--, 79/1])

> They have been <tormented>, being destitute, since men were arrogant against them while they walk in hunger and thirst. (38.5 [XXVII 8, 81/4])

> He who loves me and finds fault with those who do not do my commandments, these will thus be hated and persecuted. (50.1 [--, 90/9])

It is hard to avoid the conclusion that a present struggle is reflected here. Therefore it is required that the Lord return to the earth, for this is where the community's ordeal is taking place. Near the end of the writing (50.4 [--, 91/1]), those who suffer for their faith are identified as "martyrs": "Those who have endured this *will be as martyrs with the Father*" (*kama 'enta samā't yekawwenu ba-xaba 'ab*). Thus the disciples' question in *Ep. apost.* 15.8 ("Is it perhaps necessary again that we take the cup and drink?") may be understood as an explicit reference to martyrdom.[69]

---

[68] Syriac text and ET in John Gwynn, "Hippolytus and his 'Heads against Caius,'" *Hermathena* 6 (1888) 403–4, 415–16. The Syriac for the phrase "with his slain (pl.)" is ʿm qtylwhy. In the Peshitta (the "vulgate" Syriac Bible) the same passive participle (in the singular) renders τραυματίας in Deut 21:2 where, as noted, the Coptic version has ⲍⲱⲧⲃ.

[69] 15.8 is possibly an allusion to the martyrdom of Peter. With this verse Erik Peterson ("Das Martyrium des hl. Petrus nach der Petrus-Apokalypse," in *Frühkirche, Judentum und Gnosis* [Rome/Freiburg/Vienna: Herder, 1959] 89 n. 7) has compared *Apoc. Pet.* 14 (in the Rainer fragment; text in M. R. James, "The Rainer Fragment of the Apocalypse of Peter," *JTS* 32 [1931] 271; ET in *NTApoc* 2. 679 n. 3): "Go thou [Peter] to the city that ruleth over the west, and drink the cup which I promised thee." Cf. Mark 10:39; Matt 20:22–23; *Mart. Poly.* 14.2: "that I may share, among the number of your martyrs, in the cup of your Christ"; and *Asc. Isa.* 5.13: "For me alone the Lord has mixed the cup."

This evidence may lend support to the original suggestion by Cyril C. Richardson ("A New Solution to the Quartodeciman Riddle," *JTS* n.s. 24 [1973] 74–84) that the Quartodeciman controversy in some circles (for Richardson, in Asia Minor) concerned an attempt "to conform the Easter celebration to a *martyr's festival*" (p. 81). Thus, "if one considers the section on Easter in the *Epistle of the Apostles* not as an account of what has always been done, but as an innovation, being urged on the churches under an apostolic fiction, we can view the matter in a new light. It is a story of persecution and reflects Acts xii. Peter is in prison; he manages to escape and to celebrate Easter as a martyr's festival with a vigil and cock-crow Mass. The implication seems to me to be: this is how you ought to keep Easter *because of persecution*" (p. 82).

Hornschuh (*Studien*, 93) rightly questions the extent to which "martyr" is a technical term in

In light of the passages quoted here, and with regard to the meaning now derived from *Ep. apost.* 15.9, a translation problem in *Ep. apost.* 38.1 may be resolved. Duensing's translation is as follows (--, 80/9):

> But those who desire to see the face of God and who do not regard the person of the sinful rich and who do not fear the men who lead them astray, but reprove them, *they will be crowned* (text: *wounded*) *in the presence of the Father*, as also those who reprove their neighbours will be saved.[70]

The emphasized phrase may be retranslated, in line with 15.9, as follows:[71]

'ellu qʷesulāna yekawwenu ba-xaba 'ab.
They, *the wounded* [*slain*], will be with the Father.''

Ep. apost. 17.1 – 19.4:
The Lord's Parousia and the Disciples' Preaching

Ep. apost. 17.1 – 3 (IX 11, 59/9)

Ethiopic	Coptic
1 And we said to him, "O Lord, how many years yet?"	1 But we said to him, "O Lord, after how many years yet will this happen?" 2 He said to us,
2 And he said to us, "When the hundred and fiftieth year is completed, between Pentecost and Passover will the coming of my Father take place."	"When the hundredth part and the twentieth part is completed, between Pentecost and the feast of unleavened bread, will the coming of the Father take place."
3 And we said to him, "O Lord, now you said to us, 'I will come,' and then you said, 'He who sent me will come.'"	3 But we said to him, "Here now, what have you said to us, 'I will come,' and how do you say, 'It is he who sent me who will come'?"

The question of the date of the parousia was one with which both the first and the second century were concerned: "the end is not yet" (Mark 13:7); "the end will not be at once" (Luke 21:9). Ps 90:4, in which Hippolytus took refuge in his *C. Gaium* frg. 5 quoted above, is called to witness also in

---

the *Epistula*; cf. Paul Peeters, "Les traductions orientales du mot Martyr," AnBoll 39 (1921) 50 – 64, esp. pp. 54, 58.

[70] *NTApoc*, 1. 217 (emphasis added).

[71] The thematic connection between 38.1 and 50.1, 4 seems to have been overlooked by previous translators, who (with the exception of Duensing in *Epistula Apostolorum*, 31: "diese werden beim Vater verwundet sein") have accepted Guerrier's emendation of *qʷesulāna* (wounded) to *qʷeṣṣulāna* (crowned), though it is without any manuscript support.

2 Pet 3:8. It is therefore unfortunate that *Ep. apost.* 17.2 (IX 13, 59/9), which reads like a specific response to the disciples' question in 17.1, has found no consensus of interpretation. *Ep. apost.* 17.2 has frequently been claimed as the writing's temporal autograph;[72] but beyond the general range of date indicated (120 – 180 CE) there has been no firm advance.[73]

---

[72] See Schmidt, *Gespräche Jesu*, 397.

[73] The numerous proposals for interpreting this verse are reviewed by Vanovermeire, "Livre que Jésus-Christ a révélé," 220 – 39. Eight approaches to *Ep. apost.* 17.2 may be distinguished and summarized as follows. (1) The Latin fragment possibly offers support for the Ethiopic reading ("hundred and fiftieth") against the Coptic ("the hundredth part and twentieth part"). To this figure should be added the thirty years of Jesus' life, hence the terminus ante quem of 180 CE; cf. Justin *1 Apol.* 46.1, where the author shows awareness of the one hundred and fifty years since Jesus' birth (Schmidt, *Gespräche Jesu*, 397 – 98). (2) The Coptic figure is original, as is the striking expression, "between Pentecost and the feast of unleavened bread." The Ethiopic figure is the result of a scribal error. The author of the *Epistula* would not announce the parousia to his own generation, hence the terminus ante quem is 130 – 140 CE (Ehrhardt, "Eine neue apocryphe Schrift," 722 – 23). (3) Scribes faced an inevitable temptation to bring a prediction up to date. The text behind the Ethiopic reading simply added a generation to the received text; hence the terminus ante quem is 140 – 170 CE (Hans Lietzmann, review of Schmidt, *Gespräche Jesu*, in *ZNW* 20 (1921) 174). (4) The odd Coptic phrase, "the hundredth part and the twentieth part," can be understood to mean "a century and 1/20 of a century," i.e., 105; hence a possible terminus ante quem is 105 + 30 (the life of Jesus) = 135 (Anton Baumstark, "Alte und neue Spuren eines außerkanonischen Evangeliums [vielleicht des Ägypterevangeliums]," *ZNW* 14 [1913] 244 and n. 2). (5) The Coptic text really says "1/100 + 1/20." This is the same as 1/100 + 5/100, and from a figure such as this it is not possible to derive a date of composition (Hugo Duensing, review of Schmidt, *Gespräche Jesu*, in *GGA* 184 [1922] 248; see also Duensing, *Epistula Apostolorum*, 14 n.7). (6) Matt 24:37 ("As were the days of Noah, so will be the coming of the Son of man") is a probable allusion to the prophecy in Gen 6:3: "His days shall be a hundred and twenty years." Hence the Coptic figure in *Ep. apost.* 17, and the terminus ante quem of 120 + 30 = 150 CE (Delazer, "De tempore compositionis," 260 – 61, 272, 291 – 92). (7) Ps.-Philo and *2 Baruch* offer evidence of speculation as to the date of the end. The *Epistula* attempts the same precision. The original Greek read: ὡς τοῦ ἑκατοστοῦ καὶ εἰκοστοῦ ἔτους πεπληρωμένου, τοτ' ἐν τῇ ἑορτῇ τοῦ πάσχα (var. τῶν ἀζύμων). This text was corrupted (note the order: Pentecost and Passover) by dittography: ΤΟΤΕΝΤΗ[Π]ΕΝΤΗΚΟϹΤΗ, deriving from ΤΟΤΕΝΤΗΕΟΡΤΗ. Hence the terminus ante quem is as in (1) above (Léon Gry, "La date de la fin des temps, selon les révélations ou les calculs du Pseudo-Philon et de Baruch [Apocalypse syriaque]," *RB* 48 [1939] 337 – 56; idem, "La date de la parousie d'après l'Epistula Apostolorum," *RB* 49 [1940] 86 – 97). (8) Dio Cassius 57.18.3 – 4; 62.18 and *Orac. Sib.* 8.50 – 53 (Hadrian), 65 – 68 (three rulers after Hadrian), 148 – 149 (948 years) show the pagan and Jewish world's concern with the date of the end. *Orac. Sib.* 8.65 – 67 was revived when Antoninus Pius prepared for the celebration of Rome's 900th anniversary in 147 – 48 CE; and 8.148 – 150 allows a further forty-eight years. This time frame was familiar to the *Epistula*'s community, and both the Coptic (120 + 30) and the Ethiopic (150 = 120 + 30) reflect it. Hence the terminus ante quem is 130 – 140 CE (H. J. Cladder, review of Schmidt, *Gespräche Jesu*, in *TRev* 18 [1919] 452 – 53; Vanovermeire, "Livre que Jésus-Christ a révélé," 233 – 39).

As Hornschuh (*Studien*, 118 – 19), following Duensing, concludes, a more secure ground for the dating of the *Epistula* must be sought outside chap. 17.

It is tempting to build on the observation that two dates are given in 17.2: (a) the year, and (b) the time of the year. The Coptic does not have "year" but "part" (ογων [IX 13], = μέρος [Crum, 483a]). This word, in connection with "Pentecost," is similar to a phrase in Hippolytus

It will be noticed, however, that in the context of *Ep. apost.* 17 what is of concern is not so much the date as the nature of the coming; what is startling to the disciples in 17.2 is the fact that the coming is to be the Father's, and it is to this point that they respond in 17.3. To be connected with this is the Lord's prediction, near the end of the writing, in which the disciples are informed that "after three days and hours he who sent me will come that I may go with him" (51.1 [--, 92/1]). This concluding promise maintains a distinction between the sender and the sent one which is never fully relaxed; in fact, it is this very distinction which *Ep. apost.* 17 uses the occasion of the parousia question to explore. Thus the issue of date and time fades completely as the disciples pursue their question of the relation between the Lord and the Father in 17.3 (X 1, 59/11).

Ep. apost. 17.4 – 8 (X 3, 59/12)

Ethiopic	Coptic
4 And he said to us, "I am wholly in the Father and the Father in me."	4 Then he said to us, "I am wholly in my Father and my Father is in me
5 Then we said to him, "Will you really leave us until your coming? Where will we find a teacher?"	
6 And he answered and said to us, "Do you not know that until now I am both here and there with him who sent me?"	
7 And we said to him, "O Lord, is it possible that you should be both here and there?"	
8 And he said to us, "I am wholly in the Father and the Father in me (after?) his image and after his form and after his power and after his perfection and after his light, and I am his perfect word."	with regard to the resemblance of form and of power (?) and of perfection and of light and of full measure and with regard to voice. I am the word."

The first response to the parousia tradition comes in the form of an "I am" saying (17.4) which is a tour de force from the Johannine tradition.

Comm. in Dan. 4.55.3 (on Dan 12:11 – 12), and suggests that items (a) and (b) in *Ep. apost.* 17 may originally have been distinct traditions. Hippolytus speaks of the coming of the *antichrist* (variant: the *Christ*) εἰς μέρος πεντηκοστῆς; and it is a cultic point of reference, rather than a precise date, that seems most applicable to the discussion in *Ep. apost.* 15 – 17. Cf. Bernhard Lohse, *Das Passafest der Quartadecimaner* (Beiträge zur Förderung christlicher Theologie 2/54; Gütersloh: Bertelsmann, 1953) 78 – 81; Joachim Jeremias, *The Eucharistic Words of Jesus* (Philadelphia: Fortress, 1977) 123.

This, of course, is very similar to Jesus' utterances in John 10:38 ("The Father is in me and I am in the Father") and 14:10 ("I am in the Father and the Father in me"; cf. 14:20; 17:21, 23). However, two considerations urge caution in describing *Ep. apost.* 17.4 as a quotation from John: (1) in the *Epistula* the saying stands alone, the explicit object neither of knowledge (cf. John 10:38: "that you may know . . .") nor of belief (cf. John 14:10: "Do you not believe that . . ."), and there is no other hint of awareness of the Johannine context;[74] (2) this saying, already a strong statement of "indwelling" in John, is found in the fuller ("wholly") form, and probably independent of the Johannine gospel, in *Acts John* 100:

τῶν οὖν πολλῶν ἀμέλει καὶ τῶν ἔξω τοῦ μυστηρίου καταφρόνει·
γίνωσκε γάρ με ὅλον παρὰ τῷ πατρὶ καὶ τὸν πατέρα παρ' ἐμοί.

Therefore ignore the many and despise those who are outside the mystery; for you must know that I am wholly with the Father, and the Father with me.[75]

But for a community facing suffering, even this reassurance will not suffice. Therefore the saying is challenged by the disciples in 17.5 with a question that reinforces the picture of the Lord as teacher.[76] Who, in the interim between the ascension and the parousia, will serve as the guide and guardian of the community? The question is reminiscent of *Gos. Thom.* (NHC 2, 2) 12a: 34.25 – 27: "The disciples said to Jesus, 'We know that you will depart from us. Who is to be our leader?' " But for the *Epistula*'s author it is not a matter of reestablishing a chain of apostolic authority. For this writer there is but one teacher, the Lord alone, and there can be no successor in the foundational role of teacher *of the disciples*. And so it is that the community is offered another reassurance from the tradition, in the form of another "I am" saying put into the form of a question (17.6 [--, 60/2]).

The issue of the presence and absence of divine figures was of course not a new one. Perhaps from the time of Homer, heroes living and dead had been the subject of such speculation. Of Heracles, Homer—or an interpolator[77]—had written (*Odyssey* 11.601 – 603):

---

[74] Regarding the function of this saying in John 14, D. Bruce Woll (*Johannine Christianity in Conflict* [SBLDS 60; Chico, CA: Scholars Press, 1981] 47) has observed that "the introductory words, *ou pisteueis hoti* . . . (vs. 10), and *pisteuete moi hoti* . . . (vs. 11), as well as the use of the formula in the argument (as something Philip was expected to believe already), suggest the possibility that the formula, *ego en to patri kai ho pater en emoi*, may have had confessional status in the Johannine community."

[75] Greek text in Lipsius-Bonnet, *Acta apostolorum apocrypha*, 2/1. 201; ET in *NTApoc* 2. 234.

[76] All commentators are agreed that the Coptic has omitted 17.5 – 8a, since both the Ethiopic and the fragmentary Latin read these verses; see Schmidt, *Gespräche Jesu*, 178; Vanovermeire, "Livre que Jésus-Christ a révélé," 121.

[77] Setting *Odyssey* 11.602 on one side as an interpolation, Ugo Bianchi ("Docetism: A Peculiar Theory about the Ambivalence of the Presence of the Divine," in Joseph M. Kitagawa and Charles H. Long, eds., *Myths and Symbols: Studies in Honor of Mircea Eliade* [Chicago/London:

After him [Sisyphys] I [Odysseus] marked the mighty Heracles—his phantom; for he himself among the immortal gods takes his joy in the feast.[78]

It was a proposition that raised the serious exegetical question given voice by Plotinus in the 3d c. CE (*Ennead* 1.1.12): "The poet seems to be separating the image with regard to Heracles when he says that his shade is in Hades, but he himself among the gods."[79]

Christological discussion, especially in exegesis of the Fourth Gospel, could find a solution much like that offered in *Ep. apost.* 17.6. Hippolytus, for example, comments on John 3:3 ("Unless one is born anew, he cannot see the kingdom of God") as follows: "Who, then, was in heaven but the fleshless Word—he who was sent for the purpose of showing that he who is on earth is in heaven too?" (*C. Noet.* 4.11).[80] To the same end, within the popular, apocalyptic frame of *Gos. Bart.* 31–32, this exchange is found:

> Bartholomew asked: "Lord, when you lived among us, did you receive the sacrifices in paradise?" Jesus answered: "Verily, I say to you, my beloved, even when I taught among you, I sat at the right hand of the Father and received the sacrifices in paradise."[81]

But the *Epistula*'s Johannine formula, though dogmatically watertight, does not satisfy, and here as five times elsewhere in the writing the disciples ask: "Is it possible . . . ?" What is called forth is an interpretive commentary on the traditional saying in 17.4, the result being a saying + list combination

---

University of Chicago Press, 1969] 267) finds the oldest western example of "the ambivalence of the presence of the divine" in the legend of Helen in the *Palinode* of Stesichorus (7th-6th c. BCE). As Bianchi notes, precisely this legend and personality (Helen's) were later adopted by Simonianism.

[78] Greek text and ET in A. T. Murray, *Homer: The Odyssey* (2 vols.; LCL; London: Heinemann; Cambridge, MA: Harvard University Press, 1960) 1. 428–29.

[79] Greek text and ET in A. H. Armstrong, *Plotinus* (6 vols.; LCL; London: Heinemann; Cambridge, MA: Harvard University Press, 1979–83) 1. 120–21.

[80] Greek text and ET in Butterworth, *Hippolytus: Contra Noetum*, 54–55.

[81] ET in *NTApoc* 1. 491; reference in Hornschuh, *Studien*, 50. On the date of this work, see Felix Scheidweiler and Wilhelm Schneemelcher, "The Gospel of Bartholomew," *NTApoc* 1. 484–86. Cf. Clement of Alexandria *Excerpta Theodoti* 4.2: "For on high, too, he [the Lord] was Light and that which was manifest in the flesh and appeared here is not later than that above nor was it curtailed, in that it was transplanted hither from on high, changing from one place to another, so that this was gain here and loss there" (Greek text and ET in Robert Pierce Casey, ed., *The Excerpta ex Theodoto of Clement of Alexandria* [SD 1; London: Christophers, 1934] 42–43). In a third, hymnic, genre the same concern is given exalted expression (if not practical resolution) in Melito *Pass. Hom.* frg. 14 (Hall, *Melito of Sardis: On Pascha*, 81–82):

> He was seen as a lamb, but remained a shepherd; . . .
> treading the earth, and filling heaven; . . .
> He stood before Pilate, and sat with the Father;
> He was fastened to the tree, and held the universe.

(17.8 [X 3, 60/4]), in which the attributes shared by the Father and the Son are catalogued as follows: (1) form (ⲙⲟⲣⲫⲏ, 'ar'ayā); (2) power (ⲝⲓⲛ, xāyl);[82] (3) perfection (ⲙⲟⲩⲍ, feṣṣāmē); and (4) light (ⲟⲩⲁⲉⲓⲛⲉ, berhān). As the translations above show, neither reading is straightforward. The Ethiopic seems to understand the "resemblance" or "likeness" ('amsāl) to be itself the first of the attributes uniting the Lord with the Father.[83] The list's conclusion is a more serious problem; the awkward Coptic "and of full measure and with regard to voice" now seems on the basis of Ethiopic fam. 1 manuscripts to stand for "and regarding perfection of voice."[84]

Leaving aside the fifth element in the list ("voice"), it is therefore in the likeness of four qualities that the Lord's unity with the Father is said to reside. These four terms, all found elsewhere in the *Epistula*, are of the author's own choosing, and they serve to interpret the saying which introduces them. In a general way, of course, each might be identified in other early Christian literature as an attribute by which the Father's presence is mediated to the people of God. But the immediate context, namely the question about the parousia, has influenced the selection here. This is because items (1) *form* and (2) *power* correspond to the disciples' question in *Ep. apost.* 16.2: "In a *power* of what sort or in an *appearance* of what order will you come?" Items (3) *perfection* and (4) *light* correspond to the Lord's prediction in *Ep. apost.* 19.8 (XI 1, 62/5): "You will see a *light* <that> is more exalted than all that shines, . . . the *accomplishment* [*perfection*] that accomplishes. . . ." This statement appears to be a reformulation of *Ep. apost.* 16.3 – 5 in abstract terms. The consequence of the list may therefore be judged to be this: inasmuch as the Lord comes to the earth to judge the living and the dead (16.5), he comes in the power of those attributes in which he is wholly in the Father. The Son is to be known in the parousia of the Father, and the Father in the coming of the Son.

However, one important element in the author's reassurance remains unaccounted for. In *Ep. apost.* 17.6 the author reported the presence of the Lord "both here [on earth] and there with him who sent me"; but this was presented as a state of affairs valid "until now" (Eth.: 'eska ye'ezē).

---

[82] Coptic ⲝⲓⲛ, "power, capacity" (Crum, 773b) is rare; it is defined on the basis of Ethiopic xāyl.

[83] In 17.8, where the Coptic (X 4) reads "with regard to the resemblance" (ⲁⲃⲁⲗ ⲍ̄ⲛ̄ ⲡⲓⲛⲉ) the Ethiopic, as quoted above from *NTApoc* 1. 201, has "?after? his image" ('esma 'amsālu). The Ethiopic word 'esma, which usually is equivalent to the Greek γάρ, here probably = τοῦτ' ἔστιν (that is) as in Rom 9:8 (Dillmann, *Lexicon*, s.v. 'esma 2.c [747]).

[84] This leaves the last phrase in the Coptic of 17.8 ("I am the Logos") with no Ethiopic counterpart. This suggests that it is either a gloss on "voice," or the beginning of the biographical sequence in *Ep. apost.* 18, all of which the Ethiopic has in indirect discourse. The latter is virtually certain since the phrase "I am the Logos" begins a similar speech in 39.12 (XXX 4, 83/1): "I am the Logos; I became flesh, labouring and teaching. . . ."

"Now," the interim between the resurrection and the parousia of the Father, is the turning point, the moment of the Lord's imminent departure. How then are the disciples to proceed? How is the author's community to realize in its midst the continuing presence of the Lord?

Ep. apost. 18.1 – 6 (X 7, 60/6)

Ethiopic	Coptic
1 This is, when he was crucified, had died and risen again, as he said this, and the work that was thus accomplished in the flesh, that he	1 "I have become to him a thing, i.e. . . .
	completed according to the type;
2 was crucified, and his ascension— this is the fulfilling of the number.	2 I have come into being on the eight(h day) which is the day of the Lord.
3 "And the wonders and his image and everything perfect you will see in me with respect to redemption which takes place through me, 4 and while I go to the Father and into heaven.	3 But the whole completion of the completion you will see through the redemption that has happened to me, 4 and you will see me, how I shall go to heaven to my Father who is in heaven.
5 But look, a new commandment I give you, that you love one another and obey each other and (that) continual peace reign among you.	5 But look now, I give you a new commandment; love one another and" [Coptic missing one page]
6 Love your enemies, and what you do not want done to you, that do to no one else."	

The movement towards the new commandment is momentarily interrupted by an "I am" saying (18.1 – 4) which summarizes (a) the Lord's place of origin,[85] (b) the Lord's accomplishment and its manifestation (Coptic: "the whole completion of the completion"; cf. Ethiopic: "the work that was thus accomplished in the flesh"), and (c) the Lord's manifest return. (The Ethiopic in effect reduces the speech to a catalogue of christological events.) But such language as this still does not respond to the communal question at hand, and therefore the metaphysical reflections cease as the Lord addresses his disciples in the present of the author's community (18.5 – 6 [X 13, 60/9]). The affinity between this form of the love command and its form in numerous canonical and extracanonical writings is amply illustrated by

---

[85] Understanding κγριακη with Hornschuh (*Studien*, 35 – 37) to be shorthand for ἡ κυριακὴ ἀνάπαυσις (the eighth rest or heaven): cf. *LPGL*, *s.v.* κυριακός 4.d.x (786b), and *s.v.* ὀγδοάς 3, 4 (934b).

Schmidt.[86] Here there are essentially five commands collected as one, three referring to love of the brethren and two to love of enemies. (This is the first of fifteen references to the commandment[s] in the Epistula.) The key to understanding the present passage is its location: it follows the announcement of the Lord's departure. Indeed, a threefold pattern is found, which closely parallels John 14:11 – 15:

John 14	Ep. apost. 17–18
I am in the Father and the Father in me. (vs 11)	I am wholly in the Father and the Father in me. (17.4)
. . . (greater works than these will he do, because) I go to the Father. (12)	. . . (you will see me, how) I go to my [Eth. the] Father. (18.4)
If you love me, you will keep my commandments. (15)	I give you a new commandment. (18.5; cf. John 13:34)

In both writings the testamentary legacy of a new commandment is bestowed in connection with the ascent of the Lord to the Father. The moment of departure becomes the moment of law-giving.

Ep. apost. 19.1 – 4 (--, 61/4)

19.1 "And both preach and teach this to those who believe in me, and preach concerning the kingdom of my Father, and as my Father has given me power (MSS CN add: so I give it to you) that you may bring near the children of the heavenly father. 2 Preach, and they will believe. You (it is) whose duty is to lead his children into heaven." 3 And we said to him, "O Lord, it is possible for you to do what you have told us; but how will we be able to do it?" 4 And he said to us, "Truly I say to you, preach and teach, as I will be with you."

As the author's focus shifts from command to commission, so too for the first time in the *Epistula* the succession is extended, from the Lord to the disciples and thence to all who believe. For the *Epistula*, no one comes to the Lord except through the disciples (19.2); and this procession into heaven is seen as the highest goal. As the Lord told the disciples even before the dialogue's inception, "My <Father> has given me the power to take up you and those who believe in me" (12.4 [V 3, 56/5]). But here in chap. 19 the disciples object, in the third of the "How/Is it possible . . . ?" questions.[87] With all the authority the introduction commands, the Lord's Amen saying

---

[86] *Gespräche Jesu,* 62.
[87] With *Ep. apost.* 19.3 cf. *Ap. Jas.* 6.22–25: "Lord, how shall we be able to prophesy to those who request us to prophesy to them?"

provides a mandate to the author's community: "Preach and teach, *as I will be with you*" (19.4).

The crisis of the Lord's departure is resolved in the Fourth Gospel by the coming of the Spirit:

> . . . the Spirit of truth . . . dwells with you and will be in you. (John 14:17)
>
> He will teach you all things, and bring to your remembrance all that I have said to you. (John 14:26)

In the *Epistula* it turns on the presence of the risen Lord among the disciples, as *preacher* and *teacher*. It is a situation quite foreign to the Gospel of John, where, though the Father (8:28), the Son (6:59) and the Spirit (14:26) are said to *teach*, there is no mention of their *preaching*; indeed, there is no occurrence of either of the standard NT verbs for preaching, εὐαγγελίζεσθαι and κηρύσσειν.

In the *Epistula* the Lord is presented as the Teacher *par excellence*, a role to be exemplified for this author and community in the present of the revelation dialogue: the risen Lord (chap. 10) and the departing Lord (chap. 17) is the Teacher. The question becomes whether in this writing there is also a dominical precedent for *preaching*; that is, whether or not the Lord's preaching ministry is clearly presented as a precedent for the author's circle.

At the start of this chapter it was pointed out that the antidocetic thrust of the miracle collection (*Ep. apost.* 4–5) and of the post-resurrection appearance account (*Ep. apost.* 9–12) seems to be threatened by the Lord's association with the angels (*Ep. apost.* 13–15). The case of Gabriel, however, throws important light on the preaching ministry of the Lord both before and after the resurrection. The Lord is said to have taken the form of the angel Gabriel and thus to have "brought the message" to Mary (14.1 [VI 12, 57/10]). In the same chapter this idea becomes more explicit, as the angel's part in the annunciation is deliberately excluded (14.6–7 [VII 10, 58/3]): "I became flesh, for I alone was servant (ⲆⲓⲀⲔⲞⲚⲞⲤ, *lāʾk*) to myself with respect to Mary in an appearance of the form of an angel."[88]

---

[88] In other writers, too, the description of the Lord as "messenger," a concept which is already possible on the basis of the Greek διάκονος (cf. LSJ, *s.v.* διάκονος 1 [398a]), is made explicit. For example, Hippolytus writes (*C. Noet.* 12.1):

> Now while he found a home in these [prophets], the Word was giving utterance about himself. For he himself was already acting as his own herald (ἑαυτοῦ κῆρυξ) in revealing that the Word was going to appear among men.

(Butterworth, *Hippolytus: Contra Noetum*, 70–71.) With the first phrase cf. *Ep. apost.* 19.19: "But if all the words that were spoken by the prophets are fulfilled in me—for I was in them. . . ." Cf. *Pistis Sophia* 1.62, where Mary, reflecting upon the annunciation, states: "That is the time when thou didst do service (ⲆⲓⲀⲔⲞⲚⲓ) to thyself" (Carl Schmidt, ed., Violet MacDermot, trans., *Pistis Sophia* [NHS 9; Leiden: Brill, 1978] 125).

The Gabriel motif persists in *Ep. apost.* 15; indeed, chaps. 13 – 15 may be styled a "Gabriel cycle" within the writing. Whether or not the prophecy about the disciple's imprisonment and rescue is directly borrowed from Acts 12, the appearance of the Lord, or rather, "of my δύναμις in the <form> of the angel Gabriel" (15.5), is the goal of the mission. For the disciple's release for the *agape* celebration prefigures the time when "he comes out from there and preaches what I have delivered to you" (15.7).

Finally, in *Ep. apost.* 27.1 the Lord reports on his mission to the dead:[89] "I have descended to <the place of> Lazarus, and have preached <to the righteous and> to the prophets." A dominical precedent for preaching is thus established for the *Epistula*. The Lord is to be considered less as χριστὸς ἄγγελος than as χριστὸς κῆρυξ or χριστὸς εὐαγγελιστής. And this adds weight to the view of *Ep. apost.* 19.1 – 3 offered above, that the Lord's presence with the disciples is promised in their preaching and teaching. The crisis prompted by the Lord's departure, and the hope of his return, are bound together in the mission charge, the fulfillment of which guarantees the Lord's abiding company.[90] The connection is made again, with greater clarity, in *Ep. apost.* 29 and 30, where the disciples' question is answered with an immediate and repeated charge:

> O Lord, in what way will one be able to believe <that you> will go and leave us, as you <said> to us, "A day will come <and an hour> when I shall go up to my Father?" (*Ep. apost.* 29.8 [XXV 8, 71/9])
>
> Go you and preach to the twelve tribes and preach also to the Gentiles. . . . <Go> and preach the mercy <of my> Father; and what he has done through me <will I my>self do through you in that *I am in* (or: *with*) *you*. (*Ep. apost.* 30.1, 3 [XXV 12, 72/1])

That this connection is the theological goal and communal mandate of *Ep. apost.* 16 – 19 receives confirmation in the appearance of two further "I am" sayings, which consolidate the foundation upon which the next great block of dialogue (chaps. 20 – 33) is to be built. The first is a restatement of the Lord's unity with the Father (19.10 [XI 4, 62/7]): "I am fully the <right hand> of the <Father>." The second saying extends the "I am" to "you are," as the disciples are told (19.15 [XI 15, 63/2]): "<As I> am in him, so <will you be> in me." With this declaration the center of gravity has now moved to the disciples, and to an exploration of their exemplary salvation.

---

[89] Numerous parallels from early Christian writers are cited in Schmidt, *Gespräche Jesu*, 453 – 576; to these add Hippolytus's designation of the Christ as "evangelist of the dead" (*frg. in Ps 90*; ET in ANF 5. 239).

[90] Cf. 2 Tim 4:1 – 2, where the expected, if distant, ἐπιφάνεια (appearing) becomes a stated motive for preaching.

Summary

1) The analysis above suggests that *Ep. apost.* 15.9 – 19.4 is the product more of compositional skill than of theological invention. Almost nothing in these chapters is novel, either in content or in form. But the arrangement of the materials is grounded in the author's insight that the parousia can be the starting point for a chain of ideas, each of which (in the argument of the *Epistula*) derives from its predecessor.

2) The question of the parousia is addressed directly by means of a traditional piece (*Ep. apost.* 16.3 – 5) which is edited to specific ends: an emphasis on the Lord's return to the earth; the exclusion of the angelic host; and the exalted status of the community's "slain" (15.9).

3) But the parousia is also the Father's, a statement made tolerable by a Johannine statement of indwelling. Under the pressure of the notion of the double presence of the Lord, the traditional saying is qualified with a list of attributes within the divine Father/Son community.

4) The assurance of the Lord's presence on earth as in heaven is said to be valid "until now" (i.e., until his departure). Therefore the Lord makes provision also for a continuing communal life, under a new commandment.

5) This commandment is not only to be lived, it is also to be preached and taught, for this is the way the disciples are to fulfill their duty to the children of God. In both of these responsibilities the Lord has set the abiding example.

6) The dominical mission, now in the disciples' hands, is the guarantee of the Lord's continuing presence with the disciples. Thus, it is at the fullest sense of parousia that the author of the *Epistula* arrives.

5

Epistula Apostolorum 41 – 42:
A Commission to Baptize

The *Epistula* declares its audience to be the universal church (2.2: "to the churches of the East and West, towards North and South"). It appears to quote a baptismal creed, the fourth article of which is "the holy Church" (5.22). But the writing disappoints the reader in search of clues about the organization within the community from which it springs.

It is possible, of course, that in chap. 13 the reader is given a glimpse of Christian and earthly, as well as of angelic and heavenly, worship: ". . . I adorned the archangels with a wondrous voice that they might go up to the altar of the Father and serve and complete the service until I should go to him." Similarly, there seem to be echoes in chap. 21 of a possible liturgical source common to the *Epistula* and to the *Liturgy of St. Mark*.[1] In addition,

---

[1] See Schmidt, *Gespräche Jesu*, 74; Hornschuh, *Studien*, 104. In *Ep. apost.* 21.9 the Lord says: "I am the hope of the hopeless, the helper of those who have no helper, the treasure of those in need, the physician of the sick, the resurrection of the dead." The intercessory prayer of the *Liturgy of St. Mark* includes the following: ". . . for you our God are the one who sets free those who are bound, who restores the broken, *the hope of the hopeless, the helper of those who have no help, the resurrection of the fallen* (ἡ ἀνάστασις τῶν πεπτωκότων), the harbor of the storm-tossed, the advocate of the oppressed" (Greek text in F. E. Brightman, ed., *Liturgies Eastern and Western* [Oxford: Clarendon, 1896] 127; cf. also the *Liturgy of the Coptic Jacobites* [Brightman, ibid., 166], where, however, the phrase "the resurrection of the fallen" is lacking). Duensing (*NTApoc* 1. 206 n. 2) cites the *Acts of Paul and Thecla* 37: "To the storm-tossed [God's Son] is a refuge, to the oppressed relief, to the despairing shelter" (ET in *NTApoc* 2. 363). The combination of "hope," "helper," and "resurrection" seems, therefore, to be peculiar to the *Epistula* and the *Liturgy of St. Mark*, and presumably to their source. Several phrases quoted from the *Liturgy* are apparently inspired by OT verses, e.g., Ps 142(143):10; Ps 145:7 – 8; and Jdt 9:11; but these verses are not reflected in *Ep. apost.* 21.

two references to baptism (27.2; 42.3) and mention of the disciples' *agape* or eucharist (15.7) suggest that both incorporation and communal celebration were recognizably sacramental. The apostles are told that Paul will set out from the land of Cilicia "to tear asunder the Church which you must create" (33.2). What, then, may be learned of the ministry of the leaders of this church?

Nowhere in the *Epistula* is there any indication of a hierarchy among the community's members.[2] The priority of the apostles is one of time only. As the Lord's disciples they are the first messengers of his revelation, but what is promised to them is promised to all who believe. Among the disciples complete mutuality is prescribed ("Love one another and obey each other . . . ," 18.5 – 6), presumably the ideal of the author's circle; and this is consistent with the writing as a whole. Nevertheless, in chaps. 41 – 42 there are indications of a rudimentary division of labor within the community. This is less the establishment of an officer class than an apparent necessity brought about by missionary effort. Here, and perhaps here alone in the writing, a distinction in authority emerges, corresponding to three phases of incorporation into the community: between those who preach and those who hear, between the baptizers and those who are baptized, and between the teachers and those who are taught.

This threefold distinction is not stated as a simple forecast of what is to be, although given the dialogue's post-resurrection setting the author might have been satisfied with merely putting a prediction into the mouth of the risen Lord: "you will preach, baptize, and teach." Instead the distinction is achieved as the result of discussion of the command, "Go and preach," with which *Ep. apost.* 41 begins, and it is sustained only after the resolution of a challenge to the words of Jesus familiar from Matt 23:8 – 10. The latter saying, or group of sayings, is by no means the only traditional material reflected in these chapters, however, and the task once again is to discern how the author's compositional method and message have reshaped the traditions at hand.

Ep. apost. 41 is connected with what precedes by a familiar expression of what I have termed "dialogical rhetoric," in *Ep. apost.* 40.5a: "But when he had said this to us, we said to him, 'O Lord, in all things you have taught us . . . and pitied us and saved us. . . .' " To this acknowledgement of the Lord's saving revelation is added an important thematic summary of the dialogue which follows (40.5b [XXXI 5, 83/7]): ". . . that we may preach to those who are worthy to be saved, and that we may earn a reward with you."

The command to preach, which both inaugurates and dominates the dialogue in *Ep. apost.* 41 – 42, is met eight times in the *Epistula*. Three times it is connected with the command to teach (19.1, 2; 46.1); and three times with

---

[2] Schmidt (*Gespräche Jesu*, 376) notes: "There is no hierarchy in the Catholic sense."

the imperative, "Go" (30.1, 3; 41.1). Preaching is to be the occupation of the released prisoner in *Ep. apost.* 15.7. Paul's mission is to preach and teach (*Ep. apost.* 31.5). The Lord himself is pictured as both preacher and teacher, and it is in imitation of the Lord that the disciples are to preach. Indeed, the *Epistula* claims that it is the very preaching ministry of the disciples (and hence presumably of the author's community) that generates the continued parousia, or presence, of the risen Lord. Thus, in these chapters an issue is explored that is thematically central to the writing and of practical as well as theoretical significance within the community.

As in previous sections, so in *Ep. apost.* 41–42 exegesis is dogged by issues of text and translation; a glance at the two recensions in the following pages shows something of the problem. On the other hand, the reader can be more than usually confident about the precise extent of the section. In *Ep. apost.* 43 there begins an exposition of a form of the parable of the wise and foolish virgins. There is also an *inclusio* in the term "reward," which appears in *Ep. apost.* 40.5 and again in 42.7.[3]

Ep. apost. 41.1–2:
The Command to Preach

Ethiopic	Coptic
1 And he said to us, "Go and preach and be good ministers and servants."	1 <But> he answered and said to us, "Go, and preach; thus you will become workers . . . and servants."
2 And we said to him, "O Lord, you are our father."	2 But we said to him, "You it is who will preach through us."

Here for the first time in the *Epistula* the more concrete particulars of title and office are added to the command to preach. But here too—and not for the last time in these chapters—the text's obscurity, enhanced by a sizeable lacuna in the Coptic manuscript, for a moment denies us the key to the connection between the disciples' statement in 40.5b and the Lord's command.

Duensing's translation of *Ep. apost.* 40.1, quoted above, is based on the following text (XXXI 8, 83/9):

Copt.: ⲃⲱⲕ ⲧⲉⲧⲛ̄ⲧⲁϣ[ⲉⲁⲉⲓϣ ⲁⲟⲩ] ⲧⲉⲧⲛⲁⲥ̄ⲱⲡⲉ ⲛ̄ⲉⲣⲅⲁⲧⲏⲥ
        [. . . ⲁ]ⲟⲩ ⲛ̄ⲁⲓⲁⲕⲟⲛⲟⲥ
Eth.: *ḥoru wa-sebeku wa-kunu xĕrāna lāʾkāna wa-ʾagberta*

---

[3] The word occurs nowhere else in the *Epistula*. The Ethiopic of *Ep. apost.* 38.4 (81/4) includes the phrase, "great is their reward"; but this is only one of several additions in the Ethiopic of chap. 38 inspired by the Matthean beatitudes.

In his attempt to fill the lacuna in the Coptic text, Schmidt supplies [ⲁⲟⲩ ⲛⲉⲓⲱⲧ ⲁ], and translates the whole command: "Go and preach, <thus> you will be workers <and fathers> and servants."[4] Schmidt notes that [ⲁⲟⲩ ⲛ̄ⲥⲁⲍ ⲁ], "und Meister" ("and masters"), would also be a suitable restoration, but later quotes the passage in full, without editorial marks, according to the first restoration.[5] Schmidt is followed by James: "Go and preach, and ye shall be labourers, and fathers, and ministers."[6]

As for the Ethiopic, Guerrier, its first editor, translates the text as follows: "Go and preach, be good ministers and good servants."[7] Similarly Isaak Wajnberg, Schmidt's colleague, gives the translation: "Go and preach and be good messengers and laborers!"[8] However, persuaded that Schmidt's restoration of the Coptic lacuna is correct, Wajnberg points to the fact that in two of the Ethiopic MSS[9] there is a superfluous conjunction, *wa-* (and), between the adjective "good" and the first noun (translated "ministers" above). This *wa-* Wajnberg takes to be a vestige of another noun, *ʾabawa* (fathers). He therefore concludes that the Ethiopic must itself be reconstructed, as follows:

ḥoru wa-sebeku wa-kunu xērāna ʾabawa wa-lāʾkāna wa-ʾagberta
Go and preach, and be good apostles, fathers, and servants.[10]

By Schmidt's and Wajnberg's admission the persuasive force of the Coptic reconstruction, "and fathers," lies in the anticipation thereby secured both of the Lord's next speech (in 41.3) and of the discussion (in 41.5–42.7) of the disciples' threefold status as fathers, servants, and teachers. But there are problems with using the context in this way to fill the lacuna. To be sure, had the nouns surrounding the lacuna been "servants" and "teachers," this understanding of the text would have had much to commend it. As it is, the following objections stand in its path, and call for a new proposal.

1) In the Coptic text the Lord's next speech (41.3) is not about three offices (or titles) but about two.
2) In these chapters, wherever "fathers" are mentioned they are the *first* in a pair or triad of terms.
3) The reconstruction virtually ignores the majority Ethiopic reading, a

---

[4] Schmidt, *Gespräche Jesu*, 19* (text), 131 (translation).
[5] Ibid., 131 n. 9; 257.
[6] James, *Apocryphal New Testament*, 500.
[7] Guerrier, "Le testament," 83.
[8] Wajnberg, in Schmidt, *Gespräche Jesu*, 130.
[9] MSS AS; the extra "and" is read also in MS CNT.
[10] Wajnberg, in Schmidt, *Gespräche Jesu*, 130 n. 4.

reading which offers plain sense in itself and permits a satisfactory and parallel restoration of the Coptic.

4) The size of the Coptic lacuna will not accommodate Schmidt's proposal, which requires nine characters.[11]

Apart from the intrusive conjunction *wa-* (and) in some witnesses, and some variation in the manuscripts as to the form of the second noun, the Ethiopic text is stable and sensible. Indeed, the second noun, translated "servants" above, is a good starting point for a fresh review of the text and its translation. Guerrier's text, as quoted, has the noun *'agberta*, the accusative form of *'agbert* which is the plural of *gabr* (servant). The new manuscript evidence favors the collective noun *gabbār* (workers, laborers), as read by MSS BKNO.[12] In the Ethiopic NT this collective noun twice stands for the Greek plural, ἐργάται (Matt 9:37–38; Luke 10:2), and therefore corresponds in *Ep. apost.* 41.1 to the Coptic ⲚⲈⲢⲄⲀⲦⲎⲤ already quoted. A similar correspondence can be claimed for the first Ethiopic noun, *lā'kān*, the plural of *lā'k*, which in the Ethiopic NT regularly translates Greek διάκονος,[13] and which here exactly matches Coptic ⲚⲆⲓⲀⲔⲞⲚⲞⲤ .

With these equivalences established, it is next necessary to acknowledge and, if possible, to explain the reversal of these two nouns in the Ethiopic (διάκονοι and ἐργάται) over against the Coptic (ἐργάται and διάκονοι). In the first place, transposition is a familiar feature of scribal accident and design. Even in the texts of the OT and NT, the writings perhaps least liable to editorial tampering,[14] transposition of words or phrases is especially common in the oriental versions, where nuance and idiom can result in a new word order in the vernacular.[15] A number of examples of Coptic/Ethiopic disagreement in word order can be collected in the *Epistula*,[16] and there is

[11] Examination of a microfilm of the Coptic text shows that there is space for six or seven characters. As is customary in ancient manuscripts, the Coptic text is written in continuous script. For this reason no account has been taken of the editorial spaces between words.

[12] Other variants are as follows: MSS AT read *gabarta* (plural of *gabāri* [maker, craftsman]); MS C has *gabr* (the singular noun, but presumably understood as a collective); and MS R has the singular form of the noun read in MSS AT. It will be noted that all readings derive from the same verbal root; see Dillmann, *Lexicon, s.v. gabra* (1159), for the entire word group.

[13] See Dillmann, *Lexicon, s.v. la'aka* (47).

[14] Of the many *cruces interpretum* in *1 Enoch*, e.g., Black (*Book of Enoch*, vii) states that "these are more numerous in Enoch than in the more protected texts of canonical scripture." But cf. the assertion of Ephraim Isaac (*A New Text-Critical Introduction to Maṣḥafa Berhān* [Leiden: Brill, 1973] 27 n. 6) that "the Ethiopian church has no official canon because it never distinguished between heretical or non-heretical, authentic or non-authentic, scriptures. This is why it has preserved so many early apocryphal and pseudepigraphic works suppressed and lost elsewhere."

[15] Examples from the Ethiopic version of the NT and of *Hermas* are given in George H. Schodde, *Hêrmâ Nabî: The Ethiopic Version of Pastor Hermae Examined* (Leipzig: Brockhaus, 1876) 14–15.

[16] E.g., (1) the order of the archangels in *Ep. apost.* 13.5; (2) 13.8: "the wisdom of the like-

usually no need to ascribe the difference to any ulterior redactional motive. Secondly, in this particular verse there is the issue of the status of the ἐργάτης in the communities of transmission: few scribes would hesitate to place a διάκονος before an ἐργάτης. In light of these considerations the verbal agreement between the Coptic and Ethiopic nouns may safely be accepted.

The modern translator is left, then, with the Coptic lacuna on the one hand, and the Ethiopic adjective, *xērāna*, on the other. This adjective, the plural of *xēr*, is blandly but accurately rendered "good" in Duensing's translation quoted above. It regularly translates many Greek adjectives—Dillmann lists ten in the NT alone.[17] But since it is found only twice elsewhere in the *Epistula*, there is little internal evidence for its Coptic equivalent here. However, one of these two occurrences of the word is so near to *Ep. apost.* 41.1 in spirit and letter that it may be of value. In *Ep. apost.* 23.1 (XVII 2), one of the speeches of dialogical rhetoric in the mouth of the disciples, the following is found:

> O Lord, there is a necessity upon us to inquire through you, for you command us to preach, that we ourselves may learn with certainty through you and be *profitable preachers. . . .*

For "profitable preachers" (ⲛ̅ⲣⲉϥⲧⲁϣⲉⲗⲉⲓϣ ⲉⲩⲣ̅ϣⲉⲩ) the Ethiopic text (67/2) has *xērāna mazēnewāna* (*good* preachers). Coptic ⲣ̅ ϣⲉⲩ (to be useful, prosperous, virtuous),[18] like Ethiopic *xēr*, has many regular Greek equivalents. The meanings of the two words coincide in verbal or adjectival forms of ἀγαθός, χρηστός, καλός. Therefore both versions in *Ep. apost.* 23.1 yield the sense "profitable preachers," even though the original Greek cannot confidently be conjectured.[19]

A new restoration of the Coptic lacuna may now be attempted: ⲁⲟⲩ ⲧⲉⲧⲛⲁⲍⲱⲡⲉ ⲛ̅ⲉⲣⲅⲁⲧⲏⲥ [ⲉⲩⲣ̅ϣⲉⲩ ⲁ]ⲟⲩ ⲛ̅ⲇⲓⲁⲕⲟⲛⲟⲥ "and you will be profitable ἐργάται and διάκονοι." This is a reading which makes good sense and approximates the Ethiopic closely, except for the transposition of the nouns. It also comfortably fits the space available.

On the basis of this reconstruction a further step may be taken. When the

---

ness'' (Coptic) = "the likeness of his wisdom" (Ethiopic); (3) 15.7: "the remembrance . . . and the Agape" (Copt.) = "my Agape and my remembrance" (Eth.); (4) 30.1: "from <South to> North" (Copt.) = "North and South" (Eth.).

[17] Dillmann, *Lexicon, s.v. xēra* (610).

[18] Crum, *s.v.* ⲣ̅ ϣⲁ ⲩ (599b).

[19] It is worth mentioning that in Attic Greek the word ἐργάτης can serve as an adjective, "hard-working, strenuous" (LSJ, *s.v.* ἐργάτης [682b]). Conceivably, therefore, the Coptic (and underlying Greek) ἐργάται in *Ep. apost.* 41.1 could itself be reflected in the Ethiopic adjective *xērān* (good, useful, profitable, efficient).

end of chap. 40 and the beginning of chap. 41 are brought together, the following sequence (quoting direct speech only) is observed:

> ... that we may *preach* to those who are worthy to be saved, and that we may earn a *reward* with you. (40.5)
> Go and *preach*, and you will be [Eth.: Be] good ἐργάται and διάκονοι. (41.1)

In the context of a mission charge, the mention of "reward" together with the epithet ἐργάτης suggests at least the possibility that behind this exchange lies the proverbial saying attached to the commissioning of the disciples in Q (Matt 10:10; Luke 10:7): "The laborer is worthy of his reward."[20]

The earthy comparison of mission to labor entered the sayings tradition at an early stage, as another saying, in Q (Matt 9:37–38; Luke 10:2) and in *Gos. Thom.* 73: 46.6–9, indicates: "The harvest is plentiful, but the laborers (ἐργάται) are few; pray therefore the Lord of the harvest to send out laborers (ἐργάται) into his harvest." The term ἐργάτης, its cognate verb forms, and other terminology associated with manual work, enjoyed wide currency, especially in connection with the maintenance of Christian missionaries. In 1 Cor 3:8 Paul speaks of the right of each to "receive his wages according to his labor." Later in the same letter (9:3–14) the figure is again appealed to.[21] With a more domestic orientation, but still retaining the strength of the original analogy, 1 Tim 5:17–18 bids the community:

> Let the elders who rule well be considered worthy of double honor, especially those who labor in preaching and teaching; for the scripture says, "You shall not muzzle an ox when it is treading out the grain," and, "The laborer deserves his wages."[22]

[20] Matthew has τροφή for Q's μισθός, the form found also in *Dial. Sav.* 139.9–10.

[21] See Dieter Georgi, *The Opponents of Paul in Second Corinthians* (Philadelphia: Fortress, 1986) 40, for the use of the term ἐργάτης in Paul (of his opponents) and elsewhere in the NT. Georgi notes that "the opponents saw themselves as apostles of Christ, as ἐργάται, as διάκονοι" (p. 64 n. 33). Cf. also *Ep. apost.* 39.12: "I became flesh, *labouring* and *teaching* . . ."; and John 4:35–38; 5:17.

[22] Cf. also 2 Tim 2:15: "Do your best to present yourself to God as one approved, a workman who has no need to be ashamed, rightly handling the word of truth." In the *Didache* the right of the "laborer" is applied, by extension, to the prophet and the teacher (*Did.* 13.1–2; cf. *1 Clem.* 34.1). In *Thom. Cont.* 138.21–34 Thomas asks the Lord for help in speaking and hearing about the hidden things (24–25) and in performing the truth (26–27). The Savior answers:

> If the things that are visible to you are obscure to you, how can you hear about the things that are not visible? If the deeds of the truth that are visible in the world are difficult for you to perform, how indeed, then, shall you perform those . . . which are not visible? And how shall you be called "Laborers" (ⲉⲣⲅⲁⲧⲏⲥ)? In this respect you are apprentices, and have not yet received the height of perfection.

See John Douglas Turner, *The Book of Thomas the Contender* [SBLDS 23; Missoula, MT: Scholars Press, 1975] 10–11; 132–33. Cf. *Thom. Cont.* 144.38–39: "those who are [ignorant] will *labor* at preaching [instead of you]."

Given the breadth of possible application of the ἐργάτης figure, it is unlikely that the term ever became a technical one for a specific office or function. The "laborer" remained within the realm of figurative allegiance to the "Lord of the harvest," rather, perhaps, than to a specific congregation or community; hence the enduring vigor of the model and the frequent use of the dominical proverb. The early connection with preaching was possibly never lost. But as far as *Ep. apost.* 41 is concerned, it is not yet possible to move from the general association of the term with preaching to a precise connection between the ἐργάτης and the διάκονος. At this point it is enough to point out that neither term has any perceptible technical connotation.[23]

The challenge presented to the translator by *Ep. apost.* 41.1 is renewed in the complete disagreement between the versions in 41.2. The Ethiopic reading, "O Lord, you are our Father," answers well to the sense (deriving from Schmidt's reconstruction) of what precedes, and on formal grounds is recommended by the presence of the vocative address, "O Lord." But although the distinction between the Father and the Son is at times blurred in the *Epistula*, the two are never completely identified, and the author is usually content with statements of mutual indwelling[24] qualified according to specific attributes. The Coptic, "You it is who will preach through us," serves both the immediate and the wider contexts well, recalling, for instance, the injunction "Preach and teach, as I will be with you" (*Ep. apost.* 19.4) and the repeated "through me" of the apostolic functions to be outlined in 41.6 – 42.4.[25] As will soon be seen, there is no necessity to bind *Ep. apost.* 41.1 – 2 with the *threefold* scheme of 41.5.

Ep. apost. 41.3 – 6:
The Lord's Saying Questioned

Ethiopic	Coptic
3 And he said to us, "Are all fathers and all servants, all teachers?"	3 Then he answered us saying, "Do not be all fathers nor all masters."

---

[23] However, that the ἐργάτης and διάκονος were later a recognizable pair is suggested by their reappearance in the *Statutes of the Apostles* 22. In giving the following summary of a deacon's duties this *Statute's* lexical similarity to *Ep. apost.* 41.1 is remarkable: "Andrew said: Let the deacons be doers of good works" (Copt.: ⲡⲉⲭⲁϥ ⲛ̄ϭⲓ ⲁⲛⲇⲣⲉⲁⲥ ϫⲉ ⲛ̄ⲇⲓⲁⲕⲟⲛⲟⲥ ⲙⲁⲣⲟⲩϣⲱⲡⲉ ⲛ̄ⲉⲣⲅⲁⲧⲏⲥ ⲉⲍⲉⲛⲍⲃⲏⲩⲉ ⲉ ⲛⲁⲛⲟⲩⲟⲩ; Eth.: *yebē ꞌEndreyās diyāqonāt yekunu gabāreyāna megbāra sannāy*). Coptic text in Paul de Lagarde, *Aegyptiaca* (1883; reprinted Osnabrück: Zeller, 1972) 247; Ethiopic text and ET of both versions in Horner, *Statutes*, 304, 8, 136.

[24] See *Ep. apost.* 17.8: "I am wholly in my Father and my Father is in me."

[25] See also *Ep. apost.* 28.3 (Coptic): "O Lord, . . . will you yourself now preach these things?"

4 And we said to him, "O Lord,
did you not say, 'Do not call
(anyone) on earth father and master,
for one is your father and teacher,
he who is in heaven'?

5 Now you say to us that[26] we should
like you[27] become fathers to many
children and also teachers and
servants."

6 And he answered and said to us,
"You have rightly said.
Truly I say to you, all who have
listened to you and have believed
in me will receive the
light of the seal that is in my hand,
and through me
you will become fathers[28]
and teachers."

4 We said to him, "O Lord,
it is you who said, 'Do not call
(anyone) father upon earth,
for one is your father who is in
heaven and your master.'

5 Why do you now say to us, 'You
will be fathers of many
children and servants and
masters'?"

6 But he answered and said to us,
"As you have said.
For truly I say to you, whoever will
hear you and believe
in me, he <will receive from> you the
the light of the seal through <me>
and baptism through me;
you will <become> fathers and servants
and also masters."

The author's introductory ⲧⲟⲧⲉ (then) in 41.3 (XXXI 11, 83/10) marks a new moment in the dialogue. In view of the Coptic reading and forthcoming discussion there is no reason to consider the Ethiopic "and all servants" as other than an addition. On the other hand, Schmidt is probably right to accept the question form, as in the Ethiopic: "Are you not ... ?"; his suggestion that the Coptic translator read the indicative ἐστέ for its identical imperative counterpart (ἔστε) possibly explains the difference.[29] The

[26] The Ethiopic here is in indirect discourse after the word *kama* (that), possible because an original Greek ὅτι was not understood as ὅτι *recitativum*.

[27] The translation "like you" results from the misplacing, in family 2 MSS only, of the pronoun "you." This pronoun belongs, as in family 1 MSS, with the verb ("*you* say"); without the pronoun, the word "like" (*kama*) simply means "that."

[28] The Ethiopic manuscript tradition lacks "and servants." In its place, the strongest family 1 witnesses have the plural adjective *xērāna* (without the conjunction, "and"), which has already been met in 41.1 ("*good* ministers . . ."). These MSS thus read: "You will become fathers and *good* teachers" (or possibly "fathers and teachers *of good things*"). The omission of "and servants" is probably deliberate, because in *Ep. apost.* 42.3, where the Coptic has "and you will be called servants," the Ethiopic omits the entire phrase. The reason for the omission in 41.6 may be the translator's wish to bring the *Epistula* in line with the *Constitutions of the Apostles*, a church order authoritative in the Ethiopian church; in *Const. apost.* 3.11.1 and 8.46.11 deacons are forbidden to baptize (references in *LPGL*, *s.v.* διάκονος II B.7.o.vii [353a]).

A singular attempt to restore "servants" to the Ethiopic of *Ep. apost.* 42 is found in MS N. At the end of 42.7, after the words "a share of the kingdom," this manuscript continues: *wa-lāʾka baʾenta ʾaššanaykemu la-kʷellu ba-temhert* ". . . and [you will be called] servants, since you have completed [or: perfected, beautified] all things through your teaching."

[29] Schmidt, *Gespräche Jesu*, 131. The Greek negative particle μή is therefore understood (a) as introducing a question whose implied answer is no (in Eth.) and (b) as negating the imperative (in Copt.). For the indicative/imperative inconsistency see also *Ep. apost.* 21.7; 45.2.

question is a completely artificial construction, designed to bring the titles "father" and "teacher" into the discussion. The stage is set for the disciples' counterquestion in 41.4–5, which erects the obstacle to be cleared before the Lord can give the unchallenged directions in chap. 42.

By now the reader is prepared for this questioning of the Lord's words. But this is the first time in the *Epistula* that the quoted saying is known also from a canonical source, here Matt 23:8–10. Whether the Coptic or the Ethiopic is nearer to the originally quoted form, the saying appears to conflate the prohibitions in Matt 23:8 and 9. However, unless the heaven/earth antithesis is specifically Matthean redaction in Matt 23:8–10,[30] it is by no means certain that the author of the *Epistula* is quoting (or paraphrasing) the text of Matthew's gospel. Nor is this question the principal one, for the essential point is the author's affirmation of the apostles' (and hence the community's) right to challenge a saying of the earthly Jesus ("it is you who *said* . . .") in light of the revelation of the risen Lord ("Why do you *now say* to us . . . ?").[31]

Even with the threefold pattern of ministry (fathers, servants, teachers) at last in view, it remains for the Lord to affirm the new formulation. This is done in two stages, comprising the two parts of *Ep. apost.* 41.6. The first is a brief statement of approval which, though part of the traditional rhetoric of the dialogue, is here well placed: "You have rightly said."[32] The second is an Amen saying, the special authority of which needs no elaboration. The saying stresses the complementary roles of the Lord and the disciples. The Lord indeed acts through the disciples (cf. the Coptic of 41.2), but the disciples' agency is decisive: "Whoever will hear *you*. . . ." There is nothing in the content of the verse to suggest a traditional antecedent, except for the term "light of the seal," on which the Coptic phrase "and baptism" is probably a gloss.[33] The whole is in the author's own words, in line with the recurring concern with belief through the disciples:

---

[30] So, e.g., Gundry, *Matthew*, 458.

[31] The exegetical difficulty persists, that the words the Lord is said to have spoken "now," in the present of the revelation (41.5: "You will be fathers of many children . . ."), are a quotation neither of what has gone before nor of what follows. Possibly it is for this reason that the Ethiopic translator has put *Ep. apost.* 41.5 into indirect speech. But previous examples of this kind of present quotation by the disciples ("he who sent me will come," 17.3; "A day will come <and an hour> . . . ," 29.8) are also unanticipated, as is a further example in 49.4.

[32] This is the Ethiopic reading, which probably presupposes the Greek καλῶς ἐλαλήσατε. The Coptic translator apparently read καθὼς ἐλαλήσατε, hence "As you have said." Cf. the same variant in Esth 6:10 LXX.

[33] G. W. H. Lampe (*The Seal of the Spirit* [2d ed.; London: S.P.C.K, 1967] 115) will say only that here "the seal may be synonymous with Baptism," i.e., it need not stand for an additional rite. Cf. Irenaeus *Epideixis* 3: "This baptism is the seal of eternal life"; *Testim. Truth* 69.7–14.

My Father has delighted in you and in those who will believe in me *through you*. (*Ep. apost.* 19.5 [--, 62/1])

... (that) those who will be instructed *by us* may believe in you. (23.2 [XVII 7, 67/3])

... <you> ... I have redeemed ... and all who *through you* will believe <in> me. (28.1 [XXII 10, 70/3])

The new and special emphasis of this saying, however, becomes clear only in light of *Ep. apost.* 42.2 – 4, to be considered below.

Ep. apost. 42.1 – 4:
The Disciples as Fathers, Servants, and Teachers

The solidarity of the disciples is such that all, as the Lord has announced in *Ep. apost.* 41.6, will become fathers, servants, and teachers. This, of course, is in addition to the relationship which obtains among the disciples themselves and with their Lord:

I am well pleased to be with you, that you may become joint heirs with me of the kingdom of heaven.... (*Ep. apost.* 19.4 [--, 61/9])

You will be my brothers and companions. (19.5 [--, 61/10])

You are my brothers, companions in the kingdom of heaven. ... (32.4 [--, 74/8])

This equality of status needs no reinforcement. But there is an almost inevitable tension between the new titles of *Ep. apost.* 41 – 42 and the earlier talk of equality and fraternity. On the basis of a dominical saying the disciples have objected to their new description. Their objection has been overruled. A new concern arises, in the form of another "How?" question, the last in a series of such questions (42.1 [XXXII 10, 84/6]):

Ethiopic	Coptic
And we said to him, "O Lord, how is it possible for these three to be in one?"	But we said to him, "O Lord, how now (is it possible) that each one of us should become these three?"

It cannot be said that what follows directly answers the disciples' question. These things are so because the Lord has spoken. But as has been suggested by previous questions of this kind, a large measure of the questions' point is to reduce the disciples to a level of disbelief or misunderstanding from which only the Lord can lead them. A further difficulty is raised by this question, namely the conflict between the prohibition in *Ep. apost.* 41.4 ("Do not *call* [anyone] ...") and the references to *becoming* in 41.6 and 42.1. It is the former, *being called* fathers, teachers, and servants, that is taken up by the Lord's reply in 42.2–4. It is therefore a reasonable conjecture that the appellation at least has become for the author of the *Epistula* a communal reality.[34]

The heart of these chapters, appropriately given as the answer to the disciples' "How?" question, is the Lord's speech in which the nature of the three offices is set before the disciples. *Ep. apost.* 42.2–4 is best viewed not simply as a consecutive discourse, but as the threefold use of a literary pattern whose elements are as follows:

a) "You will be called" + a title;
b) the connective, "for";
c) the principal action in the ministry (revelation; reception; giving);
d) an adverbial statement of means or manner;
e) the gift given in the ministry.

The order of items (d) and (e) is not entirely consistent, but the pattern as a whole is sufficiently secure to permit the certain delimitation of the final office ("teachers") at the end of *Ep. apost.* 42.4; that is, the clauses which follow (beginning with "You have warned them" in 42.5) are related not to the "teachers" only, but to all. Filled out with the specifics of the Lord's speech, the compositional pattern appears as follows:

Ep. apost. 42.2	*Ep. apost.* 42.3	*Ep. apost.* 42.4
a) You will be called fathers,	a) You will be called servants,	a) You will be called masters,
b) for	b) for	b) for
c) you have revealed to them	c) they will receive	c) you have given them
d) with seemly hearts and in love	d) by my hand through you	e) the word
e) the things of the kingdom of heaven.	e) baptism of life and forgiveness of sins.	d) without grudging.

The first of these promises echoes the Lord's words in *Ep. apost.* 12.3 (IV 14, 56/4): "Rise up, and I will reveal to you what is above heaven and what is in heaven. . . ." This fulfillment is no surprise, for in the *Epistula* the ministry of the disciples is in every respect anticipated by that of the Lord. As the disciples reported in *Ep. apost.* 6.1 (--, 52/12): "These things our Lord . . . revealed to us, and likewise we to you." There seems, however, to be

---

[34] A further possibility, that "fathers" in *Ep. apost.* 41–42 is a designation, retrospective from the author's time, of the apostles as "the generation(s) of deceased Christians" (BAG, *s.v.* πατήρ, 2d [635b]; cf. 2 Pet 3:4; *1 Clem.* 23.3; *2 Clem.* 11.2) is unlikely given that the same argument cannot be made for "servants" and "teachers."

little that requires the epithet "father," unless it is the manner of revelation, "with seemly hearts and in love." Hornschuh suggests that for this author "through the preaching of the revelations the apostles found holy families," of which the disciples are considered the fathers.[35] Suspecting Essene influence here as elsewhere in the *Epistula*, he compares 1QH vii 20–21: "I sought support in Thy truth, and I. . . . And Thou hast made me a father unto sons of kindness and a nursing-father to men of wonder. . . ."[36] Clearly for the *Epistula* the activity designated "revelation" is understood as preaching. But at this point in the Lord's speech the specific sense in which this preaching is to be understood cannot be determined.

Leaving aside for the moment *Ep. apost.* 42.3, concerning "servants," we come to the third sentence, which speaks of the disciples as "masters," or better, "teachers," who deliver the word. Again it is not specified in what context the teaching has taken place. But by making reference to the teachers' manner, "without grudging" (XXXIII 6 ογϣⲛⲣ̄ⲫⲑⲟⲛⲉⲓ, 84/10 *za-ʾenbala ḥemām*), the author again alludes to a dominical precedent set earlier in the writing (24.5 [XVIII 3, 67/8]): "What you wish, say to me, and I will tell it to you *without grudging*" (ογϣⲛ̄ⲣ̄ⲫⲑⲟⲛⲉⲓ, *za-ʾenbala ḥemām*).

When we move back to *Ep. apost.* 42.3, and to the announcement, "You will be called servants," it becomes clear in light of the statements already examined that there are several differences to be collected and assessed.

1) The *subject* of the subordinate clause, item (c) in the pattern outlined above, is not the disciples but an unidentified "they" ("they will receive . . .").

2) The *object* of this clause has not one member (as in 42.2: "the things of the kingdom of heaven"; and in 42.4: "the word") but two: "baptism of life and the forgiveness of their sins."

3) Noteworthy, though probably of minor significance, is the fact that the *adverbial phrase*, item (d) in the pattern, expresses not manner (as in 42.2, 4) but agency: "by my hand through you."

4) In 42.3 (XXXIII 2, 84/8) the *tense* of the disciples' action is not past (as in 42.2 [XXXII 15, 84/8]: "you have revealed" = ⲁⲧⲉⲧⲛ̄ϭⲱⲗⲡ, *kašatkemu*; and in 42.4 [XXXIII 5, 84/9]: "you have given" = ⲁⲧⲉⲧⲛ̄ϯ, *ʾaʿlawkemu*) but future: "they will receive" = ⲥⲉⲛⲁⲭⲓ, *yenaššeʾu*.

This latter point, the discrepancy between the tense of the disciples' action as "servants" and as "fathers" and "teachers," recalls *Ep. apost.* 41.6. There, receipt of "the light of the seal" was singled out in anticipation of the threefold promise, "You will <become> fathers and servants and also

---

[35] Hornschuh, *Studien*, 72.

[36] Mansoor, *Thanksgiving Hymns*, 150–51. Cf. perhaps 1 John 2:13, 14, though the precise meaning of "fathers" in these verses is disputed.

masters.'' In 41.6, as here in 42.3, receipt of the gift of baptism was placed in the future: ''Whoever *will* hear . . . *will receive.*'' Baptism, which alone of the three functions of the disciples is yet to happen, is as it were the new *and as yet unfulfilled* charge. To put it another way, inasmuch as the disciples are to baptize, they *will be* the διάκονοι of the Lord. And for this new commission the two other functions, preaching and teaching, are the accomplished (and doubtless continuing) preparation within the author's community.

The objection can be raised, however, that it is because of the immediate post-resurrection setting of the dialogue that baptism is placed in the future. ''They *will* receive'' baptism, it might be argued, because for the *Epistula* these chapters amount to something of a Great Commission, in which the future ministry of the disciples is foretold. This is almost certainly the case with the threefold future common to the promise of the three titles (''you will be called,'' i.e., element [a] in 42.2, 3 and 4) which presumably affirms and legitimates such actual calling within the author's circle; for the community's ministers the author in effect asserts: *You are rightly called. . . .* For this reason the ministries of teaching and preaching might similarly have been cast in the future, given the universal scope of the mission (''from <sunrise> to sunset and from <South to> North,'' 30.1) and further, given the forecast of the preaching of Paul in *Ep. apost.* 31. But they are not set in the future, as the continuation of chap. 42 serves to emphasize: ''You *have warned* . . . you *were not* afraid'' (42.5 – 6).[37]

Therefore it is necessary to emphasize the difference in tense, and to undertake to explain it. As it happens, an explanation can be attempted in light of the verses which follow, since they will be found to supply the missing link: information about the people identified only as ''they'' in *Ep. apost.* 42.3.

Ep. apost. 42.5 – 8:
At the Threshold of Baptism

Ethiopic	Coptic
5 ''And (you) have warned them and they have turned back in the things for which you rebuked them.	5 ''And (you) have warned them; and when you warned them they turned back.
6 And you were not afraid of their riches and did not respect the face,	6 You were not afraid of their riches <and of> their face,

[37] The question persists why it is that the prospective ministry (baptism) is the second rather than the third of the three in 42.2 – 4. There are two possibilities. Either (1) the author retains a traditional (hierarchical?) order of the communty's offices; or (2) teaching is understood to be both pre- and post-baptismal, i.e., it will continue after the imminent completion of the second charge of the disciples.

but you kept the commandment of the Father and did it.	but you kept \<the commandment\> of my Father and performed them.
7 And you have a reward with with my heavenly Father; and they shall have forgiveness of sins and eternal life and a share of the kingdom.''	7 And you will have \<a\> great reward with my Father who is in heaven, and they shall have forgiveness of sins and eternal life, and will have a part in the kingdom of heaven.''
8 And we said to him, ''O Lord, if they had a ten-thousandfold mouth they would not be able to give thanks to you as it is fitting.''	8 But we said to him, ''O Lord, even if each one of us had ten thousand tongues to speak with, we would not be able to give thanks to you, for you promise us such things.''

In *Ep. apost.* 42.5 – 6 (XXXIII 6, 84/10) the author brings together a group of motifs which are more or less tightly connected elsewhere in the work: (a) the disciples' warning or reproof; (b) the absence of fear; (c) the absence of partiality; (d) the ignoring of others' riches; and (e) the keeping of the commandments. Five times elsewhere in the *Epistula* three or more of these ideas are present:

Only *keep my commandments*, and do what I tell you, . . . *without fear* . . . (and) *without respect of persons* serve in the way that is direct and strait and narrow. (*Ep. apost.* 24.6 [XVIII 5, 67/9])

Men will follow them [= the followers of ''vain teaching''] and will submit themselves to their *riches*, their depravity, their mania for drinking, and their *gifts of bribery*; and *respect of persons* will rule among them. (37.5 [--, 80/7])

But those who desire to see the face of God and who *do not regard the person* of *the sinful rich*, and who *do not fear* the men who lead them astray, but *reprove* them, they, the wounded, will be in the presence of the Father, as also those who *reprove* their neighbours will be saved. (38.1 [--, 80/9])

Preach and teach in uprightness (and) well, *hesitating before no one* and *fearing no one*, but especially (not) *the rich*, for *they do not do my commandment* but revel in their *riches*. (46.1 [XXXVIII 9, 88/2])

Whoever *regards the person* for \<their\> sake, \<he will be like\> the two, as the pro\<phet said\>, ''Woe to those *who regard the person* and \<justify the ungodly\> *for the sake of gifts*, whose \<God is\> their belly.'' (47.5 [XL 3, 89/2])

The fivefold occurrence of this group of ideas puts it beyond doubt that there is a communal reality in the author's mind. The question arises whether this is merely an ideal or perceived reality or an actual one; whether the connection of false teachers with bribery, for example, is part of the real experience of the author or simply a literary *topos*, designed to discredit the opponents of the author's community.

On the basis of the appearance of this material as commands (*Ep. apost.* 24 and 46), as predictions (37 and 38), and as communal casuistry (47), it would be possible to argue that the implied situation and therefore the prescribed ethic, though edifying enough in its own right, are but ideal constructs. And it is certainly correct to observe that in each case, including *Ep. apost.* 42.5 – 6, the modern reader would welcome more specificity in the charges and commands. Full weight, then, has to be given to the typical nature of the characterizations of the opponents.[38]

Nevertheless in *Ep. apost.* 42 the father-servant-teacher[39] disciples are said already to have revealed the things of the kingdom; to have delivered the word; to have warned (successfully: "they turned back" [42.5]); to have faced others' riches and status without fear; and to have done the commandments, that is, the five-clause communal command which first appeared in connection with the first charge to preach and teach (*Ep. apost.* 18.5 – 19.1). Unless these accomplishments too are but the fictions of the author, there is no reason to doubt that the individuals referred to as "they" and "them" in *Ep. apost.* 41 – 42 are throughout the same people: former followers of the "vain teaching" who have been won, by preaching, teaching, and censure, for the author's group, and who are one with the author's community in every respect *except baptism*, at the threshold of which they now stand.

It is for this reason that the reward of the disciples, the concern to which chaps. 41 – 42 were seen initially to respond, is quickly passed over: "And you will have <a> reward with my Father who is in heaven."[40] This is indeed a cursory response to the statement with which the section began: "... that we may earn a reward with you" (40.5; Ethiopic: "Will there be for us a reward with you?"). The effect is to highlight the three part reward of those who have turned back: forgiveness of sins and eternal life and a part in the kingdom (42.7).

These, of course, are the stated fruit of baptism, the first of which has already been specified in 42.3 as "baptism of life and the forgiveness of their sins." And for the granting of this reward there is a satisfactory dominical

---

[38] Cf., e.g., 2 Chr 19:7: "Now then, let the fear of the Lord be upon you; take heed what you do, for there is no perversion of justice with the Lord our God, or partiality, or taking bribes"; Jer 9:23: "Let not the rich man glory in his riches"; and among early Christian writers *Herm. Vis.* 1.1.8; 3.9.6; Polycarp *Phil.* 6.1; *Acts Pet. 12 Apost.* (NHC 6, 1) 11.26 – 12.14: "The rich men . . . who reveled in their wealth and pride—do not dine in [their] houses, . . . lest their partiality influence you."

[39] With these three offices in one cf. 1 Thess 5:12: "those who labor among you and are over you in the Lord and admonish you," a description not of three distinct roles but of "three functions of one role" (Wayne A. Meeks, *The First Urban Christians* [New Haven: Yale University Press, 1983] 134); so already J. B. Lightfoot, *Notes on Epistles of St. Paul* (1895; reprinted Grand Rapids: Baker, 1980) 79.

[40] The Coptic has "*great* reward" and, at the end of the verse, "kingdom *of heaven*," both probably additions in line with Matt 5:12.

precedent in the *Epistula*. It was to offer such baptismal incorporation that the Lord is said to have descended to preach to "your fathers the prophets": in order that they might be given "the right hand of the baptism of life and forgiveness and pardon for all wickedness" (27.1 – 2).[41] Just as the *preaching* of the Lord was seen (in Chapter Four) to be characteristic of the Lord as διάκονος, so here the Lord's precedent in conferring the gift of *baptism* is taken up by the disciples explicitly as διάκονοι.

Ep. apost. 41 – 42 may also be used to define further the function of the *Epistula* within its community. It was suggested (in Chapter One) that the broad range of materials presented, and the special emphasis upon the Lord as Teacher, allowed the possibility that the document is a manual of instruction of some sort. It was further shown (in Chapter Two) that the five-part formula at the end of *Ep. apost.* 5 not only has parallels in baptismal contexts in other early Christian literature but is also introduced with an explicit reference to the status of baptized persons. This raised the possibility that the *Epistula* might comprise material from which teachers of catechumens might draw; indeed, that the *Epistula* might itself be a "catechism."

Such possibilities would remain entirely contextless, however, were it not for *Ep. apost.* 41 – 42, in which motifs central to the author's polemic, now ordered with a particular temporal emphasis, allow the conjecture already hinted at: the opponents are among those at whom the *Epistula*'s mission of preaching and teaching is aimed, and the writing's temporal goal, for these and for others who have responded to the message of the successors of the disciples, is *baptism*. Baptism signifies eternal life and a part of the kingdom, as well as the forgiveness of sins; and baptism is the sign and seal of that full salvation which, as the disciples have announced in *Ep. apost.* 34, it is the task of this literary "revelation" to effect.

Therefore it is hard to agree with Hornschuh when he writes that for the author of the *Epistula*

> baptism seems to have no constitutive significance for the Christian's salvation. To be sure, there is occasional talk of "baptism of life" (27[38] and 42[53]); so too "the forgiveness of sins" is connected with the sacrament of baptism (42[53]; cf. also 27[38]). But it seems that the phrase "baptism of life" is a fixed expression, which the author has taken over and which for him is of use as nothing other than an edifying flourish.[42]

Hornschuh's estimate of the position of baptism in the theological scheme of the author is based, then, upon "baptism of life" being a "fixed expression." But so too is the five-clause confession which concludes the description of "what our Lord Jesus Christ did" in *Ep. apost.* 4 – 5; and it is clear

---

[41] The text quoted here is the Ethiopic. The Coptic is fragmentary.
[42] Hornschuh, *Studien*, 64.

that there is very little elsewhere in the writing which the author has formulated in fresh vocabulary, in word or in phrase. The *Epistula* is no *creatio ex nihilo*: composition, not theological creativity, is the key to the author's method and message. In the case of *Ep. apost.* 41–42 the author has shown a preference for a particular group of communal ideals, and with these ideals baptism has unambiguously been connected.

These chapters encourage a further development of these observations. In Chapter One my concern was to isolate the special redactional vocabulary which forms the compositional glue between the various sections of diverse doctrinal and ethical exposition. Among the terms to surface was the verb "to reveal," whose appearance in every instance was in a stereotyped, inherently contextless remark of the disciples. The special emphasis then placed upon the cluster of terms attracted to "revelation" may now be lifted to show a new emphasis, whose detection is occasioned by *Ep. apost.* 41–42: an emphasis upon *the disciples*, on "we" and "us" as recipients of the revelation. This second emphasis confirms the we/they distinction recently outlined in *Ep. apost.* 41–42. *Ep. apost.* 34.1–2, the fullest example of the author's preferred vocabulary in the mouth of the disciples, now shows a striking exclusiveness:[43]

> O Lord, such meaningful things you have spoken and preached to *us* and have revealed to *us* great things never yet spoken, and in every respect you have comforted *us* and shown yourself gracious to *us*. For after your resurrection you revealed all this to *us* that *we* might be really saved.

The disciples, and by implication their successors, are the only legitimate ministers of this saving revelation and of its seal, baptism.

The present section (*Ep. apost.* 42.5–8) concludes with an example of the rhetorical speech with which the reader is by now familiar: "O Lord, even if each of us [Eth.: even if they] had ten thousand tongues to speak with, we [Eth.: they] would not be able to give thanks to you, for you promise us such things [Eth.: as it is fitting]." However, there may be more here than mere rhetoric.[44] In *Ep. apost.* 19 the author employed a long quotation from Psalm 3 to illustrate the fulfillment of the prophet's words in the Lord's resurrection. There is nothing unusual in this, because the third psalm is often found

---

[43] The other texts gathered in Chapter One have the same character.

[44] The rhetorical image of the tenfold tongue goes back to Homer *Iliad* 2.489, and reappears frequently in ancient authors, e.g., in Ovid *Fasti* 2.119–21; Virgil *Aeneid* 6.625–27; Valerius Flaccus *Argonautica* 6.36; and among Christian writers in Theophilus *Ad Autolycum* 2.12. For an inventory and discussion of instances of the figure in literature down to the 12th century CE, see Pierre Courcelle, "Histoire du cliché virgilien des cents bouches (*Georg.* II, 42–44 = *Aen.* VI, 625–627)," *Revue des études latines* 33 (1955) 231–40; and G. Pascucci, "Ennio, *Ann.*, 561–62 V² e un tipico procedimento di ΑΥΞΗΣΙΣ nella poesia latina," *Studi italiani di filologia classica* 31 (1959) 79–99.

in early Christian literature, supplying as it does a convenient proof-text for resurrection in vs 5:[45]

ἐγὼ ἐκοιμήθην καὶ ὕπνωσα
ἐξηγέρθην ὅτι κύριος ἀντιλήψεταί μου

I lie down and sleep;
I wake again, for the Lord sustains me. (*RSV*)

But the *Epistula* is unique in quoting so much of the psalm. And since there is nothing in the quotation, other than the resurrection proof-text, that corresponds to the discussion in *Ep. apost.* 19–21, a broader view of the psalm's relevance to the author's situation may be attempted. In particular, in vss 1 and 6 the psalmist speaks of salvation from the multitude that have oppressed him:

O Lord, how many are my foes!
many are rising against me. . . .
I am not afraid of ten thousands of people
who have set themselves against me round about.

For the author of the *Epistula*, who are these "thousands" but the majority, to whom the minority, the author's group, have witnessed, and from whose number some, when warned, have turned back? Thus in *Ep. apost.* 42.8 the disciples speak for the minority in declaring: "Even if each one of us had ten thousand tongues . . . ," that is, even if we had the numerical strength of the majority, whose oppressive ways are for the author lamented in the words of Psalm 3.

Summary

1) Two traditional sayings have determined the shape of the dialogue in *Ep. apost.* 41–42: the saying about the worthy "laborer" and the prohibition of titles familiar from Matt 23:8–9. The former is not quoted as a whole, but is presupposed. The latter, standing in the way of the threefold description of titles and functions espoused by the author, is now revised by the Lord himself in light of the community's missionary activity.

2) In *Ep. apost.* 42 the Lord describes the three apostolic responsibilities, the way now being clear for the use of the forbidden titles. As "fathers," the responsibility is preaching or revelation; as διάκονοι, baptism; and as "teachers," delivering the word. The chapter is of the author's design,

---

[45] See, e.g., *1 Clem.* 26.2; Justin *1 Apol.* 38.5; *Dial.* 97.1; Irenaeus *Adv. haer.* 4.33.13; *Epideixis* 73; Clement of Alexandria *Strom.* 5.105.

and it reflects at many points the author's preferred theological vocabulary.

3) Of the three ministries outlined, one is placed in the future, that is, baptism, the importance of which has already been signaled in *Ep. apost.* 41.6. The baptism of those who have heard the Lord's words appears to be imminent. This observation, together with references to baptism elsewhere in the writing, suggests again the function of the document as a teaching manual for instructors of those preparing for baptism.

4) Yet the *Epistula* also has a marked polemic. It may further be conjectured, from the use elsewhere in the writing of terms central to *Ep. apost.* 42, that the strong we/they dichotomy reflects a real situation of competing Christian groups. The community of the *Epistula* has made its appeal to the rival group, who are possibly in the majority. Of those "warned" at least some have "turned back." It is they who await baptism, by the Lord through the agency of the disciples—the leaders of the *Epistula's* community.

6

Epistula Apostolorum 43–45:
The Community Defined

Ep. apost. 43–45 constitutes one of the largest blocks of material in the writing which may reasonably be considered self-contained. This is not to say that these chapters are thematically or formally divorced from the rest; the exchange of the dialogue continues with its characteristic rhetorical features, and editorial motifs shape the composition as in earlier and later chapters. But in *Ep. apost.* 43–45 there is a single point of reference, namely the fate of five wise and five foolish virgins.

Inevitably the modern reader is drawn to a comparison with Matthew's parable, and modern commentators have taken as their starting point the dependence, variously described, of the *Epistula* upon Matt 25:1–13.[1] However, the differences between the two are more than superficial and would suggest only a thematic indebtedness to Matthew's parable rather than direct literary dependence.[2] The following features of Matthew's story are not present in the *Epistula*: lamps, oil, flasks, the delay of the bridegroom, and the midnight cry. The most significant difference between the two is that in Matthew 25 *all* the virgins sleep, in the *Epistula* only the foolish.

To bring together *Ep. apost.* 43–45 and Matt 25:1–13 is in any case to compare unequal partners. Matthew's parable of the kingdom, whatever its origin, includes but one verse of what modern opinion unanimously regards as secondary matter (25:13): "Watch therefore, for you know neither the day

---

[1] Schmidt, *Gespräche Jesu*, 223; Hornschuh, *Studien*, 21.

[2] Hornschuh (ibid., 21) suggests that the departure from the text of Matthew is characteristic of the author's technique of "Wechselrede."

nor the hour."[3] In *Ep. apost.* 43–45 the story is thoroughly enmeshed with discussion and interpretation which borders on exegesis: the allegory is decoded even as the story is being told.

Therefore both Schmidt and Hornschuh have been quick to move on to the question of the point of the dialogue for the author of the *Epistula*. Schmidt sees the whole as concerned with whether or not the intercession of the righteous for the wicked can be effective.[4] It is the same question, he suggests, as emerges in 4 Ezra 7:102–103:[5]

> I answered and said, "If I have found favor in thy sight, show further to me, thy servant, whether on the day of judgment the righteous will be able to intercede for the ungodly or to entreat the Most High for them, fathers for sons or sons for parents, brothers for brothers, relatives for their kinsmen, or friends for those who are most dear."

The answer for the author of the *Epistula* is no: "Whoever <is shut out> is shut out" (43.14).[6] Thus Schmidt gleans the historical information that the author's community as yet knows no system of penitential discipline. Schmidt proceeds to compare lists of names in *Herm. Vis.* 3.8.3–5; *Sim.* 9.15.2; and *Barn.* 2.2 similar to the lists of virtues in *Ep. apost.* 43.6 and 16; equally, the names of the wise in the *Epistula* could derive from Paul's triad in 1 Cor 13:13 together with Grace and Peace from the Pauline greetings (e.g., Rom 1:7; 1 Cor 1:3; 2 Cor 1:2) or the Pastoral Epistles (cf. 1 Tim 1:2; 2 Tim 1:2; Tit 1:4).[7]

Hornschuh, like Schmidt noting the differences between Matt 25:1–13 and *Ep. apost.* 43–45, pursues the interpretation of the latter with reference to the writing's religious environment: the struggle between orthodoxy and heresy. For Hornschuh the essential problem of interpretation is the contradiction between the names of the second group of virgins (in *Ep. apost.* 43.16) and their designation, "foolish."[8] He finds an explanation in the Jewish-Gnostic myth of Sophia, as recoverable from the *Apocryphon of John*, the

---

[3] See, e.g., Joachim Jeremias, *The Parables of Jesus* (rev. ed.; New York: Scribner's, 1967) 52; 110–11; Dan Otto Via, *The Parables: Their Literary and Existential Dimension* (Philadelphia: Fortress, 1967) 123.

[4] Schmidt, *Gespräche Jesu*, 378.

[5] Ibid., 381. Schmidt also cites *2 Bar.* 85.12: "[At the coming of the times,] there will not be an opportunity to repent anymore, . . . nor opportunity of repentance nor supplicating for offenses, nor prayers of the fathers, nor intercessions of the prophets, nor help of the righteous" (*OTP* 1. 651–52); and *2 Enoch* 53.1: "Let us not say, 'Our father is in front of God; he will appear [in front of God] for us on the day of judgment.' For there a father cannot help a son, nor yet a son a father" (*OTP* 1. 180).

[6] Schmidt, *Gespräche Jesu*, 381.

[7] Ibid., 383.

[8] Hornschuh, *Studien*, 23.

Acts of Thomas, the *Gospel of Philip,* and as reported by Irenaeus and Hippolytus.[9] This myth represents the figure of Sophia as twofold: upper and lower.[10] She is presented in *Gos. Phil.* (NHC 2, 3) 60.10–15 as follows:

> Echamoth is one thing and Echmoth another. Echamoth is Wisdom simply, but Echmoth is the Wisdom of death which is the one which knows death, which is called "the little Wisdom."

In the *Epistula* this mythological framework is invoked for polemical purposes; yet for the author the distinction between saving wisdom and fallen wisdom also serves a parenetic intent.[11] This is a fundamental insight into the author's treatment of the parable. But in an attempt to build upon it the following analysis will differ from those already reviewed in that the larger church historical (Schmidt) and religious-historical (Hornschuh) backgrounds will take second place to a more detailed investigation of the text itself. The results already presented remain important in the larger frame; but what is lacking to date is a coherent explanation of the present shape of the text in light of the writing as a whole. Indeed, to an extent unprecedented in this study the decisive evidence must be recovered by establishing the original text and its translation.

It is therefore necessary to ask again whether or not the theory of simple literary paraphrase of Matt 25:1–13 provides an adequate account of these chapters; to ask for which portions of *Ep. apost.* 43–45 the *Epistula*'s author was directly and solely responsible; and not least to ask what new contribution these chapters can make to our understanding of the author's communal situation and theological vision.

That the author was working with a source of some kind is certain; despite the best editorial efforts the dialogue remains an incomplete amalgam of story, elaboration, and interpretation. It is also certain that *Ep. apost.* 43–45 is not the product of the simple combination of a single source and the author's editorial expansion. There are additional materials, intermediate between the source and the author, which are neither required by the core narrative nor central to the author's redactional message. In *Ep. apost.* 43–45 there are several detectable layers of material, each of which is

---

[9] Ibid., 26–28.

[10] Cf. G. C. Stead, "The Valentinian Myth of Sophia," *JTS* n.s. 20 (1969) 75–104; and George W. MacRae, "The Jewish Background of the Gnostic Sophia Myth," *NovT* 12 (1970) 86–101, esp. 90–91: "One must bear in mind that Sophia is an ambivalent figure in Gnosticism: through her fall she is blamed for the existence of evil matter, but because she belongs to the world of light as an Aeon of the Father and is sometimes in the myth reinstated to it, she is credited with the presence of the divine or of revelation in man."

[11] Hornschuh, *Studien,* 28; 123–24, esp. p. 124: "The whole [section] is a parenesis to the faithful, an admonition, to keep away from heresy."

separable from the rest and promotes a distinct theological interest. At the compositional level there is one clear sign of a seam between two layers: in *Ep. apost.* 43.5 a narrative comment ("But we wept and were sad about those who had fallen asleep") separates the Lord's introduction of the names of the wise ("Now hear their names" [43.4b]) from the names themselves ("He said to us, 'The five wise are . . .' "[43.6]). This is but one of several clues to the structure of these chapters.

Ep. apost. 43.1 – 2, 8b – 9, 14(?):
The Story of the Wise and Foolish

The disciples' questions in *Ep. apost.* 43.3 ("Who are the wise and who are the foolish?") and 43.15 ("Who are the foolish?") indicate that the "parable" of the wise and foolish is for the *Epistula* an allegory. As such it is not merely a figure or extended metaphor. Rather there is a given story, at points hidden by the dialogical overlay, which may be reconstructed as a two-stage history representing the periods before and after the bridegroom's arrival. (The arrival is not explicitly mentioned.) It is not necessary to assume that the story was already known to the readers, still less that the Matthean version was known. Unlike Matthew's simile ("The kingdom of heaven shall be compared to ten maidens" [25:1]) the *Epistula* makes its point of comparison the second person plural, "you": "You will be [Eth.: Be] like the wise virgins" (43.1), as in the nearest Synoptic parallel to Matt 25:1 – 13, Luke 12:35 – 40:[12] "Let your loins be girded and your lamps burning, and *be like* men who are waiting for their master to come home from the marriage feast. . . ."

The narrative begins as follows (43.1 – 2):

Ethiopic	Coptic
1 Be as the wise virgins who kindled the light and did not slumber and who went with their lamps to meet the lord, the bridegroom, and have gone in with him into the bridegroom's chamber.	1 You will be like the wise virgins who watched and did not sleep, but <went> out to the lord into the bride-chamber.
2 But the foolish ones who talked with them were not able to watch, but fell asleep.	2 But <the foolish> were not able to watch, but fell asleep.

[12] See C. H. Dodd, *The Parables of the Kingdom* (rev. ed.; London: Nisbet, 1961) 121. In the NT, ὅμοιος is used with a second-person-plural referent only at Luke 12:36. Richard Bauckham ("Synoptic Parousia Parables Again," *NTS* 29 [1983] 132) speaks of the exhortation in *Ep. apost.* 43.1 as a "mildly deparabolizing step" in the application of the story to Christian eschatological teaching.

The contrast between the two groups is complete: watched/did not watch; did not sleep/slept.[13] The story resumes in 43.8b-9, with the second and final stage: the history of the wise and foolish after the arrival of the bridegroom. As in the first stage, two parallel accounts are given, concerning the wise and the foolish respectively. Since the intervening material (43.3–8a) has introduced questions of interpretation, including the identity of the bridegroom ("I am the Lord and I am the bridegroom" [43.8a]), first-person references continue to appear; but the Ethiopic text preserves the third-person form presumably in the source:[14]

Ethiopic	Coptic
8b [The wise] have gone with me into the house of the bridegroom, and laid themselves down (at table) with the bridegroom and rejoiced.	8b [The wise] have gone into the house of the \<bridegroom\> and have laid themselves down with me in my \<bride\>chamber \<and rejoiced\>.
9 But the five foolish slept, and when they awoke they came to the house of the bridegroom and knocked at the doors, for they had been shut.	9 But the five foolish, when \<they\> had fallen asleep, they awoke, came to the door of the bridechamber and knocked, for they had been shut out.

To this point the narrative (43.1–2, 8b-9) is spare but coherent. It is free from interpretation but clearly invites it. No editorial theology is apparent. A conclusion similar to that in Matt 25:13 ("Be awake!" or "Watch!") would be appropriate here—more so than in Matthew, where all the virgins sleep. Instead the reader is left with the sobering fact of the exclusion of the foolish. But to this should probably be added the pronouncement in *Ep. apost.* 43.14, "Whoever \<is shut out\> is shut out," a saying which may originally have come from the mouth of the bridegroom.[15] For the rest, we are left with a narrative in which, as Claude G. Montefiore remarked of Matt 25:1–13, "the virgins are half bridesmaids, half bride."[16]

---

[13] The Ethiopic additions may be influenced by Matthew 25, but there is no verbatim borrowing. With the phrase "who kindled the light" in the Ethiopic of 43.1, cf. *Gos. Phil.* 85.32–33: "Every one who will [enter] the bridal chamber will kindle the [light]. . . ."

[14] Alternatively, 43.8b and the phrase "But the five foolish, when \<they\> had fallen asleep" in 43.9 belong with *Ep. apost.* 45.3–4; see below on *Ep. apost.* 43.3, 5, 10–13; 45.3–6.

[15] For the original ending of Matthew's parable, Via (*Parables*, 124) conjectures: " 'Sir, open to us.' But he replied, 'I tell you, I will not.' "

[16] Montefiore, *The Synoptic Gospels* (2d ed.; 2 vols.; London: Macmillan, 1927) 2. 316.

Ep. apost. 43.6, 16:
The Names of the Wise and Foolish

Even before the Lord has finished relating the story, the disciples ask to know the identity of the virgins. The names are given in two lists:

> The five wise are Faith and Love and Grace, Peace and Hope. (43.6)
>
> [The foolish] are Knowledge and Insight, Obedience, Forbearance, and Mercy. (43.16)

It is important to recognize that such lists as these are found frequently in early Christian literature, either thematically integrated with their contexts or as separable catalogues of virtues. The following are typical:[17]

> We rejoice in our sufferings, knowing that suffering produces *endurance*, and endurance produces *character*, and character produces *hope*, and hope does not disappoint us, because God's *love* has been poured out into our hearts. . . . (Rom 5:3–5 [cf. Jas 1:3])

> The fruit of the Spirit is *love, joy, peace, patience, kindness, goodness, faithfulness, gentleness, self-control.* (Gal 5:22–23 [cf. 2 Cor 6:6–7])

> We give thanks to God . . . remembering before our God and Father your work of *faith* and the labor of *love* and steadfastness of *hope* in our Lord Jesus Christ. (1 Thess 1:2–3 [cf. 1 Cor 13:13; 2 Thess 1:3–4])

> Aim at *righteousness, godliness, faith, love, steadfastness, gentleness.* (1 Tim 6:11)

> Make every effort to supplement your *faith* with *virtue*, and virtue with *knowledge*, and knowledge with *self-control*, and self-control with *steadfastness*, and steadfastness with *godliness*, and godliness with *brotherly affection*, and brotherly affection with *love*. (2 Pet 1:5–7)

> How blessed and wonderful, beloved, are the gifts of God! *Life* in immortality, *splendor* in righteousness, *truth* in boldness, *faith* in confidence, *continence* in holiness: and all these things are submitted to our understanding. (*1 Clem.* 35.1–2)

> We have touched on every aspect of *faith* and *repentance* and *true love* and *self-control* and *sobriety* and *patience*. . . . (*1 Clem.* 62.2)

> *Fear* then, and *patience* are the helpers of our faith, and *long-suffering* and *continence* are our allies. While then these things remain in holiness towards the Lord, *wisdom, prudence, understanding*, and *knowledge* rejoice with them. (*Barn.* 2.2–3)

---

[17] See J. N. D. Kelly, *The Epistles of Peter and of Jude* (HNTC; San Francisco: Harper & Row, 1969) 305, on these and similar "catalogues" of virtues in the NT and other hellenistic literature.

From *Faith* is born *Continence*, from Continence *Simplicity*, from Simplicity *Innocence*, from Innocence *Reverence*, from Reverence *Knowledge*, from Knowledge *Love*. (*Herm. Vis.* 3.8.7 [cf. *Sim.* 9.15.2])

Lists are found which agree in number, and very closely in content, with *Ep. apost.* 43.6 or 43.16:

Peace [be with you from] Peace, [*love* from] Love, [*grace* from] Grace, [*faith*] from Faith, *life* from Holy Life! (*Ap. Jas.* 1.2 – 7)

And in the midst of the immeasurable deep there are five powers which are called by these unutterable names:
<1> The first is called *love*, . . .
2. The second (is called) *hope*, . . .
3. The third is called *faith*, . . .
4. The fourth is called *gnosis*, . . .
5. The fifth is called *peace*, . . .[18] (*The Untitled Text* [Bruce Codex] 10)

Now the existence of such lists in itself tells us little about the particular lists in the *Epistula*.[19] Even the characterization of the names of virtues as "maidens" in *Hermas* shows only the easy personalization of feminine abstract nouns. But the presence of lists of virtues in contemporary writings does raise the question, whether the author of the *Epistula* attached the names to the five wise and foolish, or the names/virtues were already attached to the virgins, albeit secondarily, in the author's source. To explore these possibilities it is necessary to assess the relationship of the specific virtues in the *Epistula* to the rest of the document.

The first group of names, together with Duensing's translation of the Coptic (*NTApoc* 1. 222), is as follows (43.6 [XXXV 2, 85/11]):

Copt.: ⲧⲡⲓⲥⲧⲓⲥ ⲁⲟⲩ ⲧⲁⲅⲁⲡⲏ ⲙⲛ̄ ⲧⲭⲁⲣⲓⲥ ⲧⲣⲏⲛⲏ ⲙⲛ̄ ⲧⲍⲉⲗⲡⲓⲥ ·
Eth.: 'amin wa-feqr feššeḥa wa-salām wa-tasfā
Faith and Love and Grace, Peace and Hope.

The third name in the Coptic text, ⲭⲁⲣⲓⲥ , has as its Ethiopic parallel the word *feššeḥa*, which represents Greek χαρά (joy).[20] Otherwise there is

---

[18] Coptic text and ET in Carl Schmidt, ed., Violet MacDermot, trans., *The Books of Jeu and the Untitled Text in the Bruce Codex* (NHS 13; Leiden: Brill, 1978) 245. MacDermot compares Epiphanius *Panarion* (= *Adversus haereses*) 31.5.8. Cf. also *Untitled Text* 2 (p. 228): gnosis, life, hope, rest, love, resurrection, faith, rebirth, the seal; and 15 (p. 256): praise, joy, gladness, pleasure, peace, hope, faith, love, truth.

[19] The author's interest in and repeated use of lists was pointed out in Chapter One above; but in Chapter Two (on the miracle list in *Ep. apost.* 4 – 5) it was observed that the simple collection of formal parallels to the *Epistula*'s lists is only the first step towards interpretation.

[20] Schmidt, *Gespräche Jesu*, 136 n. 3; Duensing, *Epistula Apostolorum*, 36 n. 6. Scribal and semantic confusion between the two terms is common; indeed, "it seems that χάρις is not always clearly differentiated in mng. fr. χαρά" (BAG, *s.v.* χάρις [877a]). E.g., the Ethiopic of

complete agreement. However, in other places in the *Epistula* the nouns do not perfectly correspond in the two versions. As it is, these Greek words are found transliterated in the extant Coptic text (including chap. 43) five times, four times, once, twice, and once respectively; the Ethiopic nouns are found three, three, (three), four, and six times. Allowance must be made for the presence of numerous cognates, especially verbal forms, in both versions. The Greek verb πιστεύειν (to believe), for instance, is represented twenty-three times in the Coptic, fifty times in the Ethiopic. But nowhere except in *Ep. apost.* 43 does the author imply the special desirability of these virtues above others, nor, indeed, above the five to be called "foolish."

The names of the foolish, together with Duensing's translation of the Coptic, are as follows (43.16 [XXXVI 11, 86/10]):

Copt.: ΓΝΩϹΙϹ ⲁⲟⲩ ⲦⲘⲚⲦⲢⲘⲚⲌⲎⲦ· ⲦⲘⲚⲦϹⲘⲎⲦ· ⲦⲘⲚⲦⲀⲢⲰⲎⲦ· ⲘⲚ ⲠⲚⲀⲈ·
Eth.: *labbewo ʾaʾmero samiʿ teʾgešt meḥrat*
Knowledge and Insight, Obedience, Forbearance, and Mercy.

These Coptic nouns are found only here in the *Epistula*; the Ethiopic, three times, once, twice, twice, and five times respectively. Again the lack of correspondence between the two versions is not easily explained; in only two cases is some consistency found. The Ethiopic term *meḥrat*, which is the standard equivalent of the Greek word ἔλεος (mercy), is found twice with the transliterated Greek οἰκονομία (Duensing: "plan," "arrangement") in the parallel Coptic text (*Ep. apost.* 13.8 [VI 11, 57/8] and 21.2 [XIV 12, 65/6]). Similarly, the fourth Ethiopic noun is found elsewhere in parallel with the transliterated Greek ὑπομονή (*Ep. apost.* 44.4 [XXXVII 4, 87/3]; Duensing: "perseverance") and ὑπομονεῖν (38.4 [XXVII 4, 81/2]; Duensing: "persevered").

However, in the case of the "foolish" virtues, as conversely in the case of the "wise," it is impossible to find any trace of the negative connotations which presumably would be attached to names of foolish virgins. That is, it cannot be shown that the author has carefully distinguished the "wise" virtues from the "foolish," and it is therefore impossible to strive for a distinction in the *Epistula* between wise virtues and foolish vices.[21] And it is here,

---

1 Enoch 5.7 promises that the elect shall have "light, joy, and peace," where for "joy" (= Ethiopic *feśḥ*) the Greek Syncellus fragment has χάρις. For other examples see the manuscript variants in Tob 7:18; Sir 30:16; 2 Cor 1:15; Phlm 7; 3 John 4; Ignatius *Eph.* (Long Recension) *proem.*; 12.1; Melito *Pass. Hom.* 661.

[21] This is not to deny that at the hands of another author the second group of attributes might be portrayed negatively. Reinhart Staats ("Die törichten Jungfrauen von Mt 25 in gnostischer und antignostischer Literatur," in Walther Eltester, ed., *Christentum und Gnosis* [BZNW 37; Berlin: Töpelmann, 1969] 98–115, esp. 113) has pointed to a remarkable parallel to the *Epistula*'s list of foolish virgins in a homily of Pseudo-Macarius (*Serm.* 49.3.1) on Matt 25:1–13, where αἱ πέντε λογικαὶ αἰσθήσεις τῆς ψυχῆς ("the five reasoning senses of the

as already noted, that Hornschuh locates the central exegetical issue in these chapters: the designation of otherwise laudable virtues as foolish. Hornschuh's resolution of this tension is achieved with reference to the notion of a divided Sophia. But perhaps it is not necessary even to posit a distinction between the higher and the lower. All depends on just what the story and its interpretation were designed to achieve, not only as a theological statement but also as an ethical mandate to this community.

Ep. apost. 43.7 – 8a:
The Identification of the Wise

To this point the attempt has been made to reach the earliest levels of tradition in *Ep. apost.* 43 – 45, that is, the simplest form of the narrative and the lists of names attached to the two sets of virgins. Whether or not the kernel of the story derives directly from the written text of Matthew's gospel, the author was working with a source, itself written or oral. Similarly, in the lists of virtues secondarily connected with the primary narrative (and probably prior to the writing of the *Epistula*), we are dealing with an ethical commonplace, the list form, which is widely attested in contemporary literature.

It is only at the third stage, at which individuals or groups (i.e., real people rather than the abstraction of the virtues' names) are associated with the wise and the foolish respectively, that the author's purpose in all of this can begin to be discerned. The connection previously reviewed, consisting of virgins and names, is not immediately extended into an identification of virgins (together with their names) with individuals or groups. Just as the allegory begins with a *comparison* ("You will be *like*"; Eth.: "Be *as*" [43.1]), so now in 43.7 – 8a the wise virgins and their names are not so much *identified* with a specific Christian group, as Hornschuh[22] implies, as *associated* with them, whether actively or inactively. Therefore it is not to be presumed that the virgins and their names are in either case synonymous with or ciphers for a particular group.

---

soul"), understood as lesser virtues, are named σύνεσις, γνῶσις, διάκρισις, ὑπομονή, and ἔλεος (understanding, knowledge, discernment, endurance, mercy). Staats (pp. 108, 113) also compares Tertullian *De anima* 18 (on the distinction between the bodily sense and the intellectual faculties): "[This] distinction they [= "the Gnostics and the Valentinians"] actually apply to the parable of the ten virgins: making the five foolish virgins to symbolize the five bodily senses, seeing that these are so silly and so easy to be deceived; and the wise to express the meaning of the intellectual faculties, which are so wise as to attain to that mysterious and supernatural truth, which is placed in the pleroma" (ET in ANF 3. 198). In the *Epistula*, however, it will be seen that the author is concerned with the essential *unity* of the two groups.

[22] *Studien*, 26 – 28.

The place of the wise is described as follows (43.7−8a [XXXV 3, 86/1]):

Ethiopic	Coptic
7 As soon as[23] they who believe in me have these, they will be leaders to those who believe in me and in him who sent me.	7 Among those who believe they who have these will be guides to those who have believed in me and in him who sent me.
8 I am the Lord and I am the bridegroom; they have received me.	8 I am the Lord and I am the bridegroom whom they have received.

It becomes clear that the group involved here is not composed of the believers over against the unbelievers, nor of those who have received the Lord over against those who have not. Instead the author is concerned with the *leaders* among those who believe: those who are in possession of these specific virtues. This fits the larger context well, for in the previous section (*Ep. apost.* 42−43) it seems all but certain that the leaders (i.e., the father-servant-teacher disciples) held center stage. Who, then, are the foolish? Before the second identification can be made, the text and translation of *Ep. apost.* 43.17−44.2 must be investigated.

Ep. apost. 43.17; 44.1−2a:
Text and Translation

The text of these verses are as follows (XXXVI 12, 86/11):

Ethiopic	Coptic
ʾella nomā ba-dibēhon[24]	ⲛⲉⲓ ⲅⲁⲣ ⲛⲉⲧⲁⲍ̄ⲛ̄ⲕⲁⲧⲉ ⲍ̄ⲛ
la-ʾella ʾamnu[25]	ⲛⲉⲧⲁⲍ̄ⲣ̄ⲡⲓⲥⲧⲉⲩⲉ
wa-yeʾammanuni[26]	ⲁⲟⲩ ⲁⲩⲣ̄ⲍⲟⲙⲟⲗⲟⲅⲉⲓ ⲛ̄ⲙⲁⲓ
wa-ʾenza ʾi-yegabberu teʾzāzeya	ⲛ̄ⲡⲟⲩⲉⲓⲣⲉ ⲁⲉ ⲛ̄ⲛⲁⲉⲛⲧⲟⲗ︦ⲏ
ba-[27] ʾella nomu[28]	ⲍⲓⲧ︦ⲛ ⲛⲉⲧⲁⲩⲛ̄ⲕⲁⲧⲉ
ʾafʾa yeqawwemu ʾem-mangešt[29]	ⲥⲉⲛⲁ6ⲟⲩ ⲅⲁⲣ ⲛ̄ⲡ︦ⲃ︦ⲗ︦ ⲛ̄ⲧⲙⲛ̄ⲧⲣ̄ⲣⲟ

[23] For "among" (Copt.) the Eth. has "as soon as." The Coptic translator presumably read ἐν τοῖς πιστεύουσιν. If the Eth. translator read ἐν οἷς, it is conceivable that this relative phrase was understood to be a simple resumptive, e.g., "and so," as C. F. D. Moule (*An Idiom Book of New Testament Greek* [2d ed.; Cambridge: Cambridge University Press, 1959] 197) has suggested in Acts 26:12, Luke 12:1 (possibly), and elsewhere; cf. BAG, *s.v.* ὅς I.11.c (585a): "under which circumstances."

[24] Variant reading: MSS BKMQR: *ba-dibēhomu* (= masculine suffix).

[25] MSS LMPS (= Guerrier): *yaʾammenu* (= imperfect tense for perfect).

[26] MSS CN: *taʾamnuni* (= perf. for imperf.).

[27] MSS AT: *bo-* (= "there is/are..."); LMPQRS omit.

[28] MSS BKQR: *nomā* (= fem. for masc.).

[29] MSS AT omit "the kingdom."

Duensing's translation of the Coptic (in *NTApoc* 1. 223) is as follows:

These are they which slept in those who have believed and acknowledged me. (43.17)

But my commandments were not fulfilled by those who slept. (44.1)

Consequently they will remain outside the kingdom. (44.2a)

Duensing's rendering of the Ethiopic text differs only in that 44.1 and 44.2a are more closely connected: "And since those who slept did not fulfil my commandment, they will be outside the kingdom."

In his edition and translation of the Ethiopic, however, Guerrier had suggested a translation in which 43.17 and the first part of 44.1 are joined as follows:

Ce sont (les virtus) qui ont dormi en ceux qui croient, et qui ont confiance en moi, (43.17)

mais qui n'ont pas accompli mon commandement. (44.1)

(Il y en a) qui ont dormi et sont tenus en dehors du royaume.[30] (44.2a)

Schmidt's translation is closest to that of Guerrier in that the clause which refers to failure to keep the commandments is connected by him, as by Guerrier, directly with what precedes:

Diese nämlich (γάρ) sint es, die geschlafen haben unter denen, die geglaubt (πιστεύειν) haben, und haben bekannt (ὁμολογεῖν) mich, (43.17)

aber (δέ) meine Gebote (ἐντολή) nicht getan. Wegen derer (durch die), welche geschlafen haben, (44.1)

werden sie nämlich (γάρ) bleiben außerhalb des Reiches.[31] (44.2a)

In all three translations both linguistic and logical problems are squarely addressed. The principal logical question is this: Where are those referred to as "they" to be understood as *virtues*, and where as *a class of believers*? For Duensing the answer is twofold: as virtues in 43.17 (i.e., the virtues that "slept" in some believers) and as believers (albeit excommunicate) in 44.1–2. Duensing therefore pays a small price in logical consistency for a smooth rendering of the clause whose second word is ⲁⲉ (but); however, his translation of the third-person plural takes it quite naturally as a passive whose agent ("by") is expressed, as regularly in Coptic, with the preposition ⲍⲓⲧⲛ̄.[32]

---

[30] Guerrier, "Le testament," 86–87.

[31] Schmidt, *Gespräche Jesu*, 141, 143.

[32] Without the expression of agency ("by"), the verb is the normal third-person-plural active, here negated.

The merit of Guerrier's and Schmidt's translations of 43.17–44.1 is their understanding of the subject of the three actions (believing, acknowledging, not keeping the commandments) as the same: the believers *in whom* the foolish virtues slept. Structurally this interpretation well matches the description of the wise in *Ep. apost.* 43.7–8a. It is ingeniously maintained by Schmidt in 44.2 as well. Since he no longer requires the prepositional phrase ("by those who slept") to express the agent of a passive verb (as in Duensing), Schmidt now takes it causally: "*Through* those who slept, that is, they will remain...."

Not every issue is resolved, however. In whichever way the connection is made between 43.17 and 44.1, a more serious difficulty arises in connecting 44.1 and 44.2. This difficulty is not readily visible in any of the translations quoted above, in each of which there is the appearance of a progression from (a) the *identification* of the virtues (43.17) to (b) the *charge* of failure to keep the commandments (44.1) and thence to (c) the *consequence* of that failure (44.2). The implication, therefore, is that the penalty for failure to keep the commandments will be exclusion from the kingdom (and also from the "sheepfold" [44.2b]). And it is implied that from this arises a *second* consequence and penalty: destruction by the "wolves" and a painful death (44.3–4).

There is no doubt that *Ep. apost.* 44.3–4 speaks of the painful end of those outside the kingdom. What is at issue here is whether exclusion from the kingdom is itself to be understood as punishment—or as *consequence* at all. In grammatical terms, the question is whether or not the ⲅⲁⲣ in 44.2 will bear the weight of a description of the consequence of the action censured in 44.1. To answer this it must be determined first with what probability the original text read γάρ, a word whose regular meaning is that of the English explanatory "for," secondly whether or not the range of meaning available for this conjunction can include expressions of consequence, and finally whether or not the term's use elsewhere in the *Epistula* suggests an alternate rendering.

In Chapter One it was seen that the adverbs ⲧⲟⲧⲉ (then) and ⲡⲁⲗⲓⲛ (again) appear with some frequency in the *Epistula*, and that their appearance probably reflects the original Greek text. The same can be claimed, for internal and external reasons, for ⲅⲁⲣ. Outside of this writing the Coptic translation of the NT offers a useful control.[33] In the Sahidic version of the Gospel of John, for example, with only two exceptions the sixty-four occurrences of

---

[33] The Coptic NT is not the only control. The use of ⲅⲁⲣ in the Nag Hammadi tractates published to date (1985) has been reviewed, and it is consistent with the conclusions presented below. See also the notes on the use of ⲅⲁⲣ in the *Treatise on Resurrection* (NHC 1,4) in Bentley Layton, *The Gnostic Treatise on Resurrection from Nag Hammadi* (HDR 12; Missoula, MT: Scholars Press, 1979) 176–77.

the word are reproduced, transliterated, in the Coptic text.[34]

The second and third questions posed, concerning the meaning of γάρ elsewhere in the *Epistula* and in contemporary Greek in general, may be taken together. This is because the use of γάρ in the one is consistent with its uses in the other. The conjunction is found in the extant Coptic forty-four times, not including reconstructions. Excluding for a moment the present passage, almost the full range of contemporary usage of γάρ is represented in the writing, including a high proportion of those uses distinctive of literary dialogues. Thus γάρ is found:

1) expressing *cause, reason,* or *explanation*:[35]

> Now keep <yourselves> away from them, *for* death is in them . . . (*Ep. apost.* 7.3 [I 5, 53/6; Eth.: ʾ*esma* = "for"])
>
> But if all the words that were spoken by the prophets are fulfilled in me—*for* I was in them—. . . (19.19 [XIII 10, 64/9; Eth.: ʾ*esma*])
>
> You do well, *for* the righteous are anxious about the sinners. (40.2 [XXX 11, 83/4; Eth.: ʾ*esma*])

2) in questions, "where English idiom leaves the word untranslated" or adds "*then, pray*":[36]

> "*For* you know that the angel Gabriel brought the message to Mary?" We answered, "Yes, O Lord." (14.1 [VI 13, 57/10])

3) as an emphatic particle, "to confirm or strengthen something said."[37] This usage is especially significant in speeches of the Lord in which no direct connection is being made with what precedes the γάρ clause. The following Amen sayings, for example, have ΓΑΡ but are not directly explanatory:[38]

---

[34] It is probable that in the case of the two exceptions (John 9:30; 18:13) the word was not read by the translator. See George Horner, ed. and trans., *The Coptic Version of the New Testament in the Southern Dialect, otherwise called Sahidic and Thebaic* (7 vols.; Oxford: Clarendon, 1911–24) 3. 161, 281.

[35] Cf. BAG, *s.v.* γάρ 1a, e; 2 (151b–52a); LSJ, *s.v.* γάρ, I.1a, b (338b).

[36] BAG, *s.v.* γάρ 1f (152a). With one exception (23.1), in none of the examples cited under (2), (3) and (4) does the Eth. text have a conjunction or adverb corresponding to ΓΑΡ in the Coptic.

[37] LSJ, *s.v.* γάρ I.3b (338b); BAG, *s.v.* γάρ 4 (152b), e.g., in 1 Cor 9:10; 1 Thess 2:20.

[38] On the other hand, two Amen sayings, responding to statements of the disciples, do seem to have an explanatory ΓΑΡ: *Ep. apost.* 41.6 (XXXII 5, 84/3): "As you have said. *For* truly I say to you . . ."; 47.7 (XL 8, 89/5): "See now that a judgment <is appointed for them.> *For* truly I say <to you . . . >."

Truly (ⲍⲁⲙⲏⲛ ⲅⲁⲣ) I say to you, I will come ... (16.3 [IX 5, 59/5])

Truly (ⲍⲁⲙⲏⲛ ⲅⲁⲣ) I say to you, <all> who have believed in me ... I will <lead> up to heaven. (28.4 [XXIII 7, 70/9])

In such contexts the Amen introduction is treated as a fixed expression, almost as an exclamation. Other nonexplanatory uses of ⲅⲁⲣ also have this formulaic quality:

On that day (ⲍ̄ⲛ ⲫⲟⲟⲩⲉ ⲅⲁⲣ ⲉⲧⲙ̄ⲙⲟ), when I took the form of the angel Gabriel ... (14.5 [VII 6, 58/1])

My son, on the day of judgment (ⲍ̄ⲛ ⲫⲟⲟⲩⲉ ⲅⲁⲣ ⲛ̄ⲧⲕⲣⲓⲥⲓⲥ) ... (26.4 [XXI 1, 69/2])

O Lord, in that day (ⲍ̄ⲛ ⲫⲟⲟⲩⲉ ⲅⲁⲣ ⲉⲧⲙ̄ⲙⲟ) they will say to you ... (39.3 [XXVIII 5, 81/9])

Twice the idiomatic ⲁⲛⲁⲅⲕⲏ ⲅⲁⲣ is found:[39]

Yes, it is necessary (ⲁⲍⲟ ⲟⲩⲁⲛⲁⲅⲕⲏ ⲅⲁⲣ) until the day when I come ... (15.9 [VIII 15, 59/2])

O Lord, there is a necessity (ⲟⲩⲁⲛⲁⲅⲕⲏ ⲅⲁⲣ) upon us to inquire ... (23.1 [XVII 3, 67/1; Eth. fam. 1: *’esma*])

4) in nominal phrases:

[It is] these (ⲛⲉⲓ̈ ⲅⲁⲣ) with respect to whom the prophet said ... (43.4 [XXXIV 12, 85/8])

I am the Lord (ⲁⲛⲁⲕ ⲅⲁⲣ ⲡⲉ ⲡⲭⲁⲉⲓⲥ) and I am the bridegroom ... (43.8 [XXXV 6, 86/2])

In uses (2), (3) and (4), most of which may be characterized as stereotyped expressions, the effect of the ⲅⲁⲣ is to add emphasis, or perhaps formality, to the saying. But even when the primary, explanatory function (i.e., usage [1]) of the conjunction is not present, there is still no hint of an alternative involving result or consequence. Therefore it is possible to speak of a resumptive γάρ or an emphatic γάρ, but not, on this evidence, of a γάρ which is synonymous with οὖν (therefore).

This conclusion has importance for the translation of *Ep. apost.* 43.17– 44.2. Despite the evidence from the NT[40] and from elsewhere in the *Epistula*, with the exception of Guerrier's translation (of the Ethiopic text only) the translations offered express or imply that the prediction "they will remain

[39] Cf. *Auth. Teach.* (NHC 6,3) 30.22 for the same phrase, again without any inferential sense. The phrase is explanatory in Matt 18:7; 1 Cor 9:16.
[40] The use of γάρ in the NT "conforms to classical" Greek usage (BDF §452).

outside the kingdom'' (44.2) is the consequence of failure to keep the commandments on the part of those who slept (44.1). This is explicitly so in Duensing's rendering of γάρ as "daher" ("Consequently," in *NTApoc* 1. 223). It is implicit in Schmidt's "nämlich." Not only this, but in taking the prepositional phrase in 44.1 ("through those who slept") with 44.2, Schmidt makes ΓΑΡ the fourth word in its clause, a position which must be considered at least unusual.[41]

Once it is recognized that it is correct to expect a γάρ clause to be one of explanation, apart from special formal and idiomatic uses (categories [2] – [4] above), the following question surfaces: How can a clause referring to the future ("they will remain") be understood as an explanation of a past occurrence (or present, if present perfect: "my commandments have not been kept")? This, of course, is a logical impossibility. The future may shed light on the past; it may reveal the consequences of past acts or states. But in itself it does not offer the *reason* for what has been or what has been done in the past. Therefore two options are open to the interpreter. Either this γάρ in *Ep. apost.* 44.2 has an infinitely weakened sense, so that it introduces neither explanation nor result, or the text is to be suspected of corruption, based perhaps on the Coptic translator's misunderstanding of the author's Greek.

It is this second possibility that is the most fruitful. The various difficulties, reviewed above at length, appear to be soluble at once if in the phrase cεNaϭoΥ ΓαΡ ("for they will remain") the translator has mistaken the Greek present for the future. The original author wrote μένουσι γάρ ("for they *remain*"); the translator, almost certainly reading a Greek text without accents, understood and translated μενοῦσι γάρ ("for they *will remain*").

The likelihood of this explanation being correct is enhanced by observations concerning the translation of μένειν in the Coptic NT. The verb ϭoΥ (Sahidic ϭω) regularly translates the Greek verb μένειν and its compounds.[42] In John's gospel, twenty-seven of the forty occurrences of the verb μένειν are translated with ϭω.[43] Of these twenty-seven, five of the six present indicative forms in the Greek of the Fourth Gospel are translated as futures in the Sahidic Coptic.[44] Since in each case the Greek form is μένει, this present form was likely mistaken—accents being absent—for the future, μενεῖ.[45] But

---

[41] In the Sahidic of John's gospel, for comparison, ΓαΡ is second in its clause forty-five times, third seventeen times, but never fourth. That the words cεNaϭoΥ ΓαΡ begin a new clause is decisive in Hornschuh's argument (*Studien*, 122 – 23).

[42] Crum, *s.v.* ϭω (803a).

[43] In Matthew, it occurs three out of three, and in Mark, in two out of two.

[44] John 3:36; 6:56; 8:35 (twice); 14:17. The fifth instance, in John 15:10, has the Coptic Qualitative.

[45] In John 8:35 the Coptic future possibly reflects an understanding of the Greek μένει as a gnomic future: "The slave does not continue in the house for ever; the son continues for ever."

the issue of the Coptic translation of John's present forms need not be settled here for the possibility to have been established that the author of the *Epistula* wrote μένουσι γάρ ("for they remain").[46]

This assessment of the text and its translation achieves two goals. First, it secures the regular, explanatory sense for γάρ in *Ep. apost.* 44.2. Second, it indicates that there is not a double punishment for the disobedient, that is, remaining outside the kingdom (44.2), and being devoured by wolves (44.3). *Ep. apost.* 44.2 makes clear not the *consequence* of disobedience, but the *reason* for it. The author is explaining how it is that the commandments were not kept: "My commandments have not been fulfilled by those who slept, *for they remain* outside the kingdom."

Therefore the author is not describing the punishment of those in the community who have failed (or will fail) to keep the commandments. Instead the author defines the community in terms of the commandments, and in this process of definition the consequence of failure to obey is only a secondary theme. Such communal definition as this is strongly reminiscent of several passages in 1 John:

> By this we may be sure that we know him, if we keep his commandments. (1 John 2:3)

> We know that we have passed out of death into life, because we love the brethren. He who does not love abides (μένει) in death. (3:14)

> All who keep his commandments abide (μένει) in him, and he in them. (3:24)[47]

There is no certain evidence in the *Epistula* of allusion to, let alone quotation from, the Epistles of John. But the marked, even pervasive, Johannine character of much of the author's language and theology is never felt more strongly than here. In both communities the issue of right doctrine is articulated on the ethical as well as on the theological plane.

Who, then, are those who have failed to keep the commandments, those who by this definition "remain outside the kingdom"?

---

[46] The verb in the Ethiopic version of *Ep. apost.* 44.2 is in the imperfect, i.e., it is capable of either a present or a future sense. As for the choice of verb, for Greek μένειν one would expect *nabara*; but the verb *qoma* (lit. "to stand") does include the meanings "to remain, stay," and is used for μένειν, e.g., in Num 30:5 (see Dillmann, *Lexicon, s.v. qoma* [451–52]).

[47] Cf. also 1 John 2:4; 3:6, 22–23.

Ep. Apost. 43.17; 44.1 – 4:
The Identification of the Foolish

Ethiopic	Coptic
17 These have slept in those who have believed and acknowledged me.	17 These are they which slept in those who have believed and acknowledged me.
1 And since those who slept did not fulfil my commandment,	1 But my commandments were not fulfilled by those who slept.
2 they will be outside the kingdom and the fold of the shepherd;	2 Consequently they will remain[48] outside the kingdom and the fold of the \<shepherd\> and his sheep.
3 and whoever remains outside the fold will the wolf eat. And although he hears he will be be judged and will die, and much suffering 4 and distress and endurance will come upon him; and although he is badly pained and although he is cut into pieces and lacerated with long and painful punishment, yet he will not be able to die quickly.	3 But whoever remains outside \<the fold\> of the sheep will the wolves eat, and he will . . . , dying in much suffering. 4 \<Rest\> and perseverance will not be \<in\> him, and he \<will\> be badly (?) tormented that he . . . \<and they will punish\> him in great \<punishment, and he will\> be under tortures.

As with the wise, so with the foolish their identification comes immediately after the recital of their names. Since "those who have believed" (43.17) must refer to a Christian group, the subject of this second identification ("These are they") is logically the second group of five vir̄tues, which are somehow lacking, absent, or dormant ("have slept") among this second group of believers. The Ethiopic translator almost certainly took it this way, because of the choice of the feminine plural verb (86/11: *nomā* = "they [fem. pl.] have slept"); the Coptic verbal system does not distinguish between male and female subjects in the plural.[49] However, if the preposition "in" ("in those"; Coptic ⲍⲛ̄ ⲛⲉⲧ-; Ethiopic: *ba-dibēhon*) is translated "among," then despite this feminine form it seems that for the sake of the allegorical interpretation of the basic narrative the names have become one with the second group of believers.[50] In favor of this reading is the fact that already in *Ep. apost.* 43.7 the preposition ⲍⲛ̄ together with the verb πιστεύειν

---

[48] This clause has now been suggested to mean: "*For they remain* outside the kingdom."

[49] Therefore if the Ethiopic derives from the Greek via a Coptic intermediary, the feminine plural represents only the translator's *ad sensum* judgment on the Coptic.

[50] The overlapping of referents is not unknown in secondary allegorical interpretation. The discrepancies in Matt 25:1 – 13 have already been noted; another celebrated case is the interpretation (Mark 4:14 – 20) appended to the parable of the sower (Mark 4:3 – 9).

has this sense: "*Among* those who believe" (XXXV 4: ⲍ︤ⲛ︦ ⲛⲉⲧⲣ̄ⲡⲓⲥ-
ⲧⲉⲩⲉ).[51]

The similarity between the phrases in *Ep. apost.* 43.7 and 43.17 has a
further contribution to make to the discussion. In 43.7 it is "those who
believe"; in 43.17 it is "those who have believed," the verbal form now
being a Coptic perfect, the usual equivalent of the Greek aorist. This difference, at first sight only a minor one, takes on new significance in light of the
accompanying verb in 43.17, also in the perfect tense: "those who have
believed and *acknowledged* me." The verb here is ὁμολογεῖν
(ⲣ̄ⲟⲙⲟⲗⲟⲅⲉⲓ), which in the perfect suggests a specific acknowledgment or
confession. If this is so, then the second group being identified is to be
located "*among those who have come to belief* (i.e., become believers) *and
have made their confession of* (belief in) *me.*" The most probable connection between these two verbs is that between conversion and initiation; and
this initiation can hardly be other than baptism.[52]

This connection must of course be tested in relation to other passages in
the *Epistula.* But the identification of the two groups has been sufficiently
established at this point to permit the following summary. In the view of this
early Christian author, there is properly speaking only one body of believers
("sisters"). Within this whole, those who possess (in special measure?) the
five virtues listed in *Ep. apost.* 43.6 are the guides, or leaders, of the majority.
Also within this whole are those in whom the five virtues of *Ep. apost.* 43.17
"slept."

It is the latter who have failed to keep the commandments. And with this
charge the argument of *Ep. apost.* 43 – 45 is brought into contact with several
other passages in the writing, passages which share, among other things, an

---

[51] It must be admitted that in *Ep. apost.* 43.7 the Eth. does not have the same preposition as in
43.17. As noted above, in 43.7 the Eth. has *'em-kama* (as soon as, when).

[52] It appears that as early as in Rom 10:9 ὁμολογεῖν can refer to baptismal confession; cf.
Bultmann, *Theology*, 2. 136; C. H. Dodd, *The Epistle of Paul to the Romans* (London: Hodder &
Stoughton, 1932) 178; Ernst Käsemann, *Commentary on Romans* (Grand Rapids: Eerdmans,
1980) 290 – 91; and Meeks, *First Urban Christians*, 152. On the noun ὁμολογία (confession) in
Heb 3:1; 4:14; 10:23, Otto Michel ("ὁμολογία," *TDNT* 5 [1967] 215) remarks that "we are to
think of an ecclesiastical confession of faith or baptismal confession to which the hearers are
already committed."

When ὁμολογεῖν (to confess) is found together with πιστεύειν (to believe), baptismal connotations seem inescapable. Cf. *LPGL, s.v.* πιστεύω D (1083a): the aorist of πιστεύειν is used
especially of "acceptance of Christian faith in connexion with baptism" (references include Clement of Alexandria *Paedagogos* 1.6; Origen *Hom. 2.3 in Jer.*; Methodius *De resurrectione* 1.41.
Cf. the discussion of the baptismal "faith" (*Ep. apost.* 5.21 – 22) in Chapter Two.

For the close association of the two concepts in the community of the Johannine Epistles, see,
e.g., 1 John 4:15 and 5:5, where the same formula ("Jesus is the Son of God") is introduced in
turn by the two verbs. In 1 John 4:15a ("Whoever confesses..."), ὁμολογεῖν represents "the
(single) basic public confession of faith that makes one a Christian" (Brown, *Epistles of John*,
524).

antagonism towards those who are portrayed as lawless opponents who face a fearful end. Only in this connection does such violent language occur. When these other passages are brought together, it can be seen that the lawless are none other than the false teachers, those about whom warning is made throughout the writing.

1) The denunciation closest in position and in content to *Ep. apost.* 43.17 – 44.4 is in *Ep. apost.* 39.7 – 13 (XXIX 4, 82/3), where the interrogation of the last judgment is anticipated:

> If there is someone who *acknowledges* that he is reckoned to the light, while he does the works of darkness—such a one has no defence to make, nor will he be able to lift up his face to <look at the> son of God, which (Son) I am. I will say to him, ''As you sought you have found, and as you asked you have received. In what do you condemn me, O man? Why did you leave me and deny me? Why did you *acknowledge* me and (yet) deny me? ...'' Now whoever has kept my *commandments* will be a son of light. . . . But on account of those who pervert my words I have come down from heaven. I am the Logos; I became flesh, labouring and teaching that those who are called will be saved, and the lost will be lost eternally. They will be <tormented> alive and will be scourged in <their> flesh and in their soul.

2) It is precisely the combination of belief and fidelity to the commandments that is declared in *Ep. apost.* 26.1 – 3 (XX 6, 68/10) to be the basis for the ''selection'' on the day of judgment:

> Truly I say to you, the flesh will rise alive with the soul, that their accounting may take place <on> that <day>, concerning what they have done, whether it is good or bad, in order that <a> selection may take place of *believers* (Coptic: ⲛ̄ⲡⲓⲥⲧⲟⲥ ; Ethiopic: ʾella ʾamnu) who have *done the* <commandments of my> Father who sent me.

3) Those, on the other hand, who pervert the words of the Lord are the ''Simon and Cerinthus'' of *Ep. apost.* 7.3 (I 4, 53/5):

> Now keep <yourselves> away from them, for death is in them and a great stain of corruption—these to whom shall be judgment and the end and eternal perdition.

4) The same fate is predicted in *Ep. apost.* 29.1 (XXIII 13, 70/12) and in 50.9 – 11 (--, 91/5):

> But those who have transgressed <my> *commandments* and have taught another teaching . . . and who work for their own glory, teaching with other words <those who> *believe* in me rightly, if <they> are brought to ruin by such . . . eternal punishment.

There will come another teaching and a conflict; and in that they seek their own glory and produce worthless teaching an offence of death will come thereby, and they will teach and turn away from my *commandment* even those who *believe* in me and bring them out of eternal life. But woe to those who use my word and my commandment for a pretext, and also to those who listen to them and to those who turn away from the life of the teaching; they will be eternally punished with them.

It is in connection with the same style of condemnation that the association of ὁμολογεῖν in *Ep. apost.* 43.17 with baptismal confession may be confirmed. In *Ep. apost.* 27.1–4 (XXI 12, 69/7) the Lord describes his sojourn in Hades:

On that account I have descended to <the place of> Lazarus, and have preached <to the righteous and> to the prophets, . . . and I have given them the right hand of the *baptism* of life. . . . But if someone *believes* <in me and> does not do my *commandments*, although he *has acknowledged* (ⲁϥⲣ̄ⲍⲟⲙⲟⲗⲟⲅⲉⲓ) my name he receives no benefit from it and has <run a> futile course. For such will be in error and in <ruin, since they> disregarded my *commandments*.

Ep. apost. 43.3, 5, 10–13; 45.3–6:
The Attitude of Those Within

Now that the story has been told, and the wise and the foolish have been identified, the remaining material is a series of apparent scraps of theology and rhetoric. A number of these verses, however, exhibit a surprising unity of concern.

First, there is in *Ep. apost.* 45.1 an example of the rhetorical feature of the disciples' approval of the words of the Lord: "O Lord, you have revealed everything <to us> well." This speech serves simply to separate the description of the fate of those outside from the summary and conclusion in 45.3–8. The response of the Lord which immediately follows belongs with this. Like 45.1, it is not by its content specifically bound to this context: "Do you not apprehend these words?" (45.2; cf. 27.1: "Do you believe that everything I say to you will happen?").

Secondly, there are four questions asked by the disciples. Although each is required by its present context, they represent little more than convenient prompts for the Lord:

Who are the wise and who are the foolish? (43.3)
On what day will [the foolish] go in for their sisters' sakes? (13)
Is this thing definite? (15a)
Now who are the foolish? (15b)

Yet even in these relatively insubstantial questions there is a hint of the author's broader theological and communal perspective. In referring to the virgins/virtues as "sisters" (43.13) the author introduces a relationship between the story's characters which has not been anticipated, either by the core narrative or by the names and their respective identifications. This relationship is a necessary consequence of the interpretative *inclusio* formed by *Ep. apost.* 43.4b and 45.6: "These [ten] with respect to whom the prophet said, 'They are children of God.'[53] . . . The ten are the daughters of God the Father."

The attitude which characterizes the remaining editorial verses is built upon this basic proposition. There is a recurring refrain of distress on the part of those who are within the community—and indeed of those outside it. What is remarkable here is the way that expressions of joy at entry into the bridechamber are tempered with grief for those who by their own action (or inaction) are excluded. The cumulative effect of these remarks is to put their importance for this writer beyond doubt:

But *we wept and were sad* about those who had fallen asleep. (*Ep. apost.* 43.5 [XXXIV 14, 85/10])

Then *they* [the foolish] *wept and grieved* that it was not opened for them. (43.10 [XXXV 12, 86/5])

And their wise sisters who were within in the house of the bridegroom, did they remain in there without opening to them, and *did they not grieve* on their account or did they not pray the bridegroom to open to them? (43.11 [XXXV 14, 86/5])

They [the wise] were not yet able to find grace on their behalf. (43.12 [XXXVI 4, 86/7])

Through the five [wise] will they come into your kingdom. Yet they who watched and were with you, the Lord and bridegroom, *will nevertheless not rejoice* because of those who slept. (45.3–4 [XXXVII 12, 87/7])

They <will rejoice> that they have gone in with the bridegroom, the Lord; and *they are troubled* on account of those who <slept>, *for they are their sisters.* (45.5 [XXXVIII 1, 87/10])

It will be remembered that in *Ep. apost.* 9–12 (the post-resurrection appearance scene) the women who visit the tomb are twice reported to be "mourning and weeping" (9.5; 10.1) over what has happened. The imprisoned disciple in *Ep. apost.* 15 is predicted to be "in sorrow and care" (15.3) because he is far from his fellow disciples at the time of the Passover. This motif of sorrow at separation has now become the central response to the *definition* of the author's community which, as has been seen, is the

---

[53] Hornschuh (*Studien*, 21) claims that this saying comes from a lost apocryphal writing.

primary function of the story of the wise and foolish virgins in the *Epistula*.

The ethical imperative resulting from this communal definition is precisely the prerequisite for the maintenance of the community: the keeping of the commandments. There is also room for hope for those as yet outside. In the Lord's words in *Ep. apost.* 43.12 there is an indication that all is not lost for them, despite the source's fateful pronouncement that "Whoever <is shut out> is shut out" (43.14). In declaring that the wise "were *not yet* able to find grace on their account" (43.12), the way is left open for their reincorporation; indeed, *Ep. apost.* 42–43 suggests that some had turned back. The disciples finally affirm: "O Lord, it suits your greatness to show grace to their sisters" (45.7).[54]

Summary

1) *Ep. apost.* 43–45 presents the longest sustained treatment of a single complex of source material in the writing. Placed immediately after a section concerned with the preaching ministry of the disciples—including a clear reference to the imminent baptismal incorporation of those who have received the word—the story of the wise and foolish serves thus as a bridge between the programmatic ministry of the disciples (chaps. 41–42) and the case studies in the rebuke of neighbors (chaps. 46–47).

2) The kernel of the *Epistula*'s story of the wise and foolish virgins, once it is extracted from the several layers of elaboration and interpretation, exhibits an outline kinship with Matthew's parable. In parallel narratives the wise and the foolish move respectively to their joy and to their fate, the single stated deficiency of the foolish being that they slept.

3) The second layer in this complex section is that at which the virgins are named. The names, probably all of them for this author positive and desirable attributes, derive from standard lists of virtues. It is likely that they were already attached to this story before its rearrangement in the *Epistula*.

4) The third layer of material marks the author's decisive association of the virtues with two Christian groups: those who are to lead the faithful, and those who (for the present at least) "remain outside the kingdom." The author never implies that it is possession of the second set of virtues that leads to the exclusion of the "foolish"; all the reader is told is that in

---

[54] This is the Ethiopic reading at 45.7; the Coptic is defective. Hornschuh (*Studien*, 123 n. 4) recognizes that if the Ethiopic is correct, *Ep. apost.* 43–45 cannot be interpreted only in terms of the struggle between orthodoxy and heresy.

that second group of believers these virtues "slept." This, the author states, led to their failure to keep the commandments.

5) For this author, exclusion from the kingdom is not a feature of the punishment of those who fail to obey. Failure to keep the commandments is the means whereby those who in reality are "outside" may be identified.

6) Those outside the kingdom include those who have previously "believed and acknowledged" the Lord in baptism. Thus baptism is not the sole hallmark of inclusion.

7) The violent punishment of the disobedient is connected elsewhere in the writing with those who are false teachers. For the community of the *Epistula* an essential connection is to be maintained between belief, confession, baptism, and the keeping of the commandments. The public yardstick is obedience, failure in which amounts to denial.

8) Finally the author makes clear the community's obligation of concern for those who are outside. Joy at entry into the kingdom is tempered with "mourning and weeping" for those without, those to whom it may yet suit the Lord's greatness to show grace (45.7).

Conclusion

In this Conclusion, anticipated in part by the summaries at the end of each Chapter, I shall attempt to present the major results of this study. By way of recapitulation the wider issues of interpretation raised in the Preface and Introduction will first be recalled, and some justification offered for the devotion of such effort to a document so far from the mainstream of early Christian studies.

The number of accessible early Christian writings has greatly increased in the past century, and especially in the past fifty years. In some scholarly circles documents until recently unknown or known only by title or from brief quotations now command attention alongside the canonical scriptures and patristic writings. Indeed, the time is perhaps approaching when all students of Christian origins will feel the need to be as familiar with these "apocryphal" texts as with the standard canon of early Christian and non-Christian sources.

But that time has not yet come. With few exceptions, apocryphal writings of all kinds—gospels, epistles, apocalypses, testaments, etc.—still wait in the wings of the theater of critical scholarship. This is partly because of the widely held conviction that exaggerated claims have been made as to the role that these "new" texts have to play; partly because the drama of the Christian church's early centuries as taught, for example, in today's college and seminary courses does not substantially reflect knowledge gained from recent discoveries; and partly too, no doubt, because it is not at all clear what contribution these other writings can make to modern Christian life and thought. A further reason, and the one that best justifies the present study, is that too little has been done to explore the *character* of these new literary *dramatis personae*, not only as theological treatises but also as witnesses to religious life.

In the *Epistula apostolorum*, as in most early Christian literature, the modern reader confronts a writing whose author and audience are unknown apart from the writing itself. To be sure, with little or no regard to author or audience the work may be analyzed according to its dominant themes, and its place assessed in the history of Christian ideas; its scriptural quotations or distinctive religious formulas may be extracted and compared with those in similar documents. At this level of inquiry an exegetical approach to the *Epistula* yields a rich harvest, and the identification of numerous points of contact—"parallels" in form or content—between this apocryphon and contemporary writings invites further tradition-historical investigation. Again, the broader religious environment, including the conflict between emergent "orthodoxy" and "heresy," is further illuminated by the appearance in the *Epistula*, a work groping for a theology of the church as "catholic," of vocabulary and concepts which would later be judged unorthodox. Similarly, a host of minor lexical observations allows us to appreciate anew the achievement of the Coptic and Ethiopic translators.

But on the assumption, generally granted in modern scholarship, that the author did more than merely transcribe earlier sources, and that the *Epistula*'s original readers and hearers were flesh-and-blood men and women rather than some imaginary theological symposium, additional questions may be asked. We may seek to establish from the intersection of *tradition*—oral and written sources—and *composition*—the way the writing has been constructed—just what it was that this particular author wished to communicate to this particular community in their particular time and place. We may seek to discover what saving "revelation" (34.1–2) of understanding and ethics this dialogue was designed to impart. In the case of the *Epistula*, a work preserved only in secondary versions, special attention is required to a further ingredient in the quest, that of *translation*. There is, in fact, an inevitable and necessary continuity between the translation of the text, the identification of its *traditions*, and the detection of the author's method of *composition*. What, then, has been learned of the character of the *Epistula*—of its traditions, its composition, and its communal situation?

In Chapter One I sought to show that, despite the formal range of its individual literary units and the thematic breadth of its theology, the *Epistula* exhibits a striking, perhaps unique, consistency with regard to its composition as a dialogue. It was suggested that this consistency was deliberate; that the author had worked to unify diverse materials in a dialogue whose conversation partners, the disciples and the risen Lord, respectively speak for and address the *Epistula*'s community. In a test-case analysis of compositional method (on *Ep. apost.* 22–26) it was seen that the dialogue, though identified in 12.3 as "revelation," has as its chief focus not the promised heavenly secrets but instructions about the regulation and maintenance of the community.

In Chapter Two, on *Ep. apost.* 4–5, my concern was to show, first, that a traditional miracle list has been expanded with dialogical features to bring out a consistent editorial theology; secondly, that in their present location these chapters are the disciples' "aretalogy" of the earthly Jesus, authenticating both the messenger and his message; and thirdly, that in 5.21–22 the "faith" symbolized by the five loaves of the miraculous feeding is quite specifically *baptismal* faith, that is, the confession of faith made by baptized persons. This latter point is of special importance for a judgment as to the *Epistula*'s intended function in its community.

In Chapter Three, on *Ep. apost.* 9–12, the post-resurrection scene was compared with those in the canonical gospels and in the *Gospel of Peter*. The *Epistula*'s account is clearly secondary, and access to independent tradition rarely evident. But as in the previous section, the literary design of these chapters shows that the author exercised considerable compositional skill. On structural grounds it could be seen that the traditional background of the Lord's appearing is separable from that of the demonstration of his body. For the *Epistula* the Lord is risen as Teacher: Teacher of the disciples and, by implication, of those whom they will teach. The saying in 11.8, which supplies the decisive "prophetic" proof for the author's antidocetic polemic, was found to have a history-of-religions background without precise analogy in the NT Gospels or the *Gospel of Peter*.

In Chapter Four, on *Ep. apost.* 16–19, the critical step in the interpretation of the parousia tradition in 16.3–5 concerned the translation of the word "slain" in 15.9. The author's community, facing persecution of some kind, lifts up its slain as those "in the presence of the Father" (38.1). Those who persevere in faithfulness can expect the same fate and reward. In the meantime the presence of the Lord is promised to the community in its preaching and teaching, activities for which repeated dominical precedent is given. The conclusion seems warranted that behind this theological reflection on preaching and teaching lay the actual situation of the author's circle, in which a fresh appeal for a missionary endeavor was being supported by the promise of the Lord's presence (or "parousia") with the teachers and preachers.

In Chapter Five, on *Ep. apost.* 41–42, it was suggested that the community's missionary activity was the background for a dialogue that explores two traditional sayings, the first concerning the "labor" of missionaries, the second concerning titles and functions. The disciples, representing the leaders in the author's church, have acted as fathers (in preaching) and as teachers; they will act as the servants of the Lord in the baptism of those who have been won, or won back, for the author's group.

Therefore baptism, the communal setting of the five-part formula in 5.21 – 22, is now explicitly denoted as the document's temporal goal. In light of this discovery it was proposed that the *Epistula* had a catechetical purpose.

In Chapter Six, on *Ep. apost.* 43 – 45, the author's dialogical expansion of the parable of the wise and foolish virgins was examined. Over against the view that these chapters promote a rigorous discipline, or that they stand principally as a warning against the deceptive powers of heresy, the explanation emerged that the author's chief concern was with the definition of the community. This definition is based not so much on doctrinal as on ethical grounds: those within the community are those who keep the commandments.

When the *Epistula* is examined in light of the editorial and compositional clues left by the author, it becomes clearer than before that the writing is not only prescriptive but also descriptive: we encounter a theological manifesto but also, and more importantly, an earnest exhortation to a particular way of seeing and living the Christian religious life. Admittedly, the yield of insights into the communal situation is small: most of what we would like to know is presupposed by the author. It is simply not yet possible to describe what it was like to be a Christian in this Ephesian, or Egyptian, or Syrian community in the middle of the second century. Nevertheless, what has been learned is sufficient to indicate that the usual introductory considerations of date and geography, of traditions and doctrines, do not exhaust the contribution made by this document to our knowledge of early Christian life; and that an attempt to describe this work's setting in life, and hence its distinctive character, is not fruitless. There is every reason to hope that what is true for the *Epistula* is true also for other apocryphal remains of Christianity's infancy.

With detailed reference to about one third of this writing I have tried to describe how the author set about his task, and how it was that for a time the *Epistula apostolorum* was a serviceable "revelation" for its community. New times and their new struggles led to its virtual disappearance. Yet among the NT apocrypha the *Epistula* enjoys a rare distinction: as part of the "Book of the Testament of our Lord" this "Epistle of the Apostles" is still copied and read in the Ethiopian Church. Accordingly it is one of the few noncanonical texts to have in the twentieth century an enduring communal existence as a witness to Christian faith and life, and thus to continue the fulfillment of its primary, confessional role. It remains to be seen whether the *Epistula* will find as significant a part to play in the life and mission of its secondary, academic community.

Bibliography

Reference Works

d'Abbadie, Antoine. *Catalogue raisonné de manuscrits éthiopiens*. Paris: L'Imprimerie impériale, 1859.

Bauer, Walter. *A Greek-English Lexicon of the New Testament and Other Early Christian Literature*. Revised by Frederick W. Danker. Translated by William F. Arndt and F. Wilbur Gingrich. 2d edition. Chicago: University of Chicago Press, 1979.

Charlesworth, James H., with James R. Mueller. *The New Testament Apocrypha and Pseudepigrapha: A Guide to Publications, with Excursuses on Apocalypses*. American Theological Library Association Bibliography Series 17. Metuchen, N.J.: Scarecrow, 1987. [See pages 168–71.]

Crum, Walter E. *A Coptic Dictionary: Compiled with the Help of Many Scholars*. Oxford: Clarendon, 1939.

Dillmann, August. *Ethiopic Grammar*. Revised by Carl Bezold. Translated by James A. Crichton. 2d edition. London: Williams & Norgate, 1907. Repr., Amsterdam: Philo, 1974.

_____. *Lexicon linguae ethiopicae cum indice Latino*. Leipzig: Weigel, 1865. Repr., New York: Ungar, 1955. Repr., Osnabrück: Biblio Verlag, 1970.

Geerard, Maurice. *Clavis apocryphorum Novi Testamenti*. Corpus Christianorum. Turnhout: Brepols, 1992). [See pages 11–12.]

Grébaut, Sylvain. *Supplément au lexicon linguae aethiopicae de August Dillmann (1865) et Édition de lexique de Juste d'Urbin (1850–1855)*. Paris: L'Imprimerie nationale, 1952.

Hammerschmidt, Ernst. *Reisebericht und Beschreibung der Handschriften in dem Kloster des Heiligen Gabriel auf der Insel Kebran*. Vol. 1 of *Äthiopische Handschriften vom Tanasee*. Verzeichnis der orientalischen Handschriften in Deutschland 20. Wiesbaden: Steiner, 1973.

Lambdin, Thomas O. *Introduction to Classical Ethiopic (Geʿez)*. HSS 24. Missoula, Mont.: Scholars Press, 1978.

Lambdin, Thomas O. *Introduction to Sahidic Coptic*. Macon, Ga.: Mercer University Press, 1983.

Lampe, Geoffrey W. H. *A Patristic Greek Lexicon*. Oxford: Clarendon, 1961.

Leslau, Wolf. *Comparative Dictionary of Ge'ez: Ge'ez-English, English-Ge'ez, with an Index of the Semitic roots*. Wiesbaden: Harrassowitz, 1987.

_____. *Concise Dictionary of Ge'ez (Classical Ethiopic)*. Wiesbaden: Harrassowitz, 1989.

Liddell, Henry George, and Robert Scott. *A Greek-English Lexicon*. Revised by Henry Stuart Jones. Oxford: Clarendon, 1940.

Macomber, William F., and Getatchew Haile. *A Catalogue of Ethiopian Manuscripts Microfilmed for the Ethiopian Manuscript Microfilm Library, Addis Ababa, and for the Hill Monastic Manuscript Library, Collegeville, Minnesota*. Collegeville, Minn.: St. John's University, 1975–.

Metzger, Bruce M. *A Textual Commentary on the Greek New Testament: a companion volume to the United Bible Societies' Greek New Testament (Fourth rev. ed.)*. 2d edition. Stuttgart: Deutsche Bibelgesellschaft, 1994.

Till, Walter C., *Koptische Grammatik. (Saïdischer Dialekt) Mit Bibliographie, Lesestücken, und Wörterverzeichnissen*. 6th edition. Leipzig: Enzyklopädie, 1986.

_____. *Koptische Dialektgrammatik. Mit Lesestücken und Wörterbuch*. 2d edition. Munich: Beck, 1961.

Wright, William. *Catalogue of the Ethiopic Manuscripts in the British Museum Acquired Since the Year 1847*. London: Longmans, 1877.

Texts and Translations

I. The *Epistula Apostolorum* and Related Texts

Beylot, Robert, ed. and trans. *Testamentum Domini éthiopien. Édition et traduction*. Louvain: Peeters, 1984.

Bick, Josef. *Wiener Palimpseste; I. Teil: Cod. Palat. Vindobonensis 16, olim Bobbiensis; Lucanus, Pelagonius, Acta Apostolorum, Epistulae Iacobi et Petri, Epistula apocrypha Apostolorum, Dioscurides, fragmentum medicum*. Sitzungsberichte der Kaiserliche Akademie der Wissenschaften in Wien, philosophisch-historische Klasse 159/7. Vienna: Alfred Hölder, 1908. (See pages 90–99 with plate 4. See also Pius Bihlmeyer's response in *Rbén* 28 (1911) 271.]

Duensing, Hugo, ed. and trans. *Epistula Apostolorum. Nach dem äthiopischen und koptischen Texte*. Kleine Texte für Vorlesung und Ubungen 152. Bonn: Marcus & Weber, 1925. [See reviews: Rudolf Bultmann in *Christliche Welt* 39 (1925) 1064–65. Carl Schmidt in *OLZ* 28 (1925) 855–59. Ernest B. Allo in *RB* 36 (1927) 305–6. Bernhard Vandenhoff in *TRev* 26 (1927) 345–46.]

Erbetta, Mario. "L'epistola degli apostoli." Pages 37–62 in *Lettere e Apocalissi.* Edited by idem. Vol. 3 of *Gli Apocrifi del Nuovo Testamento.* Turin: Marietti, 1969. Repr., 1998.

Guerrier, Louis, and Sylvain Grébaut. *Le testament en Galilée de notre-seigneur Jésus-Christ.* PO 9.3. Paris: Firmin-Didot, 1913. Repr., Turnhout: Brepols, 2003. [See review: Anton Baumstark in *TRev* 13 (1914) 165–69.]

Hauler, Edmund. "Zu den neuen lateinischen Bruchstücken der Thomas-apokalypse und eines apostolischen Sendschreibens im Codex Vind. Nr. 16." *Wiener Studien* 30 (1908) 308–40.

Hennecke, Edgar, ed. *Neutestamentliche Apokryphen in Verbindung mit Fachgelehrten in deutscher Uebersetzung und mit Einleitungen.* 2d edition. Tübingen: Mohr Siebeck, 1924. [See pages 146–49 for a brief report, with summary, by Hennecke.]   In subsequent editions:

Neutestamentliche Apokryphen in deutscher Ubersetzung. Edited by Edgar Hennecke and Wilhelm Schneemelcher. 2 vols. 3d edition. Tübingen: Mohr Siebeck, 1959–1964. [See vol. 2, pages 126–55 for Hugo Duensing's translation.]

New Testament Apocrypha. Edited by Edgar Hennecke, Wilhelm Schneemelcher, and Robert M. Wilson. Translated by Robert M. Wilson. 2 vols. 3d edition. London: Lutterworth; Philadelphia: Westminster, 1963–1966. [See vol. 1, pages 191–227 for Richard Taylor's English translation of Hugo Duensing's German translation.]

Neutestamentliche Apokryphen in deutscher Ubersetzung. Edited by Edgar Hennecke and Wilhelm Schneemelcher. 2 vols. 4th edition. Tübingen: Mohr Siebeck, 1968. [A corrected reprint of the 3d edition; no English edition published.]

Neutestamentliche Apokryphen in deutscher Ubersetzung. Edited by Edgar Hennecke and Wilhelm Schneemelcher. 2 vols. 5th edition. Tübingen: Mohr Siebeck, 1987–1989. [See vol. 1, pages 205–33 for Caspar Detlef and Gustav Müller's translation.]

Neutestamentliche Apokryphen in deutscher Ubersetzung. Edited by Edgar Hennecke and Wilhelm Schneemelcher. 2 vols. 6th edition. Tübingen: Mohr Siebeck, 1990–1997. [A corrected reprint of the 5th edition.]

New Testament Apocrypha. Edited by Wilhelm Schneemelcher and Robert M. Wilson. Translated by Robert M. Wilson. 2 vols. Revised edition. Cambridge: J. Clark; Louisville, Ky.: Westminster/John Knox, 1991–1992. [Based on the 5th and 6th German editions; see vol. 2, pages 249–84 for Robert M. Wilson's English translation of Caspar Detlef and Gustav Müller's German translation.]

James, Montague Rhodes, ed. "The Epistula Apostolorum." Pages 485–503 in idem, *The Apocryphal New Testament.* Oxford: Clarendon, 1924. Repr. with additions, 1953. Repr., 1959.

Moraldi, Luigi, ed. and trans. "Lettera degli apostoli." Pages 1669–1702 in vol. 2 of *Apocrifi del Nuovo Testamento.* Edited by idem. 2 vols. 2d edition. Classici delle religioni 5: Le altre confessioni cristiane. Turin: Unione Tipografico-Editrice Torinese, 1975.

Müller, Caspar, and Gustav Detlef. See Hennecke, Hennecke-Schneemelcher, above.

Pérès, Jacques-Noël, trans. *L'épître des apôtres et le testament de notre seigneur et notre sauveur Jésus-Christ.* Apocryphes: Collection de poche de l'Association pour L'Étude de la literature Apocryphe Chrétienne 5. Turnhout: Brepols, 1994.

_____. "Épître des apôtres." Pages 357–92 in vol. 1 of *Écrits apocryphes chrétiens.* Edited by François Bovon and Pierre Geoltrain. 2 vols. Bibliothèque de la Pléiade 442. Paris: Gallimard, 1997.

Rahmani, Ignatius Ephaem II, ed. and trans. *Testamentum domini nostri Jesu Christi.* Mainz: Kirchheim, 1899. [Latin translation.]

Schmidt, Carl, and Isaak Wajnberg. *Gespräche Jesu mit seinen Jüngern nach der Auferstehung. Ein katholisch-apostolisches Sendschreiben des 2. Jahrhunderts.* Texte und Untersuchungen 43. Leipzig: Hinrichs, 1919. Repr., Hildesheim: Olms, 1967. [See reviews: Hermann J. Cladder in *TRev* 18 (1919) 452–53. J. de Zwaan in *NedTT* 2 (1919) 281–86. Arnold Ehrhardt in *Historisch-politische Blätter* 165 (1920) 645–55, 717–29. Gustav Krüger in *Literarisches Zentralblatt* 71 (1920) 817–20. Montague Rhodes James in *JTS* Old Series 21 (1920–1921) 334–38. Gustave Bardy in *RB* 30 (1921) 110–34. Anton Baumstark in *TRev* 20 (1921) 260–65. Leopold Fonck in *Bib* 2 (1921) 244–45. Hans Lietzmann in *ZNW* 20 (1921) 173–76. Hans von Soden in *ZKG* 39 (1921) 140–47. Hugo Duensing in *Göttingische Gelehrte Anzeigen* 184 (1922) 241–52. Felix Haase in *OrChr* n.S. 10/11 (1923) 170–73. Walter Till in *ZÄS* 63 (1928) 92.]

Sperry-White, Grant, trans. *The Testamentum Domini: A Text for Students, with Introduction, Translation, and Notes.* Alcuin/GROW Liturgical Study 19; Grove Liturgical Study 66. Bramcote: Grove, 1991.

II. Other Ancient Writings Frequently Cited

Budge, Ernest A. W., trans. *The Contendings of the Apostles: Being the Histories of the Lives and Martyrdoms and Deaths of the Twelve Apostles and Evangelists: Translated from the Ethiopic Manuscripts in the British Museum.* 2d edition. 2 vols. London: Oxford University Press, 1935. Repr., Amsterdam: Philo, 1976.

Charlesworth, James H., ed. *The Old Testament Pseudepigrapha.* 2 vols. Garden City, N.Y.: Doubleday, 1983–1985.

Erbetta, Mario. "L'epistola degli apostoli." Pages 37–62 in *Lettere e Apocalissi.* Edited by idem. Vol. 3 of *Gli Apocrifi del Nuovo Testamento.* Turin: Marietti, 1969. Repr., 1998.

Funk, Francis Xavier, ed. *Didascalia et constitutiones apostolorum.* 2 vols. Paderborn: Schoeningh, 1905.

Funk, Franz X., and Karl Bihlmeyer. *Die apostolischen Väter.* Revised by Wilhelm Schneemelcher. 3d edition. Sammlung ausgewählte Kirchen- und dogmengeschichtlicher Quellenschriften 2/1/1. Tübingen: Mohr Siebeck, 1970.

Goodspeed, Edgar J., ed. *Die ältesten Apologeten.* Göttingen: Vandenhoeck & Ruprecht, 1914.

Horner, George W., ed. and trans. *The Statutes of the Apostles or Canones apostolici.* London: Williams and Norgate, 1904.

_____. *The Coptic Version of the New Testament in the Southern Dialect, otherwise called Sahidic and Thebaic.* 7 vols. Oxford: Clarendon, 1911–1924.

Lake, Kirsopp, trans. *The Apostolic Fathers.* 2 vols. Loeb Classical Library. Cambridge, Mass.: Harvard University Press, 1912–1913.

Lightfoot, Joseph B. *The Apostolic Fathers.* 5 vols. 2d edition. 1889–1890. Repr., Grand Rapids, Mich.: Baker, 1981.

Lipsius, Richard Adelbert, ed., and Max Bonnet. *Acta apostolorum apocrypha.* 2 vols. 1891–1903. Repr., Hildesheim: Olms, 1959, 1990.

The New Testament in Ge'ez. London: British and Foreign Bible Society. 1979.

Robinson, James M., ed. *The Nag Hammadi Library in English.* 3d revised edition. San Francisco: Harper & Row, 1988.

Tischendorf, Constantin. *Evangelia apocrypha. Adhibitis plurimis codicibus graecis et latinis maximam partem nunc primum consultis atque ineditorum copia insignibus.* Leipzig: Avenarius & Mendelssohn, 1853. 2d edition. Leipzig: Mendelssohn, 1876. Repr., Hildesheim: Olms, 1987.

Zuurmond, Rochus. *Novum Testamentum aethiopice: The Synoptic Gospels.* Äthiopistische Forschungen 27. Stuttgart: Steiner, 1989.

Studies

Amann, Émile. "La lettre des apôtres." Pages 523–25 in vol. 1 of *Dictionnaire de la Bible. Supplément.* Edited by Louis Pirot and André Robert. 10 vols. Paris: Letouzey et Ané, 1928–.

Amiot, François. "La lettre des apôtres." Pages 275–85 in *Evangiles Apocryphes.* Edited by idem. Vol. 2 of *La Bible Apocryphe.* Textes pour l'histoire sacrée 5. Paris: Fayard, 1952. [A summary of contents, including paragraphs from Guerrier's translation.]

Bardenhewer, Otto. "Eine 'Epistola apostolorum.'" Pages 598–98 in *Vom Ausgang des apostolischen Zeitalters bis zum Ende des zweiten Jahrhunderts.* Vol. 1 of *Geschichte der alterkirchlichen Literatur.* 5 vols. 2d edition. Freiburg: Herder, 1912. Repr., Darmstadt: Wissenschaftliche Buchgesellschaft, 1962.

Bauckham, Richard. "Pseudo-Apostolic Letters." *JBL* 107 (1988) 469–94. [Classifies the *Epistula apostolorum* and the *Apocrypyhon of James* as "letters with mainly Gospel content"; see p. 483.]

_____. "Synoptic Parousia Parables Again." *NTS* 29 (1983) 129–34.

Bauer, Johannes Baptist. "Ein Rundschreiben der elf Apostel." Page 87 in *Die neutestamentlichen Apokryphen*. Die Welt der Bibel 21. Düsseldorf: Patmos, 1968.

Baumstark, Anton. "Alte und neue Spuren eines außerkanonischen Evangeliums (vielleicht des Ägypterevangeliums)." *ZNW* 14 (1913) 232–47.

_____. "Hippolytos und die außerkanonische Evangelienquelle des äthiopischen Galiläa-Testaments." *ZNW* 15 (1914) 332–35.

Cameron, Ron. *Sayings Traditions in the Apocryphon of James*. HTS 34. Philadelphia: Fortress, 1984. Rev. ed., Cambridge, Mass.: Harvard Divinity School, 2005.

Daniélou, Jean. "Les traditions secrètes des apôtres." *ErJb* 31 (1962) 199–215.

Delazer, Jakob. "Disquisitio in argumentum Epistolae aposotlorum." *Anton* 3 (1928) 369–406.

_____. "De tempore compositionis Epistolae Apostolorum." *Anton* 4 (1929) 257–92, 387–430.

Ehrhardt, Arnold. "Eine neue apokryphe Schrift aus dem 2. Jahrhundert." *Historisch-politische Blätter* 165 (1920) 645–55, 717–29.

Frank, Isidor. *Der Sinn der Kanonbildung. Eine historisch-theologische Untersuchung der Zeit vom 1. Clemensbrief bis Irenäus von Lyon*. Freiburger theologische Studien 90. Freiburg: Herder, 1971. [See pages 100–11.]

Eijk, A. H. C. van. " 'Only that can rise which has previously fallen': The History of a Formula" *JTS* New Series 22 (1971) 517–29.

Getatchew, Haile. "The Homily of Ase Zar'a Ya'qob of Ethiopia in Honor of Saturday." OLP 13 (1982) 185–231.

_____. "The Homily of Zar'a Ya'qob in Honor of St. John the Evangelist (EMML 1480, ff. 48r–52v)." *OrChr* 67 (1983) 144–66.

_____. "A New Look at Some Dates of Early Ethiopian History." *Mus* 95 (1982) 1–12.

Gry, Léon. "La date de la parousie d'après l'Epistula Apostolorum." *RB* 49 (1940) 86–97.

Guerrier, Louis. "Un 'Testament de notre-seigneur et sauveur Jésus-Christ' en Galilée." *Revue de l'orient chrétien* 12 (1907) 1–8.

Hill, Charles E. "The *Epistula Apostolorum*: An Asian Tract from the Time of Polycarp." *JECS* 7 (1999) 1–53.

Hillmer, Mervyn Raymond. "The Gospel of John in the Second Century." Th.D. diss., Harvard Divinity School, 1966. [See pages 28–50.]

Hills, Julian V. "Apostles, Epistle of." Pages 311–2 in vol. 1 of *Anchor Bible Dictionary*. Edited by David Noel Freedman. 6 vols. New York: Doubleday, 1992.

Hills, Julian V. "The *Epistula Apostolorum* and the Genre 'Apocalypse'." *SBLSP* 25 (1986) 581–95.

_____. "Proverbs as Sayings of Jesus in the *Epistula Apostolorum*," *Semeia* 49 (1990) 7–34.

Holland, David Larrimore. "The Third Article of the Creed: A Study in Second- and Third-Century Theology." Pages 145–54 in vol. 2 of *Papers Presented to the Sixth International Conference on Patristic Studies, Held in Oxford, 1971.* Edited by Elizabeth A. Livingstone. 3 vols. StPatr 12–14; TU 115–117. Berlin: Akademie-Verlag, 1975–1976.

Hornschuh, Manfred. "Das Gleichnis von den zehn Jungfrauen in der Epistula Apostolorum." *ZKG* 73 (1962) 1–8.

_____. *Studien zur Epistula Apostolorum.* PTS 5. Berlin: De Gruyter, 1965. [See reviews: Walter J. Burghardt in ThSt 26 (1965) 443–44. M. van Esbroeck in AnBoll 83 (1965) 417–18. Otto Betz in *TLZ* 91 (1966) 516–18. Jean Daniélou in *RSR* 54 (1966) 283–85. Antonia Orbe in *Greg* 47 (1966) 125–26. Christopher G. Stead in *JTS* New Series 17 (1966) 171–73. Pedro Vanovermeire in *RHE* 61 (1966) 539–41. Robert M. Wilson in *JEH* 17 (1966) 105. Anon. in *Irén* 40 (1967) 443. Gilles Quispel in *VC* 22 (1968) 61–63.]

James, Montague Rhodes. "Epistola Apostolorum: A Possible Quotation." *JTS* Old Series 23 (1922) 56. [Suggests a literary or tradition-historical connection with Commodian's *Carmen apologeticum.*]

_____. "The 'Epistola Apostolorum' in a New Text." *JTS* Old Series 12 (1910) 55–56.

Kelly, J. N. D. *Early Christian Creeds.* 3d edition. New York: McKay, 1972.

Lake, Kirsopp. "The Epistola Apostolorum." *HTR* 14 (1920) 15–29.

Metzger, Bruce M., and Bart D. Ehrman. *The Text of the New Testament: Its Transmission, Corruption, and Restoration.* 4th edition. New York: Oxford University Press, 2005.

Loewenich, Walther von. *Das Johannes-Verständnis im zweiten Jahrhundert.* Gießen: Töpelmann, 1932. [See pages 57–59.]

Michaelis, Wilhelm. *Die Apokryphen Schriften zum Neuen Testament.* 3d edition. Sammlung Dieterich 129. Bremen: Schünemann, 1962.

Nock, Arthur Darby. "The Apocryphal Gospels." *JTS* New Series 11 (1960) 63–70.

Pérès, Jacques-Noël. "Le baptême des patriarchs dans les Enfers." *ETR* 68 (1993) 341–46.

_____. "Gabriel, qui se tient devant Dieu." *Positions luthériennes* 39.3 (1991) 247–56.

Piovanelli, Pierluigi. "Les aventures des apocryphes en Éthiopie." *Apocrypha* 4 (1994) 197–224.

Richardson, C. C. "A New Solution to the Quartodeciman Riddle." *JTS* New Series 24 (1973) 74–84.

Schmidt, Carl. "Eine bisher unbekannte altchristliche Schrift in koptischer Sprache." SPAW (1895) 705–11.

_____. "Eine Epistola apostolorum in koptischer und lateinischer Überlieferung." SPAW (1908) 1047–56.

Schnackenburg, Rudolf. *The Gospel according to St. John.* Translated by Cecily Hastings, Francis McDonagh, David Smith, and Richard Foley. 3 vols. New York: Crossroad, 1987.

Schneider, T. "Das prophetische 'Agraphon' der Epistola apostolorum" *ZNW* 24 (1925) 151–54.

Schumacher, H. "The Discovery of the 'Epistola Apostolorum'." *Homiletical and Pastoral Review* 22 (1921–1922) 856–65.

_____. "The 'Epistola Apostolorum' and the New Testament." *Homiletical and Pastoral Review* 22 (1921–1922) 967–75.

_____. "The Christology of the 'Epistola Apostolorum.' " *Homiletical and Pastoral Review* 22 (1921–1922) 1080–87, 1303–12.

_____. "The 'Epistola Apostolorum' and the 'Descensus ad Inferos.' " *Homiletical and Pastoral Review* 23 (1922–1923) 13–21, 121–28.

Stewart-Sykes, Alistair. "The Asian Context of the New Prophecy and of *Epistula Apostolorum*." *VC* 51 (1997) 416–38.

Streeter, Burnett Hillmann. *The Four Gospels: A Study of Origins.* London: Macmillan, 1924.

Vanovermeire, Pedro. "Livre que Jésus-Christ a révélé à ses disciples." Dr. Theol. diss., Institut catholique de Paris, 1962.

Vitti, Alfredo M. "De 'Epistula Apostolorum' apocrypha." *VD* 3 (1923) 367–73.

Zwaan, J. de. "Date and Origin of the Epistle of the Eleven Apostles." Pages 344–55 in *Amicitiae Corolla: A Volume of Essays Presented to James Rendel Harris, D. Litt., on the Occasion of His Eightieth Birthday.* Edited by H. G. Wood. London: University of London Press, 1933.

Harvard Theological Studies

61. Schifferdecker, Kathryn. *Out of the Whirlwind: Creation Theology in the Book of Job*, 2008.

58. Pearson, Lori. *Beyond Essence: Ernst Troeltsch as Historian and Theorist of Christianity*, 2008.

57. Hills, Julian V. *Tradition and Composition in the* Epistula Apostolorum, 2008.

56. Nickelsburg, George W. E. *Resurrection, Immortality, and Eternal Life in Intertestamental Judaism and Early Christianity*. Expanded Edition, 2006.

55. Johnson-DeBaufre, Melanie. *Jesus Among Her Children: Q, Eschatology, and the Construction of Christian Origins*, 2005.

54. Hall, David D. *The Faithful Shepherd: A History of the New England Ministry in the Seventeenth Century*, 2006.

53. Schowalter, Daniel N., and Steven J. Friesen, eds. *Urban Religion in Roman Corinth: Interdisciplinary Approaches*, 2004.

52. Nasrallah, Laura. *"An Ecstasy of Folly": Prophecy and Authority in Early Christianity*, 2003.

51. Brock, Ann Graham. *Mary Magdalene, The First Apostle: The Struggle for Authority*, 2003.

50. Trost, Theodore Louis. *Douglas Horton and the Ecumenical Impulse in American Religion*, 2002.

49. Huang, Yong. *Religious Goodness and Political Rightness: Beyond the Liberal-Communitarian Debate*, 2001.

48. Rossing, Barbara R. *The Choice between Two Cities: Whore, Bride, and Empire in the Apocalypse*, 1999.

47. Skedros, James Constantine. *Saint Demetrios of Thessaloniki: Civic Patron and Divine Protector, 4th–7th Centuries* C.E., 1999.

46. Koester, Helmut, ed. *Pergamon, Citadel of the Gods: Archaeological Record, Literary Description, and Religious Development*, 1998.

45. Kittredge, Cynthia Briggs. *Community and Authority: The Rhetoric of Obedience in the Pauline Tradition*, 1998.

44. Lesses, Rebecca Macy. *Ritual Practices to Gain Power: Angels, Incantations, and Revelation in Early Jewish Mysticism*, 1998.

43. Guenther-Gleason, Patricia E. *On Schleiermacher and Gender Politics*, 1997.

42. White, L. Michael. *The Social Origins of Christian Architecture* (2 vols.), 1997.

41. Koester, Helmut, ed. *Ephesos, Metropolis of Asia: An Interdisciplinary Approach to its Archaeology, Religion, and Culture*, 1995.

40. Guider, Margaret Eletta. *Daughters of Rahab: Prostitution and the Church of Liberation in Brazil*, 1995.

39. Schenkel, Albert F. *The Rich Man and the Kingdom: John D. Rockefeller, Jr., and the Protestant Establishment*, 1995.

38. Hutchison, William R. and Hartmut Lehmann, eds. *Many Are Chosen: Divine Election and Western Nationalism*, 1994.

37. Lubieniecki, Stanislas. *History of the Polish Reformation and Nine Related Documents*. Translated and interpreted by George Huntston Williams, 1995.

— Davidovich, Adina. *Religion as a Province of Meaning: The Kantian Foundations of Modern Theology*, 1993.

36. Thiemann, Ronald F., ed. *The Legacy of H. Richard Niebuhr*, 1991.

35. Hobbs, Edward C., ed. *Bultmann, Retrospect and Prospect: The Centenary Symposium at Wellesley*, 1985.

34. Cameron, Ron. *Sayings Traditions in the Apocryphon of James*, 1984. Reprinted, 2004,

33. Blackwell, Albert L. *Schleiermacher's Early Philosophy of Life: Determinism, Freedom, and Phantasy*, 1982.

32. Gibson, Elsa. *The "Christians for Christians" Inscriptions of Phrygia: Greek Texts, Translation and Commentary*, 1978.

31. Bynum, Caroline Walker. Docere Verbo et Exemplo*: An Aspect of Twelfth-Century Spirituality*, 1979.

30. Williams, George Huntston, ed. *The Polish Brethren: Documentation of the History and Thought of Unitarianism in the Polish-Lithuanian Commonwealth and in the Diaspora 1601–1685*, 1980.

29. Attridge, Harold W. *First-Century Cynicism in the Epistles of Heraclitus*, 1976.

28. Williams, George Huntston, Norman Pettit, Winfried Herget, and Sargent Bush, Jr., eds. *Thomas Hooker: Writings in England and Holland, 1626–1633*, 1975.

27. Preus, James Samuel. *Carlstadt's* Ordinaciones *and Luther's Liberty: A Study of the Wittenberg Movement, 1521–22*, 1974.

26. Nickelsburg, George W. E. *Resurrection, Immortality, and Eternal Life in Inter-testamental Judaism*, 1972.

25. Worthley, Harold Field. *An Inventory of the Records of the Particular (Congregational) Churches of Massachusetts Gathered 1620–1805*, 1970.

24. Yamauchi, Edwin M. *Gnostic Ethics and Mandaean Origins*, 1970.

23. Yizhar, Michael. *Bibliography of Hebrew Publications on the Dead Sea Scrolls 1948–1964*, 1967.

22. Albright, William Foxwell. *The Proto-Sinaitic Inscriptions and Their Decipherment*, 1966.

21. Dow, Sterling, and Robert F. Healey. *A Sacred Calendar of Eleusis*, 1965.

20. Sundberg, Jr., Albert C. *The Old Testament of the Early Church*, 1964.

19. Cranz, Ferdinand Edward. *An Essay on the Development of Luther's Thought on Justice, Law, and Society*, 1959.

18. Williams, George Huntston, ed. *The Norman Anonymous of 1100 A.D.: Towards the Identification and Evaluation of the So-Called Anonymous of York*, 1951.

17. Lake, Kirsopp, and Silva New, eds. *Six Collations of New Testament Manuscripts*, 1932.

16. Wilbur, Earl Morse, trans. *The Two Treatises of Servetus on the Trinity: On the Errors of the Trinity, 7 Books, A.D. 1531. Dialogues on the Trinity, 2 Books. On the Righteousness of Christ's Kingdom, 4 Chapters, A.D. 1532*, 1932.

15. Casey, Robert Pierce, ed. Serapion of Thmuis's *Against the Manichees*, 1931.

14. Ropes, James Hardy. *The Singular Problem of the Epistles to the Galatians*, 1929.

13. Smith, Preserved. *A Key to the Colloquies of Erasmus*, 1927.

12. Spyridon of the Laura and Sophronios Eustratiades. *Catalogue of the Greek Manuscripts in the Library of the Laura on Mount Athos*, 1925.

11. Sophronios Eustratiades and Arcadios of Vatopedi. *Catalogue of the Greek Manuscripts in the Library of the Monastery of Vatopedi on Mt. Athos*, 1924.

10. Conybeare, Frederick C. *Russian Dissenters*, 1921.

9. Burrage, Champlin, ed. *An Answer to John Robinson of Leyden by a Puritan Friend: Now First Published from a Manuscript of A.D. 1609*, 1920.

8. Emerton, Ephraim. *The* Defensor pacis *of Marsiglio of Padua: A Critical Study*, 1920,

7. Bacon, Benjamin W. *Is Mark a Roman Gospel?* 1919.

6. Cadbury, Henry Joel. 2 vols. *The Style and Literary Method of Luke*, 1920.

5. Marriott, G. L., ed. Macarii Anecdota*: Seven Unpublished Homilies of Macarius*, 1918.

4. Edmunds, Charles Carroll and William Henry Paine Hatch. *The Gospel Manuscripts of the General Theological Seminary*, 1918.

3. Arnold, William Rosenzweig. *Ephod and Ark: A Study in the Records and Religion of the Ancient Hebrews*, 1917.

2. Hatch, William Henry Paine. *The Pauline Idea of Faith in its Relation to Jewish and Hellenistic Religion*, 1917.

1. Torrey, Charles Cutler. *The Composition and Date of Acts*, 1916.

Harvard Dissertations in Religion

In 1993, Harvard Theological Studies absorbed
the Harvard Dissertations in Religion series.

31. Baker-Fletcher, Garth. *Somebodyness: Martin Luther King, Jr. and the Theory of Dignity*, 1993.

30. Soneson, Jerome Paul. *Pragmatism and Pluralism: John Dewey's Significance for Theology*, 1993.

29. Crabtree, Harriet. *The Christian Life: The Traditional Metaphors and Contemporary Theologies*, 1991.

28. Schowalter, Daniel N. *The Emperor and the Gods: Images from the Time of Trajan*, 1993.

27. Valantasis, Richard. *Spiritual Guides of the Third Century: A Semiotic Study of the Guide-Disciple Relationship in Christianity, Neoplatonism, Hermetism, and Gnosticism*, 1991.

26. Wills, Lawrence Mitchell. *The Jews in the Court of the Foreign King: Ancient Jewish Court Legends*, 1990.

25. Massa, Mark Stephen. *Charles Augustus Briggs and the Crisis of Historical Criticism*, 1990.

24. Hills, Julian Victor. *Tradition and Composition in the* Epistula apostolorum, 1990.

23. Bowe, Barbara Ellen. *A Church in Crisis: Ecclesiology and Paraenesis in Clement of Rome*, 1988.

22. Bisbee, Gary A. *Pre-Decian Acts of Martyrs and* Commentarii, 1988.

21. Ray, Stephen Alan. *The Modern Soul: Michel Foucault and the Theological Discourse of Gordon Kaufman and David Tracy*, 1987.

20. MacDonald, Dennis Ronald. *There Is No Male and Female: The Fate of a Dominical Saying in Paul and Gnosticism*, 1987.

19. Davaney, Sheila Greeve. *Divine Power: A Study of Karl Barth and Charles Hartshorne*, 1986.

18. LaFargue, J. Michael. *Language and Gnosis: The Opening Scenes of the Acts of Thomas*, 1985.

12. Layton, Bentley, ed. *The Gnostic Treatise on Resurrection from Nag Hammadi*, 1979.

11. Ryan, Patrick J. *Imale: Yoruba Participation in the Muslim Tradition: A Study of Clerical Piety*, 1977.

10. Neevel, Jr., Walter G. *Yāmuna's* Vedānta *and* Pāñcarātra: *Integrating the Classical and the Popular*, 1977.

9. Yarbro Collins, Adela. *The Combat Myth in the Book of Revelation*, 1976.

8. Veatch, Robert M. *Value-Freedom in Science and Technology: A Study of the Importance of the Religious, Ethical, and Other Socio-Cultural Factors in Selected Medical Decisions Regarding Birth Control*, 1976.

7 Attridge, Harold W. *The Interpretation of Biblical History in the* Antiquitates judaicae *of Flavius Josephus*, 1976.

6. Trakatellis, Demetrios C. *The Pre-Existence of Christ in the Writings of Justin Martyr*, 1976.

5. Green, Ronald Michael. *Population Growth and Justice: An Examination of Moral Issues Raised by Rapid Population Growth*, 1975.

4. Schrader, Robert W. *The Nature of Theological Argument: A Study of Paul Tillich*, 1976.

3. Christensen, Duane L. *Transformations of the War Oracle in Old Testament Prophecy: Studies in the Oracles Against the Nations*, 1975.

2. Williams, Sam K. *Jesus' Death as Saving Event: The Background and Origin of a Concept*, 1972.

1. Smith, Jane I. *An Historical and Semantic Study of the Term "Islām" as Seen in a Sequence of Qur'an Commentaries*, 1970.